PRAISE FOR
MIDLIFE, NEW LIFE

"*Midlife, New Life* is a wise and inspiring guide to living consciously for the rest of your life. It shows you it's possible to build a life that really does get better with age."

—**Richard Leider,** international best-selling author of
The Power of Purpose, Repacking Your Bags, and
Who Do You Want to Be When You Grow Old?

"Forget ageist stereotypes about retirement. *Midlife, New Life* will help retirees find what they're really looking for: purpose-driven lives full of health, vitality, supportive relationships and financial freedom."

—**Ken Dychtwald,** PhD, author of *What Retirees Want:
A Holistic View of Life's Third Age* and
Radical Curiosity: My Life on the Age Wave

"If you're eager to embrace the change, challenges and glee of your next chapter, *Midlife, New Life* is a must-read. This guide smoothly glides you through the prosaic and practical and from money matters to mindful meditation to help you discover ways to reach for the stars and find dreams that will help you get there. You will be inspired to intentionally steer your path and find meaning in who you are, what you do, and in those whose lives you touch."

—**Kerry Hannon,** workplace futurist, best-selling author of
In Control at 50+: How to Succeed in the New World of Work,
and *senior columnist at Yahoo Finance*

"The authors of *Midlife, New Life* are three remarkable life planning experts who, together, have brilliantly captured the essence of what it takes to live intentionally and consciously in the second half of life. The book not only prompts us to reflect on and reconsider our major life choices, which were often made decades earlier, it also provides a practical roadmap to help shape our futures using the comprehensive Conscious Living Wheel framework. *Midlife, New Life*, combined with the wisdom gleaned from an individual's life experience, creates a powerful resource for those entering mid-life who wish to design a generative, resilient and purposeful future."

—Elizabeth Bussman Mahler, EdD,
teaching professor, Northeastern University

"This instructive, inspiring, and concisely comprehensive book offers the most salient advice on aging, drawn from the field's wisest thought leaders, and a message: There are plenty of resources and paths for each of us who summon conscious and true self-regard to transform the diverse challenges of aging into fulfilling and wondrous possibilities."

—Bruce Frankel, author of *What Should I Do With The Rest of My Life? True Stories of Finding Success, Passion and Meaning in the Second Half of Life,* and president of the Life Planning Network

"*Midlife, New Life* will help awaken your power of attention, so you can clarify purposeful intentions that you can then translate into intelligent actions. This is a practical playbook for living a more meaningful, happy, and fulfilling life."

—Michael J. Gelb, author of *How to Think Like Leonardo da Vinci: 7 Steps to Genius Every Day and Brain Power: Improve Your Mind as You Age*

"A practical and valuable guide for everyone approaching midlife and beyond to navigate the challenges and opportunities that await us. Well researched and easy to read, this book belongs on everyone's reading list. You'll be in the know and well prepared for the road ahead. Highly recommended."

—**Joyce Cohen,** career development/mid-life transition specialist, co-founder of My Future Purpose

"If you are looking for a resource that can help you envision, anticipate, and prepare for finding fulfillment in all the dimensions of your multifaceted life on your journey from midlife to elderhood, *Midlife, New Life* is such a book. It is filled with information and inspiration to guide you in making the choices to consciously and intentionally live in balance and wholeness as you navigate the challenging yet deeply fulfilling transitions of life's second half."

—**Ron Pevny,** director, Center for Conscious Eldering and author of *Conscious Living, Conscious Aging: Claiming the Gifts of Elderhood*

"The authors of *Midlife, New Life: Living Consciously in Midlife and Beyond* combine years of experience as researchers, coaches, mentors and advisors. In their book they creatively weave together their own experiences with stories from others, help us understand and use their Conscious Living Wheel, and challenge us to explore and create our own journey. Recognizing the uncertainties of life, they offer wise and practical guidance to help us recognize the potential in the years ahead. They encourage us to develop awareness and resilience as we create a conscious, intentional and fulfilling second half of life. This book will help you look forward to this next stage of life! I highly recommend you read it!"

—**Dorian Mintzer,** PhD, co-author of *The Couple's Retirement Puzzle: 10 Must-Have Conversations for Creating an Amazing New Life Together,* and host of the monthly 4th Tuesday *Revolutionize your Retirement Interview with Expert's Series to Help You Create a Fulfilling Second Half of Life*

"Midlife, New Life is one of the simplest and most profound statements to describe a stage of human growth and development that is no longer for a lucky few. Instead of midlife being a crisis, what if it were instead a "chrysalis" period of profound transformation. With our average lifespans expanding an extra 30 years in the past 100, the stage we identify as "midlife" has now been extended into decades of opportunity for conscious growth. I am delighted to recommend *Midlife, New Life: Living Consciously in Midlife and Beyond* as a resource for anyone from their 30s to their 80s to explore. Using the Conscious Living Wheel as a wider framework to examine our lives, this book will serve as both validation, consolation, and inspiration to deeply reinforce that the best years are yet to come."

—**Kari Cardinale,** Senior Vice President,
Modern Elder Academy (MEA)

"We all have hopes and dreams, but I remember a preacher saying: "One is either about to enter a storm, one is in the midst of a storm, or one has made it through the storm." Preparation becomes essential to fulfill the journey because what lies ahead is pretty much uncharted waters. *Midlife, New Life* gathers the wisdom of experienced sailors to help prepare you to use the multidimensional pieces of the Conscious Living Wheel in order to successfully navigate the unique course into the second half of your New Life."

—**Rev. Brian McCaffrey,** chair, Northeast Forum on Spirituality and
Aging (NEFOSA) (retired); board member,
Adult Lutherans Organized for Action (ALOA) (retired);
board member, Sage-ing International (retired)

"Midlife, New Life emerges as a guiding light—a beacon of wisdom and inspiration for those standing at the crossroads of their journey through life. The authors have provided a user-friendly framework for navigating a challenging transition, resulting in a rewarding and fulfilling life."

—**David Shriner-Cahn,** founder, Smashing the Plateau

"This is a terrific book. The clue comes early in the table of contents, from the chapter headings, all expressed as active verbs such as 'Exploring Purposefully,' 'Savoring the World,' and, my favorite, 'Bouncing Forward.' The book has such a spring in its step. And it's practical both from the insights of those who are living midlife consciously and from many, many consciousness-raising exercises and questions offered by the authors. This book doesn't simply add meaningfully to the growing literature on aging well; it infuses it with great energy."

—**Fred Mandell PhD,** founder of *Creating Futures That Work* and author with Kathleen Jordan of *Becoming a Life Change Artist*

"A deep dive into the 'sprouts' of conscious living! Regardless of where you might be, this book will guide you and reveal the potential for a fulfilling second half of your life. Its embrace of the full spectrum of your lived experiences and the revelation of the 'soil, seeds and sunlight' for your Part 2 potential is stunning and something for all of us to read and absorb."

—**Mary Ann Esfandiari,** retired NASA senior executive and US Navy Commander and current researcher for Cornell Technical Services

"The authors have masterfully crafted the art of aging gracefully and well in their new book, *Midlife, New Life: Living Consciously in Midlife and Beyond*. Brilliantly conceived and crafted around the framework of the Conscious Living Wheel, this book offers wise and practical guidance for creating an abundant and fulfilling life for those in or beyond midlife or those embarking on their next life journey."

—**Craig and Patricia Neal,** co-founders, Center for Purposeful Leadership

"*Midlife, New Life* is a comprehensive companion for creating your authentic life plan in midlife and beyond. It asks profound questions that elicit mindful responses toward new directions."

—**Candy Spitz,** transition coach and founder of the
Life Planning Network Chesapeake Chapter

"Fresh, creative, well-researched, and thought-provoking are all descriptions that hit me reading this book. The authors have been studiously thorough in the way the topics are covered to stimulate one's imagination and engagement. The quality of thought and research that's gone into this work has armed us all with the information and tools to enhance the quality of our later lives. I loved the questions and "Try this . . ." suggestions at the end of each chapter."

—**Jim Currie,** reinventing retirement entrepreneur

"*Midlife, New Life* addresses transitions to what is next in life with clarity, consciousness, warmth, and well-expressed advice. Transitioning into your encore life is not as easy as it sounds, and there are particular challenges for specific demographics. Kudos to the authors for pointing out the challenges the LGBT community faces with housing, medical, and job discrimination. *Midlife, New Life* is an excellent resource for those even thinking about what is next in your life. Highly recommended."

—**Larry Jacobson,** award-winning author, circumnavigator,
motivational speaker, and thought leader in the field of retirement

"These three accomplished authors have written an excellent treatise on the delights and challenges of midlife and beyond. It is a heartfelt exploration into issues as diverse as finding your purpose and understanding your relationship to money. Among the three of them, they cover all the important angles."

—**Sara Zeff Geber, PhD,** author,
Essential Retirement Planning for Solo Agers

"*Midlife, New Life* is a comprehensive guide to optimize your next life chapter, suggesting a positive path for the journey through midlife and beyond. I resonate with key ideas of sharing your talents in making a difference in the world, and I especially enjoyed the personal touches, encouraging people who read it to make decisions by thinking purposefully. The reader has the opportunity to benefit from years of research and experience as Eileen, Sandy, and Paul use their own life knowledge plus stories from many interesting people to give the reader an experience similar to working with a life coach."

—**Dorothy Keenan,** founder of *GrandInvolve*

"If you're eager to build more purpose and meaning into your life, *Midlife, New Life* is an invaluable resource. An engaging read that is filled with insightful questions, tested advice, and inspirational stories, it will help guide you towards new possibilities for your next chapter."

—**Nancy Collamer,** author of *Second Act Careers: 50+ Ways to Profit from Your Passions During Semi-Retirement*

"*Midlife, New Life* is an engaging, comprehensive and resource rich guide that invites the reader toward deep reflection and practical action planning for living a purposeful life. This will be my go-to recommended book for every client considering what's next in midlife and beyond."

—**Barbara Abramowitz,** psychotherapist and life coach

"*Midlife, New Life* is an inspirational book that we all need as we navigate the second half of life. The authors have taken careful thought, expertise, and stories to help us intentionally evaluate and discover what's next with key areas in purpose, living well, working for fulfillment, and relationships. Happy to see a chapter dedicated to technology because of its ever-evolving significance and relevance to living, working, and aging well."

—**Dawn Pratt,** founder of Techup for Women, managing partner at Global Training and Events Group, LLC

"Don't muddle through midlife. Enjoy the benefits of this book and live consciously. Use the authors' helpful Conscious Living Wheel framework. It invites us to be grounded in our purpose and navigate the changes, challenges, and opportunities we face with resilience. This is a must-read for anyone looking to discover a joyful path that's meaningful to themselves and others."

—**Don Maruska,** author of *How Great Decisions Get Made, Take Charge of Your Talent,* and *Solve Climate Change Now*

"I have followed this book-writing journey from original concept through initial drafts and on to the final manuscript. *Midlife, New Life* has matured into a book that challenges seasoned humans to live life more consciously with joy and wonder. This resource is a MUST for professional coaches offering individual and group coaching services for those approaching the autumn of their lives."

—**Betsy Corley Pickren,** PCC, CPCC, leadership and mental fitness coach, WoodFire Leadership, LLC

"The authors offer us inspired and practical guidance in opening our mind, heart, and will—to consciously reinvent ourselves and fulfill our purpose in a context of increased longevity and greater uncertainty about the future."

—**Alain Gauthier,** author of *Actualizing Evolutionary Co-leadership: To Evolve a Creative and Responsible Society* and co-creator of The Regenerative Elder Process of the Elders Action Network

LIVING CONSCIOUSLY *in*
MIDLIFE *and* BEYOND

MIDLIFE
NEW LIFE

EILEEN CAROSCIO

SANDY DEMAREST

PAUL WARD

FOREWORD BY CHIP CONLEY

RIVER GROVE
BOOKS

2023904904

Published by River Grove Books
Austin, TX
www.rivergrovebooks.com

Distributed by River Grove Books

Design and composition by Greenleaf Book Group
Cover design by Greenleaf Book Group
Cover images used under license from
©Adobestock.com/svetlanass13; ©Shutterstock.com/Black Salmon

Publisher's Cataloging-in-Publication data is available.

Print ISBN: 978-1-63299-707-4

eBook ISBN: 978-1-63299-708-1

First Edition

CONTENTS

FOREWORD

I was delighted to hear from two of our alums (Eileen and Sandy) from the Modern Elder Academy (MEA), the world's first wisdom school for those in midlife and beyond. They have been on an exciting writing journey with their dear colleague Paul Ward, who inspired the idea of collaborating on a book to share their knowledge, experience, and wisdom on the challenges of navigating the midlife landscape.

Living consciously in midlife and beyond requires deep exploration of our inner thoughts and beliefs and our outer behaviors and practices. *Midlife, New Life* guides the reader with insights and inspiration for exploration and practical advice for taking action. The book is full of new concepts and ideas, insights from thought leaders and expert practitioners in the field, and thought-provoking questions and practical activities.

The authors are experts in the field of living consciously in the second half of life. Midlife and beyond represents a truly phenomenal opportunity and time of possibility for new growth and new life as their book title and cover image illustrate. *Midlife, New Life* aligns well with the MEA mantra to discover and grow whole.

Eileen Caroscio, Sandy Demarest, and Paul Ward provide a valuable approach to help you create a new vision for this new life chapter.

Their Conscious Living Wheel provides an excellent framework for consciously exploring the challenges we face in the second half of life. With purpose at the center, you can explore each of the ten outer elements of the wheel in sequence or in any order you choose. Whether your biggest challenges relate to health, money, or relationships, or you are seeking new ways to make a contribution, planning a new career, or wanting to develop your creativity or resilience, you'll find answers here. If you are looking for inspiration and a practical guide to embark on the second half of life, *Midlife, New Life* is the book for you.

The authors interviewed more than 50 people, who shared their experience and wisdom. They also include their own ideas as thought leaders in the field and supportive research findings to add to the depth of the book. Eileen, Sandy, and Paul are expert guides in the field of life transitions, offering coaching, facilitation, and training to a broad spectrum of clients.

It is with fondness for this exciting time in life—and for the writers—that I recommend reading *Midlife, New Life*. It will help you turn over some new leaves in your life—just like the book cover's image—and vibrantly grow and glow into this exciting new stage of life.

Chip Conley
Founder of the Modern Elder Academy
Author of seven books, including his most recent:
Learning to Love Midlife:
12 Reasons Why Life Gets Better with Age (2024)

INTRODUCTION

A ship in port is safe, but that is not what ships
are built for. Sail out to sea and do new things.
—GRACE MURRAY HOPPER

Journeying through the second half of our lives, we may find that uncertainty about the future keeps us from sailing toward new horizons or living the good life we imagined. Advancements in medicine, nutrition, and technology all mean we may live into our eighties or nineties or even beyond, and the question of *how to live well* seems more important than ever. What would it be like to keep reaching for those new horizons, confident you have made the best, most conscious choices possible, and to do things not because we have to, but because we *want* to?

Where do you find yourself on your journey through the second half of life? Are you living consciously? Are you safe in port or sailing out to sea? Are you riding out a storm and looking for calmer waters? More specifically, are you:

- Feeling unfulfilled and uncertain about the life ahead?
- Worrying about having enough money to live on?
- Disappointed you are not living the good life?
- Concerned about working after your full-time career comes to an end?
- Excited about opportunities to help others?
- Thinking about where in the world to live?
- Wanting to live a more creative life?
- Frightened about how your relationships might change?
- Scared about the future of technology?
- Anxious about the likely challenges ahead?

If you answered yes to some of these questions, read on.

We think of consciousness as moment-to-moment awareness. When we refer to *living consciously*—as we will throughout this book—we are referring to being awake and aware of what is going on in all aspects of our lives. Greater awareness of our own inner and outer worlds, the lives of others, and the world around us allows us to be more intentional about how we show up in the world, the decisions and the actions we take to realize our vision of the future, and the way we achieve our goals.

Wherever you are on your journey through life, we hope that this book will provide ideas, strategies, and examples of real-life experiences to reflect on so that you can consciously decide what resonates with you. Think of yourself as an artist or alchemist selecting the colors, the experiences, and the vision that will become your own customized version of your next life chapter.

This book is for you if you are considering a transition from a full-time career to whatever comes next, or if you are facing other choices or decisions that are causing you to reflect on the second half of life; or perhaps you have a colleague, friend, family member, or parent at that point, and you're reading this book so you can advise and help that person; or maybe you are a life transitions coach, a career coach, or a retirement coach looking for additional inspiration or information.

What can you expect? Our hope is that by reading this book:

- You will discover new ways of living consciously, creatively, and resiliently.

- You will find new and refreshing ideas that will serve as a guide for planning activities you consider essential, helping you explore, plan, and act in alignment with your own purpose, values, strengths, and resources.

- You will learn wisdom from thought leaders in the field and those who have real-life experience of navigating through midlife and beyond.

- You will be inspired by the real-life stories and begin to shape your future with mindful awareness, purposeful intentions, and responsible actions.

- You will be inspired to lead and participate in conversations that matter, making a positive difference in your own life and in the lives of others.

OUR OWN JOURNEYS TO LIVING CONSCIOUSLY

We, the authors of this book, each bring many years of experience as researchers, coaches, mentors, and advisors helping clients navigate career and lifestyle transitions. We have written this book to share insights and inspirations from our own knowledge and experience— along with stories from others navigating this terrain. In these pages you'll find a wealth of information from interviews conducted with prominent thought leaders such as Richard Leider, Dorian Mintzer,

Marc Miller, Fred Mandell, Bruce Frankel, Nancy Collamer, and Ron Pevny. Overall, we interviewed more than 50 people with expertise and experience with some of the challenges faced in the second half of life. We have included the names of our sources where permission was granted and have used pseudonyms where our sources requested anonymity. Together, we hope to provide new perspectives on how to live more consciously in midlife and beyond.

But first, a few words on our own journeys to living consciously.

EILEEN CAROSCIO

When Eileen's father died suddenly when she was a teenager, she realized that life could change unexpectedly. This steered her into a fulfilling career as a registered nurse, helping people adjust to health-status changes and achieving next-level health goals. Her deep interest in supporting people's total well-being and their potential for moving forward beyond change and uncertainty expanded into helping individuals navigate the challenges and opportunities of the second half of life. As a leader in the midlife-and-beyond coaching field, she stresses the importance of putting a life vision and plan in place along with growing one's resiliency.

SANDY DEMAREST

Sandy has spent her career helping people at all ages and stages move to new work roles, jobs, and careers. As her daughters left the nest, she went through her own midlife transition. She discovered her purpose of coaching those in midlife and beyond to reimagine what's next. She truly believes in living with intention and helping her clients discover their purpose, connect with values, and bring their dreams to center stage.

PAUL WARD

Paul's passion is around making the world a better place to live and work, helping people reach higher levels of consciousness, championing living and leading consciously, and enabling conversations that matter. Born in England, Paul's spirit of adventure has taken him around Europe and the Americas practicing his craft as designer, engineer, marketer, business leader, visioneer, facilitator, and coach. Farther afield, walking among the indigenous tribes and the animals of the Serengeti has provided deep appreciation of the need to find guides for adventures and spiritual journeys, and for personal and organizational transformations. Having gone through his own midlife transition, as a coach he helps people in the second half of life to manifest their dreams.

HOW TO READ THIS BOOK: THE CONSCIOUS LIVING WHEEL

Our Conscious Living Wheel provides a visual framework for the book and is our way of structuring the essential aspects of living consciously. Our life purpose is at the core, the heart center, from which all other aspects of the wheel radiate. In the first chapter, "Exploring Purposefully," we explain how you might discover your life purpose or calling and become aware of your core values, your identity, and the possible transitions and identity shifts you may experience in the second half of life. Our life purpose has a significant influence on all of the other aspects of the wheel. We have included a wealth of information about living consciously for each of these outer elements of the wheel.

In "Living Well" (chapter 2), we explore how to nurture our mind and body, enhance our mental and physical health, and create a personal health resource plan for living well in the second half of life.

"Appreciating Money" (chapter 3) includes ideas about how to be more conscious about our money: making it, saving it, managing it, spending it, and leaving it behind.

Insights in "Working for a Living" (chapter 4) and "Working for Fulfillment" (chapter 5) reflect how we are living and working longer and need to reimagine our working lives and the possibility of encore careers, entrepreneurial ventures, and volunteer activities.

In "Savoring the World" (chapter 6), we look at pausing to savor and appreciate the different elements of our beautiful world and making conscious choices about where to live and where to visit in the second half of life.

In "Living Life Creatively" (chapter 7), we explore the value of consciously living life with imagination, curiosity, courage, and cheer as an attitude and a way of life, and how to develop our creative potential with mindsets and practices, processes and skills, and pathways and plans.

"Minding Relationships" (chapter 8) provides insights into some of the changing relationships in the second half of life, including our relationships with a spouse or life partner and with close and extended families, the loss of a close relationship, embracing new relationships, and the challenges of going solo in midlife and beyond.

In "Helping Humanity" (chapter 9), we look at environmental sustainability, social responsibility, and leadership in governments and business, and how we can each make a contribution to making the world a better place to live and work.

"Living with Technology" (chapter 10) represents major challenges as we age, and we explore how technology impacts how we live more consciously in each of the elements of the Conscious Living Wheel.

Resilience is needed to adapt and thrive when responding to challenges in the second half of life, and in "Bouncing Forward" (chapter 11), we suggest mindsets and practices to help build your resilience muscle to help you prepare for the path ahead and bounce forward into a more positive future.

As you read, always think about how the ideas expressed in this book apply to you as you journey toward living more consciously in midlife and beyond. You'll find references and quotes from thought leaders and others we interviewed in preparation for writing this book, and questions to help you plan your own journey. Review the Conscious Living Practices at the end of each chapter, reflect on the questions, and try the activities that resonate with you.

Our Conscious Living approach embraces the three themes of noticing what is going on, setting intention, and acting responsibly, or more simply Attention, Intention, and Action (A-I-A).[1] *Attention* comes from awareness of ourselves, others, and the world around us and includes listening and learning with an open mind. *Intention* involves thinking about purpose, possibility, and priorities, leading to thoughtful choices and decisions. *Actions* are our behaviors reflecting our intention to act responsibly. We can all aspire to live more consciously and encourage others to live more consciously as well.

We have used the word "retirement" sparingly in this book. Although retirement has been traditionally a stage at the end of our working lives, people are increasingly reinventing themselves rather than retiring in any traditional sense of the term. Maintaining the philosophy of nonretirement pioneers such as Marika Stone and Howard Stone, we believe we are all "too young to retire," at least from making valuable contributions to the world around us.[2] Our hope is that by reading this book you will be inspired to dream big, plan well, and take positive steps on your evolving journey in midlife and beyond.

MIDLIFE, NEW LIFE

If you are in midlife and beyond, now may be the time for a new life. Living consciously in the second half of life enables us all to feel more vibrant and fulfilled—and doing so will change your life, if you let it. So let's focus not only on dreaming about the future—let's begin shaping that future. Remember, a vision without a plan will remain a dream, so it's time for a new journey of discovery. Now is the time to determine your emerging identity, discover your life's purpose, and to plan to live the rest of your life consciously and intentionally, making a difference for yourself and in the lives of those you care about.

Some of the transformations we have described can be challenging, and you may be reluctant to embark on some of the deep reflections needed to move forward. We invite you to read the book with an open mind and an open heart, fully prepared for these challenges. With the education, insights, and Conscious Living Practices we have provided, we hope you will be inspired to imagine a better life and go forward to live the life you imagined.

Living
Well

Bouncing
Forward

Appreciating
Money

Living with
Technology

Working
for a Living

Exploring
Purposefully

Helping
Humanity

Working for
Fulfillment

Minding
Relationships

Savoring
the World

Living Life
Creatively

CHAPTER 1

EXPLORING
PURPOSEFULLY

It doesn't matter what you do, what matters is why you do it.
—SIMON SINEK

When the caterpillar in *Alice's Adventures in Wonderland* asks Alice, "Who are you?" she replies, "I—I hardly know, sir, just at present—at least, I know who I was this morning, but I think I must have changed a few times since then."[1] We live in a time of identity shifts, continually experiencing life transitions: from parent to friend, from business leader to community volunteer, from employee to entrepreneur, from caring for children to caring for parents. Knowing our core purpose during these identity shifts can help ground us during these transformative times—which is what we need for *exploring purposefully*. Exploring purposefully is the core, the heart center from which the other aspects of the Conscious Living Wheel radiate. We begin our Conscious Living journey by asking why: Why are we here?[2]

In this chapter we explore identity and purpose, thinking about who we are, why we are here, and who we are becoming. We also look at our core values, identity shifts, and possible reinventions.

MEANING, PURPOSE, AND CALLING

Consciously living life on purpose requires clarity around our purpose or calling, and what brings meaning to our lives. Although the words *meaning, purpose,* and *calling* are often used interchangeably, they are distinct. *Meaning* refers to a subjective feeling that our lives fit into a larger context and connotes personal significance about what is felt to be important and the experiencing of life as making sense. The words *purpose* and *calling* refer to a sense of direction in life, and enthusiasm regarding the future, addressing the question, "Why am I here?"

The meaning of our existence is not invented but rather detected. So says Viktor Frankl in his classic work *Man's Search for Meaning.* He suggests three main avenues we can travel to arrive at a meaningful life: "The first is by creating a work or by doing a deed. The second is by experiencing something or encountering someone. In other words, meaning can be found not only in work but also in love. Most important, however, is the third avenue to meaning in life: even the helpless victim of a hopeless situation facing a fate he cannot change, may rise above himself, may grow beyond himself and by so doing, change himself. He may turn a personal tragedy into a triumph."[3]

In his book *Finding Meaning in the Second Half of Life,* James Hollis describes our "profound, irresistible urge towards meaning, and our anguish at the loss of meaning."[4] We may experience a feeling that has real significance, real meaning, both in the immediate situation and in the larger context of life in general. We can find meaning in our work, our writing, in our communities, and in our relationships.

Let's take a moment of reflection.

Think back to a crisis moment in your life: maybe a diagnosis of a life-threatening illness, or the loss of someone or something you cared deeply about. What was the first thing that came into your mind in that moment of crisis? You may well have asked yourself, *Why me? Why is this happening to me now?* And then you might have wondered, *What next? What am I going to do about this crisis?* We want to understand the meaning of the situation before we decide how to handle it. Now think of a moment of joy in your life: the birth of a child, a graduation, a promotion, or any feeling of accomplishment that comes to mind. What did you feel then? What was it that gave life meaning in that moment? Make a few notes about what comes into your mind as you consider these questions about moments of crisis and joy.

What does it mean to live a meaningful life? Some of the people we interviewed for this book talked about having a life of meaning and purpose. Here is what they said:

What Feels Meaningful?

Coming alive: "I come so alive when I am writing something that's meaningful to me, and making it really as good as it can possibly be. That's what I call a signature gift. Something that really helps to define who I am."
—**Ron Pevny,** founder of the Center for Conscious Eldering

A life of service: "All my life I've been living a meaningful life in service to others and I've been really lucky throughout my career in ministry and at the university to be well-loved by the people I served."
—**Steve Jacobs,** university administrator

Higher purpose: "To be myself, to be kind and encouraging, and to learn from others; my higher purpose: to love, honor, and serve God in this world and the next."
—**Ann McKerrow,** writer

Making a difference: "Being an active advocate for Alzheimer's research and development" was a life purpose chosen after watching her mother's slow decline and eventual death from Alzheimer's disease.
—**Mary Ann Esfandiari,** retired NASA senior executive and Navy Commander

---

Ask yourself the question: What is meaningful in my life right now? Maybe it's the work you do as a teacher, for example, when you see students learning. Or maybe you volunteer in a local community group where you can see firsthand how the organization helps people in need. You might have a passion for helping younger people or supporting older people, assisting victims of domestic violence, or helping people through career or life transitions. These examples relate to some of the topics in this book. Having a life of meaning is about awareness and understanding of the past and the present, allowing us to grow and flourish in alignment with our values and guiding principles.

If the word *calling* resonates with you, we invite you to consider your life as a process of calls and responses. What has called you in the past, and what was your response to those calls? What is calling you forth now? In discerning whether these calls are true or not, Gregg Levoy offers a path between two essential questions: "What is right for me?" and "Where am I willing to be led?"[5] Ask yourself, what is calling me forth today?

Purpose and calling guide our future direction and where we are headed. Some believe we are born with a calling. Whether we believe we are born with a calling or more consciously discover or choose our purpose in life, our purpose is what we say it is. Our purpose—our *why*—can be our conscious guide for who we choose to be and how we choose to live our lives. Knowing why we are here, our purpose in life provides the foundation for all other elements of living consciously in midlife and beyond.

The words *mission* and *vision* are also often used interchangeably, but it is useful to maintain a distinction between these terms. If purpose refers to the difference one wants to make in the world, *mission* is the core strategy that must be undertaken to fulfill that purpose, and *vision* is a vivid, imaginative description of how the world will look once that purpose has been realized.

A major milestone in Paul's journey through life was an inventure in East Africa led by Richard Leider, where the adventure of a walking safari across the Serengeti was combined with an inner journey of discovery. Leider, a pioneer in the world of purpose, describes purpose as an expression of the deepest dimension within us—of our central core or essence, where we have a profound sense of who we are, where we came from, and where we are going. Purpose is what gives life meaning, our reason for being, our reason for getting up in the morning.[6]

Leider talks about Purpose with a big P and purpose with a little p: Purpose with a big P is about having a big cause or a calling, while purpose with a little p refers to the everyday, asking why you are here and how you can make a difference in somebody's life today. Purpose with a big P may be more aligned to "soul purpose," sometimes considered a deeper or more spiritual purpose connected to a cause where we can have a significant impact in the world, and purpose with a little p is more aligned to purpose we define. In other words, we have an opportunity to not only *have a purpose*, but also to *live purposefully*.

Larry Ackerman, a fellow traveler on Paul's inventure in Africa, offered eight essential questions for finding your purpose and place in the world. He believes that our identity is at the root of who we actually are. Although the way we express ourselves may change any number of times throughout our lives, who we are at our core does not change. Larry sees identity and purpose as one and the same but suggests a distinction: you cannot necessarily get to identity through purpose, but you can always get to purpose through identity. He offers eight identity mapping questions for finding our purpose and place in the world:[7]

1. Who am I?
2. What makes me special?
3. Is there a pattern in my life?
4. Where am I going?

5. What is my gift?

6. Who can I trust?

7. What is my message?

8. Will my life be rich?

We asked other people how they defined their purpose. Here are examples from the interviews:

What Is My Life Purpose?

- "To unlock the power of purpose (big P purpose) and to make a positive difference in one person's life every single day (little p purpose)." —**Richard Leider,** author of *The Power of Purpose*
- "To create, integrate, and make a difference." —**Fred Mandell,** author, life transition expert
- "To advance and build up women in technology and to be a resource advocate for professional women." —**Dawn Pratt,** founder of Tech Up for Women
- "To reach as many people in as many different cultures as possible through music." —**Kathy Holly,** TV producer, vocalist/actress/musician
- "To make a practical difference to the lives of others." —**Jim Currie,** reinventing retirement entrepreneur
- "To be the joyous midwife of peace, harmony, and unity." —**Alain Gauthier,** international leadership consultant, coach, and educator
- "To create environments to help people uncover more of what they want to be to make a difference in their world." —**Hilary Rowland,** executive coach, speaker, and facilitator
- "To build a community of those in their late-stage career to pivot to work with purpose." —**Marc Miller,** author and founder of Career Pivot
- "Living an active, well-balanced life while contributing to community and giving back." —**Kathy McEvoy,** retired executive, entrepreneur, lifelong volunteer

---

Our purpose is what we say it is—so if you haven't done this already, it is now time to discover and write down your purpose. Can you do so in ten words or less? Read on to learn how to discover your purpose.

DISCOVERING OUR PURPOSE

Dreaming may be a good place to start. Envision yourself living a life of purpose; journal about your dreams. And dream big! Reach for the stars. As the saying often attributed to C. S. Lewis goes, you are never too old to set another goal or to dream a new dream. Before writing a first draft of your purpose statement, sit quietly and contemplate the purpose questions shown in the box.

Purpose Questions

- What do you really care about?
- What are you passionate about?
- What makes you cry?
- Why do you do what you do?
- What gets you up in the morning?
- What is the difference you want to make in this world?

Brief purpose statements of ten words or less are easier to remember than long, rambling sentences. The statements often begin with "to be" or "to do" something: "to make a practical difference," for example, or "to build a community." Or you can phrase your statement in alignment with the present moment, as in "*making* a difference," "*building* a community," and so on. However you choose to say it, your purpose statement may evolve over time.

Paul's purpose statement evolved from his experiences as a hot-air balloon pilot. On the website and business card for his hot-air ballooning rides operation was the tagline "taking you higher." During coaching conversations, he was able to discover and write down a life purpose statement based on a realization that his passion for ballooning was a manifestation of a much larger life purpose: "Taking people higher in spirit, in business, and in life." His writing and coaching related to living and leading consciously provides a sense of fulfillment aligned with that purpose.

Can you have more than one purpose statement? Of course! You might have a number of purpose statements, each focusing on a specific aspect of life—but having one overarching statement may provide greater clarity of purpose.

Simply putting our perceived purpose into words is not enough; we also need to align our actions to our purpose. By following our true purpose, we can turn our work life into our life's work, our vocation into our avocation, what we are paid to do into what we love to do. This can be more fulfilling than simply working for personal recognition or financial gain because it is done to make a difference in the world and for the people we serve. The power of purpose cannot be overstated. Purpose can drive everything we do, if we let it. Purpose can inspire us to leap out of bed every morning to take purpose-driven action.

CORE VALUES

Values are commonly understood as the beliefs, ideals, or customs that give significance to the lives of individuals or members of a group and that are reflected in our behavior. Our core values reflect our beliefs, determine how we perceive the world around us, and serve as a guide to our decision-making. The words we use to describe our values reflect deeply held beliefs that change slowly if at all during our adult life.

For example, our core values might include honesty, loyalty, dependability, creativity, compassion, integrity, justice, positivity, service, courage, and gratitude. Our core values evolve from early stages of our lives, and each will mean something special to us. These values tend to be stable over our lifetime, although we may prioritize new values more consciously based on our experiences and new understanding of what specific words mean.

The terms *values* and *principles* are often used interchangeably, but distinctions between these two words may prove helpful. Values often reflect the beliefs of our cultural backgrounds and provide a complex map on which conscious and unconscious behaviors are based. Values may be considered as subjective and internal, whereas principles are external and objective. Principles (sometimes also referred to as *guiding principles*) may be thought of as codes of conduct that act as a compass to more consciously guide our choices and behaviors. The more our principles are in harmony with our values, the better the decisions we will make and the more inner peace we will have. With values and principles in alignment, our principles become the external manifestation of our internal values, and we're better able to make more conscious choices.

You can start articulating your own personal values by simply making a list of your values; if you'd like to deepen your exploration, refer to some of the tools and assessments in the Resources section at the back of this book.

TRANSITIONS

We all experience many transitions in our work life, our home life, our financial situation, our relationships, and many other aspects of our complicated lives. Our identities are often where we first encounter the challenges inherent in a midlife transition.

After a longtime career, for example, we may be asked by someone we meet for the first time, "So, what do you do?" We might begin our answer by saying, "I am a former teacher" or executive or engineer or whatever we have done for all those years. Being a former "something" represents the space between who we were and who we are yet to become. The challenge can be in letting go of old identities to make space for new opportunities that can inspire new directions.

The Transition Model, introduced by organizational consultant and author William Bridges, has three overlapping stages: endings, the neutral zone, and new beginnings.[8] To effectively move forward with new beginnings, we may have to consciously let go of the past. Loss of something or someone may be a feature of many transitions—both within and beyond our control—and may also represent a gift or opportunity for something new.

Mary Ann Esfandiari became co-chair of the Patient Family Advisory Council of the Memory and Alzheimer's Treatment Center at the Johns Hopkins Bayview Medical Center after retiring from federal service in 2014 after 39 years with NASA's Goddard Space Flight Center. Mary Ann shared her story of transition and purpose discovery.

Mary Ann had watched her mother suffer and eventually die from Alzheimer's disease and her husband of 44 years get diagnosed with mild cognitive impairment, eventually leading to several strokes and death. Mary Ann retired from two very active careers at NASA and in the navy, and the death of her husband severely challenged her search for meaning and fulfillment in the second part of her life. During the interview, Mary Ann said, "It was difficult to transition from a very active working life to a retired life and then to a widowed life." What had gotten her up in the morning had seemingly dissipated. She worked through some very difficult days and nights before finding the start of a path forward. Free time without meaning, purpose, and structure was incredibly challenging. Emerging from these challenges, Mary Ann made steady progress toward the transition and was able to describe her life purpose: to be an active advocate for Alzheimer research.

These transitions may feel like crossing a river or a highway where the challenge of the crossing depends on the size of the river or the number of lanes on the highway. Or it may seem even larger, like crossing an ocean from one continent to another. Whatever the scale of the transition, we have to let go of what is known to get into the unknown territory of the neutral zone. This neutral zone represents a time for reflection, healing, and growth. It is a necessary interim stage that can help us steer away from endings before embracing the new beginnings of the future. It's important to note that although the metaphors suggest a linear process, the three phases are not always separate stages with clear boundaries; we may find ourselves stepping into new beginnings before completing the endings and neutral zone phases. Exploring purposefully can help us with knowing who we are and with navigating these life-changing transitions.

IDENTITY

Our personal identity reflects who we truly are at our core. This reflects our inner perspective of who we think we are combined with the outer perspective of how others see us. Although the perception of our identity may change, knowing our identity can be helpful.

Our identity can be described by completing sentences beginning with "I am." For example, you might say, "I am a parent, brother, friend, writer, doctor, airline pilot, or business leader." These answers express more about what we do rather than who we are, however. Another way to complete the sentence is by describing how we feel: "I am happy, sad, hopeful, depressed, loving, excited." You might also express your values: "I am caring, conscious, curious, honest, vulnerable." We could also identify ourselves by our name, age, ethnicity or nationality, social class, and many other categories.

Pause for a moment to reflect on these questions about your identity:

- Who are you?
- What is your identity?
- Who do you think you are?
- How do others see you?
- Who do you choose to be?
- What do you stand for?
- What new identity is emerging?

In many ways, our identity reflects our past and who we have become. At times we may lose parts of our identity that mean something significant to us. When we lose our job, maybe voluntarily through retirement or when being let go from a long-held position, our all-important work identity may be lost. This loss of identity can be devastating. Numerous movies with this theme have depicted someone who loses their job yet continues to pretend to go to work every day rather than admit that something significant has changed. It is common to struggle with feelings of uncertainty and apprehension following the loss of a job, which may result in a loss of self-worth or self-esteem. The grief of losing not only our identity as it relates to a job but also the day-to-day connections with work friends, customers, and other people related to our profession can result in an extended period of mourning.

Although we may experience identity crises and moments of sadness or sorrow over the loss of identity, many of us also have wonderful experiences that result in a positive change of identity. Along with moments of personal achievement, fulfillment, and joy, loss can be a launchpad for discovering initially unforeseen yet positive changes. During the early stages of the COVID-19 pandemic, 99-year-old war veteran Tom Moore began walking laps around his English garden to raise money for the staff of the National Health Service. After reaching his initial goal of 100 laps, he kept on walking. Having captured the imagination of the nation, he went on to raise more than £30 million ($25 million) and was knighted by the queen soon after his 100th birthday. Through his actions, Moore created a new identity—although at his core, his life of service remained unchanged.[9]

IDENTITY SHIFTS

As we travel through the different stages of life, we experience identity shifts, sometimes consciously choosing our identity and at other times having an identity shift imposed upon us. Changes in our work, our relationships, our health, or where we live can all bring about significant identity shifts. As we consider a conscious identity shift, here are five steps to help us face these shifts more positively:

1. **Notice moments of impact.** Take time to reflect on moments of joy and moments of sorrow you have experienced in your life. Write down what was meaningful in each experience.

2. **Reflect on these moments of impact.** Find a quiet space for contemplation or meditation on the experiences of these moments of heightened awareness. Note the thoughts and feelings that arise as you consider these experiences.

3. **Describe your current identity.** Select specific aspects of your identity such as your values, your role, your stage in life, or any other category, and complete sentences beginning with "I am. . . ." Write as many statements as you can.

4. **Consciously choose your desired identity.** Look into the future and consider who you want to become, which existing identities you want to change, and which you want to keep. Write new "I am . . ." statements as if you have already realized a new identity.

5. **Begin forming the new aspects of your identity.** Take responsible action to begin your identity formation process. Select an identity statement or group of statements and decide what needs to change to embrace a positive identity shift.

Identity shifts in the second half of life, especially as they relate to work, may involve rebranding—something we'll explore more fully in chapter 5. For now, let's keep thinking about identity as it relates to purpose (and those purpose statements you've been thinking about here in this chapter).

Identity and purpose—the who we are and why we are here—are interconnected. We may sense a calling from a higher power or we may choose how we describe our life's purpose. We may have a changeless core, but we can choose many aspects of our identity. Maybe it is time for us to take a fresh look and make choices about who we want to be and what we stand for.

Many of us have aspirations for making a difference in the world. Sometimes our actions change our identity in the eyes of others, as in the example of Tom Moore, yet it was perhaps his changeless core, his inner identity that inspired his actions without any idea of the huge impact he was to have on the lives of so many. Maybe it is time to consciously wake up and consider who we are and who we want to become. Who do you choose to be?

REINVENTION

Transitions in the second half of life provide wonderful opportunities for reinvention. We can consciously change our identity, create new visions of the future, and discover or reenergize our life purpose. It is never too late to change course and transform our lives.

A well-known story of transformation is that of John Newton, in the late eighteenth century. As a young man he had a reputation for violent and angry behavior. He worked on slave ships and was himself a slave before eventually becoming a captain on his own slave ship, the *Duke of Argyle*, making trips from the islands off the west coast of Africa to America, where he sold the slaves. The beginnings of his identity shift—a spiritual conversion, if you like—resulted from his experiences of a storm off the coast of Ireland. He later renounced his role in the slave trade and became an abolitionist and an Anglican priest. He is now best remembered for composing, for a New Year's Day sermon in 1773, the words to the hymn "Amazing Grace." He spent many years campaigning for the abolition of slavery, and died in 1807, the year it was abolished by the British Parliament. His story affirms that we can consciously choose to turn around or redirect our lives and establish a new identity consistent with emerging values and guiding principles. We should never give up on ourselves, no matter where we have come from or what we have experienced. It is possible to choose our new identity and discover our new purpose.

There are many examples of personal transformations, both positive and negative. Stalwarts of society held in high regard can quickly fall from grace due to moments of poor judgment. Convicted felons, having served their time, can transform to live a life of service to others. In her recent book *Who Do We Choose to Be?* Margaret Wheatley asks, "Who do we choose to be for this time?"[10] Consciously exploring our purpose, choosing our identity, setting intentions, and taking responsible actions present a significant opportunity as we transition from adulthood into elderhood.

In this chapter we have explored purpose and meaning, core values and guiding principles, and identity shifts and life transitions—representing the center of our Conscious Living Wheel. Your purpose,

vision, mission, values, and identity can be encapsulated in a Personal
Conscious Living Manifesto referenced in the Resources section at the
end of this book. In the following chapters we'll visit each aspect of
the wheel in turn: living well, appreciating money, working for a living
and working for fulfillment, savoring the world, living life creatively,
minding relationships, helping humanity, living with technology, and
bouncing forward. Before moving on, we invite you to reflect on your
identity and purpose with the questions here.

CONSCIOUS LIVING PRACTICES

Questions for Reflection

- What is your life purpose? Why are you here? What gets you up in the morning?

- What is your vision of what the world will look like when you are truly fulfilling your purpose?

- What is your identity? Who do you think you are? How do others see you?

- Who do you choose to be? What new identity is emerging?

- What do you have to let go of to make space for your new identity?

Try This

- Describe your purpose in ten words or less.

- Develop a Conscious Living Manifesto referenced in the Resources section at the end of this book.

Living
Well

Bouncing
Forward

Appreciating
Money

Living with
Technology

Working
for a Living

Exploring
Purposefully

Helping
Humanity

Working for
Fulfillment

Minding
Relationships

Savoring
the World

Living Life
Creatively

CHAPTER 2

LIVING WELL

We don't beat the reaper by living longer, but by living well and living
fully—for the reaper will come for all of us. The question is what do
we do between the time we are born and the time he shows up.

–RANDY PAUSCH

L iving well is about living our healthiest, fullest, and longest life.
What does "living well and living fully" mean to you? You may be
wondering how to stay healthy and happy as you get older. The
good news is that we have more control over how we age than not, and
can take steps to support our optimal well-being.

A multitude of changes can occur in midlife and beyond, and we
want you to be well prepared for them. In this chapter, we focus on
the mental and physical health-related aspects of well-being. We share
information, perspectives, and planning guidance on nurturing both
our mind and body in the hope that you'll be inspired to take conscious
steps to your optimal well-being. Planning for now and the future is
essential for living consciously and living well.

Health defined by the World Health Organization (WHO) is "a state of complete physical, mental and social well-being and not merely the absence of disease or infirmity."[1]

Wellness refers to a conscious lifestyle intent on achieving the highest potential for well-being. *Well-being* refers to one's subjective sense of life satisfaction and balance with the many facets of one's life. We prefer the terms *wellness* and *well-being*, as they reflect dynamic intentionality and encompass multiple life dimensions of a holistic approach.

One health metric is longevity or life span. There is a distinction between our *life span*—how long we live—and our *health span*—how long we live while being healthy. A gap exists between the two, and our life span is often longer. For example, a US study revealed an average 12-year gap as being potentially unhealthy years.[2] Another health metric is *life expectancy*, or our average general life expectancy based on one's *current* age and birth year using information from the US Census and Social Security statistical data. A hundred years ago, life expectancy at birth in the United States was 55 years; roughly a century later it averages 79 years (with women living on average three to five years longer than men), a gain of 24 years.[3] Those "extra" 20-plus years gained in life expectancy are frequently referred to by healthy living and positive aging thought leaders as "bonus years," "encore years," or the "third age," to signify an emergence of a new life stage. This new life stage arrives with uncertainty and yet excitement for the infinite possibilities that can exist for each person.

Numerous studies reveal that our life span is multifactorial, influenced by our genes, our lifestyle choices, and our environment. Studies done on the general population and twins indicate that our genes account for approximately 20–30 percent influence on our life spans, leaving 70–80 percent not predetermined.[4] Although our genes can put us at risk for some diseases, our lifestyle choices can influence whether those genes "turn on" or not, impacting both our life span and health span.

We do not know precisely how long each of us will live. What we do know is that our health is foundational to supporting our overall well-being, and we can make choices that have a positive influence. These multidimensional factors can affect both the length and breadth of our lives.

Our Conscious Living approach applied to living well is based on Attention, Intention, and Action (A-I-A). Attention comes from *awareness* of ourselves, others, and the world around us and includes listening and learning with an open mind. *Intention* involves thinking about possibilities, prioritizing, and thoughtful decision-making. *Actions* are our behaviors representing our intention to act responsibly—in this context, being aware of what influences our health and making conscious and mindful decisions in alignment with our health and well-being goals.

NURTURING OUR MIND AND BODY

THE MIND

Our living well approach is being aware and conscious of our thoughts and values to help guide our actions, which is foundational to our Conscious Living Wheel concept. By making intentional decisions and engaging in activities supporting our well-being, we engage in the "inner work" of our well-being.

MINDSET MATTERS

Mindset refers to your beliefs, attitudes, and opinions you hold about the world and yourself. Research tells us mindset can influence our thoughts, decisions, behaviors, and even our physical body and health. It is a powerful area to consider as it relates to our beliefs in the second half of our lives. Pause to reflect on your beliefs: What do you think of aging? What do you think about your ability to navigate forward? What do you think of some negative cultural stereotypes of aging? How do your beliefs affect what you think, do, and experience?

Mind and body work in tandem, exhibiting "mind-body unity," explains psychologist Ellen Langer.[5] Our mind and body "talk" to each other, providing information at various levels of consciousness or awareness. Our thoughts and perceptions influence our decisions and behaviors and how we perceive and experience aging. With an *open mindset*, Langer believes that we are mindful about being aware and open to new ways of thinking, perceiving, and being, whereas being *mindless* is relying on one's usual frame of reference, habit, rule, or routine. Being mindful and open as we age allows us to be flexible and receptive to new ideas and possibilities in terms of envisioning our next life chapter, as opposed to falling into the trap of viewing aging as a downward decline. An open mindset allows us to consciously choose beliefs and behaviors that will support the journey ahead.

Another way to think about mindset is to understand the difference between a fixed and growth mindset, as explained by Stanford University Professor Carol S. Dweck.[6] An individual with a fixed mindset believes that our capacities regarding intellect and personality are set and not alterable, whereas someone with a growth mindset focuses more on continual learning and improvement. With a growth mindset, attempts and "failures" from trying something new are simply part of the process of living and provide useful information for what comes next and a sense of ease with exploring new paths. Consciously choosing a growth mindset provides us with agency and infinite possibilities for new ways of being and living well. It voids the saying "you cannot teach an old dog new tricks."

Research on positive psychology, which is focused on the science of well-being, reveals that our mindsets are powerful components in living well and aging well. Yale researchers led by Becca Levy found that thinking positively about aging extends a person's life by 7.6 years, even when taking into account other factors such as age, gender, and socioeconomic status.[7] Accepting aging as an inevitable natural process with open-mindedness about the possibilities can add interest, vitality, and life to your years ahead.

Martin Seligman, often referred to as the "father of positive psychology," developed the PERMA Model of Well-Being, which includes the five building blocks to well-being or what he calls "flourishing."[8]

The **PERMA**[9] Model encompasses

- **Positive emotions** and simply having enjoyable experiences that elicit emotions such as joy, hope, happiness, and gratitude, and savoring those emotions to keep them present and active

- **Engagement** *and* immersion in pleasurable activities where one can lose track of time, often referred to as a state of flow

- **Relationships** that provide a sense of belonging and support

- **Meaning** and purpose to one's life

- **Achieving** or accomplishing a task or project; a sense of mastery of something

Reframing is one initial way to approach problems when they develop. Using positive psychology, the reframing of a situation shifts the idea of a problem to one of a challenge by focusing on what is working, with the goal of generating solutions. Far from engaging in denial, reframing acknowledges and addresses reality with a positive focus on what is working already and possible solutions to move forward. For example, you might tell yourself, "I'm too old to learn to take a class on the computer." *By reframing*, you might instead say, "Although I'm older than I was last year, I do use the computer, and I can be resourceful and ask for help from people I know and also look up answers to questions I encounter along the way. I can try taking a computer class and see what I learn."

The positive aging movement takes into consideration the science of positive psychology in how one thinks, behaves, and experiences the challenges and opportunities as they age. The Positive Psychology Institute defines positive aging as "the process of maintaining a positive attitude, feeling good about yourself, keeping fit and healthy, and engaging fully in life as you age."[10] While challenges do occur as we move along our life journey, we can choose a positive aging approach to address those challenges for the plethora of health and well-being benefits it offers.

MINDSET AND MEANING: A POWERFUL DUO TO LIVING CONSCIOUSLY

As we explored in chapter 1, meaning is a powerful aspect for giving purpose to our lives. Fred Mandell, author, artist, and founder of Creating Futures That Work, found himself at one point in his life wondering how long he could continue doing what he was doing in a successful career that no longer engaged him in the way it had when he started. So he asked himself, "What keeps me alive?" His mindset, purpose, and meaning influenced his decision to take a financial risk. He chose a new entrepreneurial path that made him feel fulfilled and purposeful and allowed him to make a difference in the world. Health, he explained, definitely has a financial dynamic. He reported to us that if he really needed to make money, he could find a way to align that with his current interest. As it turned out, he became successful in his new path (though he did also have a backup plan, just in case). His story illuminates the inspirational pull of the envisioned vitality that arises from living life with purpose.

Shawn Perry, executive producer and host of *The Senior Zone*, a radio program dedicated to his purpose of helping the 50-plus community, states that his health *is* his wealth, and that he would rather have it more than any amount of money in the bank. He attributes his health and well-being to his DNA, mindset, healthy lifestyle, and living his life with meaning and focused intent.

As you think about mindset, pause to reflect on these questions and what you may choose: What type of mindset do you desire for your life part 2? What will provide you with the optimal mindset going forward? What mindset has helped you in the past, and how could it be helpful in the future? What role models can provide further insight? Being open-minded to possibilities, being a learner, and the acceptance of aging as a natural process are the first steps to an optimal mindset.

EMOTIONAL AND MENTAL HEALTH

Our mental health in the second half of life can be affected by many factors, including job loss, ill health, relationship breakdowns, bereavement, and money worries. Older adults make up 12 percent of the population in the US but account for 18 percent of all suicide deaths.[11] How one handles stress significantly impacts our emotions and mental frame of mind—and ultimately our health, well-being, and longevity.

Research by Elizabeth Blackburn and Elissa Epel reveals that our lifestyle choices can impact our longevity and health markers called *telomeres*.[12] Telomeres, which can be envisioned as protective shoelace caps on our chromosomes, represent our biological age: They shorten with stress and aging. Long telomeres are associated with a longer and healthier life. Their findings add to the significance of the mind-body connection and our ability to think, act, and live consciously. Our lifestyle choices can lead to telomere-shortening behavior or telomere-supporting behavior.

Supporting behaviors relate to basic nutrition, exercise, sleep, stress management, and social support. Mindfulness, meditation, and other stress management techniques such as yoga have shown to be instrumental in lengthening telomeres. Stress reduction strategies include practicing slow deep-breathing techniques, listening to music, and simply spending time out in nature.

Our mindset has a significant effect on our life span and health span as it relates to managing stress. Stress increases the stress hormone called cortisol. The overexposure to cortisol can be disruptive to many cells in our body and to other hormonal and cellular pathways that control our organs and their function.

How do we approach stress? Is it from the perspective of a negative threat, a challenge to be conquered, or a situation to avoid? Or is it from a perspective of stress being viewed as a regular part of life where we can be resourceful, tapping into supportive practices and strategies that lead to building our resiliency?

The desire to lengthen our telomeres and thus our life is really about taking responsibility for what we have influence and control over, such as our mindset and lifestyle. This can potentially earn us more time to live our lives with purpose and passion. The goal is not simply about lengthening our life but rather to embrace the totality of it—the full length and breadth. Living well and aging well is all about *applying* our knowledge of what mindsets and behaviors help us live and thrive with passion and purpose. It is Conscious Living at its best.

Let's think about and plan for ways to engage and stimulate our mind, as well as ways to soothe and rest it.

Stimulating the Mind: Self-Growth and Lifelong Learning

The self-growth aspect of the mind and brain is centered around adopting a lifelong learning mindset. It is about being curious, creative, and taking initiative to follow and pursue your interests. Self-growth is about being open to new learning and new ideas and using our critical thinking skills. One way to do that is to take classes such as those with the Osher Lifelong Learning Institute (OLLI), Road Scholar, or your local university or community colleges and recreation centers. See the Resources section at the back of the book for further ideas.

The coronavirus pandemic of 2020–2022 created more virtual paths for learning. A huge number of offerings are available online, such as those from MasterClass and the Smithsonian. An internet search will reveal a plethora of free and for-purchase classes and those that can be audited free or for a reduced fee if over a certain age (and don't hesitate to ask for that senior discount if it isn't mentioned!). Or perhaps there is something that you know and are passionate about and can teach to others. Your possibilities and choices are infinite!

Taking or teaching a class adds to our cognitive reserve. An upside of living and aging is we have accumulated knowledge and experiences, called *crystalized intelligence*,[13] that we can apply as a bridge to our future for problem solving. Crystalized intelligence relates to the continuity theory of positive aging, which means taking part of our past and applying it to the present and future to tackle new challenges in a continuous process. It is having a repertoire of experiences and knowledge to pull from. What interests do you already have that you could develop further to stimulate your mind? What are some new interests you might start to pursue? Maybe you want to volunteer in an area you've always wanted to be part of. Whatever it is that you've always wanted to do, now is the time to start.

Soothing the Mind: Practices

One way to soothe the mind from all the thinking, tasks, and tabulations we do is to engage in mindful meditation, also known as mindfulness, which is a practice of simply being aware in the moment of what you are sensing and feeling without any judgment.[14] It can include simple breathing exercises such as slow, long breaths, which have been shown to calm our minds as evidenced by participants' verbal statements as well as reduced heart rate and blood pressure.

Guided imagery and other practices keep the focus on the "now" rather than on worries about the past or the future. Mindfulness is a way of reducing stress, and many mindfulness apps are available online to try, such as Insight Timer, Smiling Mind, Headspace, and Calm. Discover what soothes your mind and integrate that into your life.

Soothing the mind can be as simple as being out in nature, whether for a few minutes or for a walk. Betty McDowall, a social justice advocate, told us that being out in nature near water is especially restorative for her. Some find music soothing, while others find a form of movement such as yoga or walking helps them to relax. Donna Kraus, a business owner and yoga instructor, shares that after losing her husband and being overwhelmed with grief, yoga became her calm, solitary sanctuary and that being with friends and family also quieted her mind and supported her well-being when she wanted company. What activity, whether active or passive, alone or with others, soothes your mind?

Our immediate environment of where we place our head to sleep at night impacts our well-being. Is our home a place of serenity and calm, or is it a Grand Central Station of activity? It does not have to be either/or; our environment can be anywhere on the continuum and can change from week to week. What is important is whether your home is what you want it to be. You may be happily focused on activities and not so much on the physical surroundings, or you may be focused on the physical structure and looks. Discover and create a home environment that meets your needs and desires. Just knowing that your surroundings impact your well-being can be helpful to seeing the big picture and how it plays a part.

Consider your outdoor environment as well. Is there a space that you can go to in your backyard, balcony, or local park that is restorative to you? "Forest bathing" or "vitamin N" are terms used for being with nature, and research reveals it can soothe our mind and support our well-being. Perhaps you might hot only walk outside but also consider bringing the outdoors inside, with a few plants or by adding a small aquarium.

THE PHYSICAL BODY

Our mind is impacted by the health of the body, especially the brain. The brain allows us to think, make decisions, and be intentionally conscious with our behaviors, as well as regulate our body. Let us look closer at the brain before moving on to the rest of the body.

Our brain's ability to process information impacts our functioning and independence. In midlife and beyond we may worry about the risk of cognitive decline. Multiple studies have revealed brain health to be supported by being mentally engaged and stimulated with a variety of interests, activities, and anything new and challenging.[15] Brain health is also related to whether we perceive situations as being a threat or a challenge and what we employ to reduce our stress levels. Yaakov Stern, a neuropsychologist and researcher, states that activity, movement, and exercise not only allow for improved circulation to the brain but also a thickened cerebral cortex and increased brain volume, which in turn improve cognition.[16] A plant-based diet such as the Mediterranean diet, with a focus on vegetables and fruit rather than a red meat–based diet, has advantages because it reduces the amount of saturated fat that can negatively affect the blood vessels and circulation. A diet rich in inflammatory-producing foods can negatively affect our health and brain. Ensuring that our hearing and vision are at their best also contributes to our overall cognitive processing. Getting adequate sleep also supports our brain health. Significant research findings reveal that deep, restful sleep helps clear toxins such as the beta amyloid, which is found in the brains of those with Alzheimer's disease.[17] Brain health is critical for making decisions and for being independent.

Brain plasticity or neuroplasticity refers to the ability of our brains to change in response to experiences and stimuli so that new connections and pathways are formed or existing ones are altered. New brain cell formation (neurogenesis) can occur, and the extent of it in adults is still being studied. Research findings reinforce that having an open or growth mindset to discovery and new learning in our thoughts and behaviors can allow for rewiring and the development of new brain pathways for cognitive enrichment.[18]

A particularly noteworthy and encouraging series of studies dealing with conscious decisions and behaviors showed that there are individuals who have the physical markings of Alzheimer's disease such as plaques and tangles, yet they do not show the symptoms of the disease and are able to adequately operate cognitively. Why is this so? Why do some show the manifestations of the disease while others do not? Studies suggest that higher levels of education or cognitive learning and social connections provide a protective factor called *cognitive reserve*, delaying the appearance or expression of outward symptoms. Individuals who remain cognitively sharp in their eighties and nineties and perform better on memory tests compared to those of similar age are referred to as "cognitive super agers."[19] Cognitive reserve provides a basis for hope, especially if cognitive decline is in one's family history.

Since restful sleep supports a vital role in clearing and "cleaning" the brain, we can utilize technology via health monitors and apps to measure and aid sleep. We will be talking more about how technology can aid in living well in chapter 10.

In addition, the general bodily aspect of well-being refers to the basics such as breathing, eating, drinking/hydrating, sleeping, and exercising/moving. These become even more important when we undergo changes as we age, and our lifestyle choices can make a big difference in *how* we age. Online life-expectancy calculators provide insight into how long you may live based on your responses to questions on lifestyle, habits, and current health. It takes a few minutes to answer specific questions, such as how often you move, whether you include vegetables with your meals and how often, and whether you smoke or drink. Project Big Life in Canada, for example, provides online life-expectancy calculators run by researchers, clinicians, data scientists, and developers to educate the public on the impact of their lifestyle choices. They also provide calculators for sodium consumption, dementia, cardiovascular disease, and more. You may find that making a few tweaks to your lifestyle choices can net you more healthy years.[20]

Assessing what we know about these basic areas and how we are doing is a good idea so we can decide what we want to continue, stop, or start doing. Although these basic body well-being aspects may not seem new to you, we encourage you to consciously reevaluate them and choose what will lead you to your optimal physical wellness.

Before starting something new, we advise you to get advice on any health-related plan from your physician. Always talk with your healthcare provider for further clarity on your own unique wellness and well-being path. Having a healthy, strong, and trustworthy patient-doctor relationship is at the core of your health and well-being. This unique relationship and rapport have been proven to improve patients' health and their overall outcomes.[21] Choose the doctor or healthcare provider you feel comfortable with; this will promote not only your physical health but also your emotional health.

EATING TO LIVE WELL

Food provides our energy to live and thrive. Having guidelines on what to eat can help us make conscious choices for the best fuel to optimize our body's functioning. From the famous Blue Zones study on the longest living communities, we know that a plant-based diet, along with the practice of stopping eating when 80 percent full, allows the satiety signal in our brain to register that we are satisfied.[22]

Low-fat, lean sources of protein such as fish or chicken are preferable over red meat. If you choose red meat, choose lower fat versions. Protein can also be obtained from beans and dairy. Lower-fat milk choices are widely available, and milk alternatives address lactose intolerance. Using egg whites can limit the amount of cholesterol in meals. Some individuals split their full egg consumption by using half egg whites and half full eggs.

As we get older, the digestive process and metabolism can slow. Diverticulosis, the development of pockets or pouches in the colon, is often the result of a diet low in fiber. It becomes problematic when food gets stuck in a pouch and it becomes inflamed (diverticulitis). Eating fibrous fruit and vegetables, along with hydration and exercise, can help keep the digestive system running smoothly. Be mindful to avoid overprocessed foods, as they are low in fiber, can cause inflammation, and are often high in calories.

Other factors to consider are the need for vitamin D and calcium. Vitamin D aids the absorption of calcium, which is needed for bone health. With the loss of estrogen, postmenopausal women are at risk for thinning bones (osteopenia), progressing to bone loss (osteoporosis). Bone density tests and blood tests for vitamin D levels can provide more information related to risks for bone breakage. Calcium and vitamin D supplements can help, and it is best to talk with your physician regarding your own situation. Salt, caffeine, and alcohol can negatively impact your bone health. You may find that certain foods affect you negatively, so you might also consider asking your healthcare provider about food sensitivities, intolerances, and allergies relating to dairy products, gluten, and more.

If you find all of the choices overwhelming, ask for more help! You may want to seek out a certified nutritionist or dietician who can examine your eating habits, food choices, and preferences to help you develop a healthy plan.

HYDRATING TO LIVE WELL

We are approximately 70 percent water, and we need it to live. Hydrating with water allows your body to smoothly process temperature regulation, digestion, elimination, and circulation. Hydration is a vital factor in staying well by circulating our fuel and enabling efficient body functioning. The Mayo Clinic states that striving for eight cups of fluid daily is still a reasonable goal.[23] Being well hydrated is particularly important while exercising, including walking on hot and humid days. Age and some medications make us more vulnerable to dehydration, which can lead to heat exhaustion, especially as we may not sense thirst as an indicator to hydrate.[24] Be mindful to limit liquids such as caffeinated or alcoholic drinks, which are diuretics that affect the balance of water in the body, as well as sugary drinks, which can add empty calories.

RESTORATIVE SLEEP

As we get older, our sleep patterns can change. Learning how to adjust so that we get the optimal quantity and quality is key. Sleep benefits our cognitive health, boosts our immune function, supports body repair, and rebalances our mood and well-being. It sets us up for a successful day. Our beds are essentially recharging units. The concept of "sleep prep" practices or rituals can also be thought of as "sleep hygiene."

They are simply the best practices for promoting a good night's sleep. Powering down by turning off our digital devices in the evening and keeping their lights out of our bedroom can make a difference, as well as darkening the room and limiting the stimuli that keep our brain awake, such as TV.

It is not unusual to have challenges with getting to sleep or staying asleep. Working late, viewing digital blue light, drinking coffee or alcohol, experiencing stress, or dealing with changing circadian rhythms, hot flashes, or the need to urinate more frequently can all be factors. Suggested sleep-inducing strategies include setting up a regular, predictable bedtime, reducing bedroom temperature, and employing powering-down strategies such as listening to music, turning down the lights, taking a shower, or having a small cup of herbal tea with catnip. (Yes, you read that right: catnip is known to soothe the mind.) Avoid checking email, exercising, eating, and drinking large amounts of fluids before going to bed. You can find apps that provide music and relaxation guides, and even apps to monitor how many hours you are actually sleeping. Discover what works for you so that you get in your zzzs.

If you still have trouble getting to sleep or staying asleep, talk with your healthcare provider. There may be other issues to check for, like sleep apnea. A whole medical specialty is dedicated to sleep-related conditions, and your healthcare provider can connect you with a sleep medicine specialist for evaluation.

FITNESS AND MOVEMENT

Movement and mobility are key to health and moving forward in life. The American Heart Association and many others cite the multiple benefits of physical activity as a mood lifter, muscle strengthener, and helper in maintaining healthy weight, bones, and circulation.[25]

Movement is considered a life extender by seven years for those who are at a healthy weight and physically active.[26] Movement contributes to our overall flexibility and our stability. Physical activity is considered so important that universities offer educational curriculum with a degree in exercise and movement science, where students learn how to teach others to integrate activity into their lives.

Just as a car generally performs best when it is driven, the same is true for our bodies. If we leave our cars unused for a period of time, the battery may lose charge and not start the engine, or the oil may thicken and the moving parts lose lubrication. The analogy applies to our bodies, too. If we do not exercise or engage our mind, we decrease our capacity for full functionality.

We involuntarily lose muscle mass as we age, starting around midlife—between 3 percent and 5 percent per decade.[27] Loss of muscle mass is accelerated by a sedentary lifestyle, unbalanced diet, inflammation, and severe stress. James Levine of the Mayo Clinic is credited with the statement "sitting is the new smoking," as it pertains to the detrimental impact upon our health. He is also credited with the treadmill desk to encourage folks to be active.[28]

Our muscles are important for strength, stability, mobility, balance, circulation, and bone health, all of which allow us to be more independent so we can walk, go up and down stairs, and be less prone to falls and injuries. It is important to secure and sustain these benefits by engaging in some form of movement. There is a type of exercise for everyone. If you are not currently active, you can begin with small steps or even exercises while sitting. The great benefit about exercise is that there is a whole continuum, and you can combine it with elements of what you already like to do. For example, if you like the idea of soothing the mind and relaxing the body, then yoga, stretching, and tai chi may be for you. If you like socializing, then seek out group classes or meetups such as walking with others.

What Gets You Moving?

- **Dorian Mintzer** (therapist, author, coach) enjoys different levels of activities to match her energy such as gardening, walking, riding her e-bike, and pickleball.
- **Jim Currie** (reinventing retirement entrepreneur) has a personal trainer, lifts weights, dances, and swims.
- **Kathy Holly** (TV producer, vocalist/actress/musician) believes in walking as a daily exercise for longevity of physical and mental health. She prays while walking and meditates to support her well-being.
- **Kathy McEvoy** (retired executive, entrepreneur, lifelong volunteer) starts her day with stretches and yoga. She and her husband chose to move to a warmer state so they both could participate in more outdoor activities.

Maintaining movement and mobility can include these choices: Start your day with it! Put exercise on your calendar like an appointment; include others in an activity or join a group; listen to music, a talk, or book while moving; get a health or exercise coach, or use an exercise app to inspire you; and walk to more places—even short walks count. Discover what works for you.

Lifestyle choices influence the length and breadth of our lives, and positive ones add up. For example, Dan Buettner, a longevity expert, identified five world regions called the "Blue Zones" where the longest-living and healthiest people live.[29] He discovered longevity commonalities and distilled them into nine key lessons highlighting movement, moderate eating, plant-focused foods, de-stressing, and more. See the Resources section at the back of the book for more information.

Darrell Green, Football Hall of Famer cornerback known as the "ageless wonder," provides us with an inspiring example of putting it all together and being a model for senior health.[30] After retiring from an amazing two decades of football, he found that he was gaining weight. Conscious of this, he built a vegetable garden and began eating plant-based, low-carb food. By choosing a healthy lifestyle, he has more energy for family, faith, and his work in the athletic program at George Mason University. Tom Brady, another ageless wonder, has actively played football for 23 years and won seven Super Bowls and also relies on plant-based meals, hydration, exercise, nightly restful sleep, and a positive mindset.

PLANNING FOR LIVING WELL

Given all that we need for healthy minds and bodies as we age, how can we best plan for living well? Being pro*active* is key. Delaying, deferring, or avoiding health concerns can potentially diminish your ability to take care of something smaller upstream, only to discover something larger and more menacing downstream.

Proactive physical health practices include getting regular physicals; wearing medic alert bracelets or identifiers, if you need them; staying up-to-date with vaccinations for flu, shingles, and pneumonia; and undergoing screening tests such as colonoscopies, mammograms, bone mineral density scans, prostate screening, and lab work for cholesterol, blood glucose, and hepatitis C. Be sure to keep your allergy records updated and your prescriptions renewed, especially any emergency medications such as epinephrine that treat anaphylactic reactions to allergens such as bees or foods. We suggest keeping a current medication list in your wallet or mobile phone and making a list of people to call in an emergency. You can also keep a record of your doctors, their specialty, and their phone numbers, as well as the pharmacy you use. Being proactive is helpful for both regular doctor visits and emergencies.

To our female readers, it is important to discuss menopause with your healthcare provider. Menopause is a spectrum, with some women having every symptom in the textbook and others sailing smoothly through it. Whatever your own experience may be, this stage of life can be an opportunity to take charge of your health and make positive lifestyle changes that promote your well-being. Don't be ashamed or afraid! Menopause is a natural process and, most importantly, one that we can't escape—so we may as well embrace it. With the right approach and support, women can manage the symptoms and reduce the risk of developing chronic health issues.

For our male readers, midlife is when the prostate can cause problems due to an enlargement or cancer. Difficult or frequent urination that interferes with sleep or activities are both symptoms to discuss with your doctor. Ensure that a PSA or prostate-specific antigen blood test is drawn to obtain a base or an updated level. Another problem that can occur is erectile dysfunction (ED), which may be related to heart disease or diabetes. Although it may feel like an uncomfortable topic, it is best to address any concerns with your doctor.

You can also be proactive about your healthcare by reviewing your health insurance plan to see what is covered. A visit for a physical may require a co-pay, for example, whereas an annual wellness visit might not. This will depend on the type of insurance you have. In the United States, annual wellness visits are generally covered under Medicare, though there are some criteria for coverage with participating providers and the length of time on Medicare.[31] Whatever your insurance may be, it will be of benefit to have a visit with your primary care physician for health assessment, promotion, and planning.

It's also a good idea to be proactive with your visits to dentists and ophthalmologists. Inflammation around our gums can affect the heart, which can negatively affect other parts of the body. Ensure that your dentist performs a visual and digital oral-cancer-screening exam of your mouth. Age is a risk factor, with diagnosis often occurring after age 40.[32] Our vision is essential for our independence and mobility too.

Some eye problems do not have symptoms until it is too late, such as glaucoma (increased eye pressure), so get those eyes checked out.

Another way to plan ahead is to consider your home environment. Certified Aging-in-Place Specialists (CAPS) can evaluate your home for safely aging in place and can make recommendations for changes and upgrades. Sometimes it is a matter of making a few adjustments, such as adding grab bars in the bath area, changing a tub to a shower, or adding lights around steps and walkways. Or you might rethink where you live altogether—for example, you might decide that you want to find a new walkable community that might fit in better with your plans of independence or upgrade to a newer home with a "universal design" approach that is accessible and usable for people of all ages and abilities.

Even if you feel a new home is not something you need at this moment, if you're active and mobile, we still encourage you to think ahead. A little planning can go a long way!

PREPARING FOR SUDDEN, UNEXPECTED HEALTH CHANGES

Even if you are a proactive planner, sudden health changes and emergencies can and do pop up unexpectedly. A car accident or a fall might change your physical condition drastically, for example, or a minor symptom, upon diagnosis, turns out to be much more serious and requires extensive treatment.

Being proactive with gathering data about your current health, your health history, emergency contacts, and doctors' names and contact information will be an advantage when time is of the essence. Identify people who have agreed to take care of family members or pets if needed. Writing the information down and sharing it with the appropriate people will prove helpful. Drawing upon your own strengths, asking for help from family and friends, and utilizing a healthcare team and support groups as needed will benefit you. You may also find yourself suddenly needing a caregiver, or being one yourself, for a partner, parent, or friend. Your healthcare team can suggest resources. Also remember that being a caregiver involves self-care.

PREPARING FOR CAREGIVING

The impact of caregiving on our health is significant if we do not take measures to support our own well-being. We often provide caregiving in addition to our usual job and are not compensated with money or stress relief. The impact becomes even greater if you are taking care of a parent as well as your own kids, or if the care receiver is residing in your home. Individuals often do not realize the full impact of caregiving until they get sick and cannot adequately fulfill caregiver duties. Eileen had the experience of understanding this dynamic, as she was a direct professional caregiver in her nursing career as well as a personal caregiver for her mother. Gleaning from what she learned, Eileen teaches classes on helping caregivers build personal and practical strategies to support their well-being. Being open to asking for help, accepting offers of help, and taking time to de-stress and find sources of joy are all important. In addition to your healthcare team, know that support groups are available for information and emotional support on a vast variety of health issues.

Some of the people we interviewed had insights to share as well. Dorian Mintzer, a therapist and founder of the interview program RevolutionizeRetirement.com, points out that if you are in any type of a relationship, you will be a caregiver or receiver or both at various times in your life. She advocates for caregivers taking time for rejuvenation and being okay with asking for help; being fiercely independent can actually be a liability. At the same time, she says that she knows having a network of friends and colleagues of different ages can be a real plus. Dorothy Keenan, founder of GrandInvolve, a volunteer organization partnering seniors with local schools to support education for vulnerable students, tells us that having her own major health incident helped change her perspective on what it means to be healthy. As a caregiver for her mother and mother-in-law, she also came to appreciate how life changes when one's health is affected and that it's important to recognize that you can decide how you will respond. Choosing to be kind despite being ill was one way they all coped.

CREATING YOUR PERSONAL HEALTH RESOURCE PLAN

We advocate creating your own personal health resource plan. This includes utilizing not only your healthcare providers but other resources such as books and educational health programs to assess and support your physical and mental well-being. Accessibility to healthcare systems is another key factor to consider in creating a plan. How far do you have to travel to your doctor's office? If you can't drive yourself, how would you get there? You might also consider complementary and alternative medicine such as meditation, biofeedback, or hypnosis, and creative outlets such as music and the arts.[33] We suggest exercising caution with any dietary supplements and discussing your considerations with your physician.

Your resource plan should also include the relevant legal paperwork such as a living will, healthcare proxy, and a health durable power of attorney that address planning for disability and eventual death. It's better to have your desires written out and voiced than not having your wishes granted when you cannot speak for yourself. Having conversations with relevant family members and your doctors can take the guesswork out of potential difficult decisions and bring clarity to decisions and actions that will be in alignment with your own wishes.[34] See Resources for help with having these conversations with family members. Because we do not know what the future entails, it is best to make these decisions consciously when your awareness, insight, and cognitive capacity are functioning well.

Additionally, there are groups that provide a discussion platform about our lives being finite called "Death Cafes," which are said to provide inspiration to live full, purposeful lives and give insight to making plans to not only leave a meaningful legacy but actively live it too. Whether you attend one of these or not, dying is part of our natural life cycle, and it can be helpful to include some thought on what would constitute "dying well" in your health resource plan.

LIVING WELL MANTRAS AND ACTIVITIES

Another way to be proactive is to create your own mottos and reminders for living well. Think of them as mantras that draw upon the wisdom you've accumulated and that can now be put into practice to best support yourself for your journey through the second part of life.

Susan O'Neil became more health-oriented as she got older. She remembers a pivotal moment at her 50th high school reunion when she saw an image of a tree with the names of individuals from her class who had passed away. As a result, her mantra became "All I can, while I can."

Bob Ruggiero describes himself as "retired and still playing" and says that "well-being is having your health and the ability and means to enjoy it and do what you want to do without worry." He was in a Cape Cod coffee shop and saw a saying on a napkin along the lines of "You don't stop playing when you get old. . . . You get old when you stop playing!" The essence of this quote is attributed to George Bernard Shaw. The statement resonated with him, providing the motivation to stay healthy and fit. And to this day his mantra is "If you can do it, do it! Don't wait!"

What might your own mantra be? A profound realization or insight relevant to an event or situation can be a prompt to develop a well-being guideline for yourself. For example, your 60th birthday or your last child getting married may prompt you to now act on your interests, creating a mantra such as "Now is my time to flourish."

Consider creating an acronym to remind you of specific key well-being ingredients. Select words that represent well-being to you and try to make a word with just the first letter of each of your gathered well-being words. You will have to play with this a bit to get it to form a new word. Once completed, this acronym can be written out and then put on your bathroom mirror or framed in your bedroom so you can see it daily. See the following example.

Dr. Nadine Hammoud, a board-certified gynecologist, shared with us her well-being reminder acronym, "Prosper":

P for pleasure to live life fully with meaning and purpose

R for respecting your body, people, and nature around you

O for being optimistic and open-minded to receiving and trying new changes

S for spirituality: having beliefs in place, values, or religion

P for having a positive attitude and perspective about life and current situation

E for empowering your body and mind through exercise and engagement

R for restoring, relaxing, de-stressing, and resilience

Another exercise we suggest is to think about developing a "life list" of activities you want to enjoy and places and people you want to visit. We prefer referring to it this way instead of the familiar term "bucket list," which suggests that these are things to do before we are "done." "Life," on the other hand, keeps the focus on what makes life delightful. It is a subtle, yet powerful, word difference.

Some activities are best enjoyed when the body is agile and flexible, so we suggest being adaptable when thinking about those things on your life list. For example, Dorian Mintzer shares that she and her husband like to bike. Over the years they have found that it takes more energy to go up a hill than it did before—so now an electric bike helps them out.

What does your own "life list" look like? Life lists are often inspired by places and experiences we want to have and the people we want to share them with. We suggest using the Conscious Living Wheel to select a specific spoke that calls to you, such as "Savoring the World," and within that ask yourself where you would like to visit and the experiences you want to have there. For example, you could select the Canadian Rockies as a destination and then riding in a gondola or hiking as activities, or a dream vacation to Norway and seeing the northern lights. Include who you want to share those experiences with. Another spoke you could select is "Living Well," and then asking yourself what would be a fun, healthy activity, where would you like to do it, and with whom. You could select the popular sport pickleball or line dancing to learn with a friend at the local recreation center.

In this chapter we explored the first dimension of the Conscious Living Wheel: Living Well. We've offered ideas and insights on health, wellness, and well-being and encouraged you to plan ahead with a positive mindset. Before we turn to the next topic, we invite you to reflect on some of the ideas you can do to enhance your mind and body.

CONSCIOUS LIVING PRACTICES

Questions for Reflection

- How can you increase your health span so it will be closer to your life span?

- What mindsets can you try out to support you in the midlife path ahead?

- What can you do to improve your emotional and mental health?

- What are some key actions you can take to support your physical body?

- How can you develop your own personal health resource plan?

Try This

- Use small time slots for activities during the day. Even a 10-minute walk will make a difference!

- Try out new activities: join a group, get a health or exercise coach, or download an exercise app to keep you motivated.

CHAPTER 3

APPRECIATING MONEY

What you appreciate appreciates.
–LYNNE TWIST

Living consciously requires us to be increasingly conscious about our money: making it, saving it, managing it, spending it, and leaving it behind. Many of us experience financial challenges in each of these areas. Thinking about and talking about financial matters can be difficult, but to develop a Conscious Living mindset and live more consciously we must embrace and face our financial challenges. In this chapter, we explore concepts of our inner money consciousness and then address the more tangible aspects of financial management— the outer world of money consciousness—along with some practical money management advice.

Some of us may feel as if we've been striving to achieve financial freedom for our entire lives. Even if we have money, we may never think that we have enough. We may also find money a difficult topic to discuss. Some of us avoid simple practices that would help us prepare for living the good life beyond our early careers without worrying about whether or not there will be enough money later on. Lynne Twist, author of *The Soul of Money*, says, "What you appreciate appreciates: In the context of sufficiency, appreciation becomes a powerful practice of creating new value in our deliberate attention to the value of what we already have."[1] We can appreciate money and how it can help us in the second half of life.

Whatever your financial situation may be, we want to bring about greater awareness of potential shifts in your thinking. For example, shifting from a sense of lack to a sense of sufficiency, from financial fear to financial confidence, and from scarcity consciousness to prosperity consciousness. We share some ideas and stories about creating wealth and growing rich with a sufficiency mindset. According to Peter Diamandis and Steven Kotler, authors of *Abundance: The Future Is Better Than You Think*, "It's not about creating a life of luxury for everybody on this planet; it's about creating a life of possibility."[2] In our view, accumulating wealth is more about the possibility of supporting a wonderful lifestyle for ourselves and our families and contributing to the well-being of others less fortunate than ourselves than about getting rich for our own indulgence.

While we are not financial advisors, investment experts, or economists, we share a Conscious Living approach based on international experience of managing personal and business finances, extensive study of retirement strategies for those in midlife and beyond, and the development of our own philosophies and practices relating to money.

COMMON BELIEFS ABOUT MONEY

Money is an integral part of our lives, yet we are often not fully aware of our beliefs around money. Our life stories influence and create our money stories. Many common beliefs around money can be limiting beliefs. So how can the energy of money be harnessed to shift away from those limiting beliefs toward beliefs based on possibility thinking, and how can we align money consciousness with our life's purpose?

In an ideal world, we would all learn about money before we left the security of our family home. Yet money can be a taboo subject, and many of us learned by listening to the words and observing the actions of our parents and other family members. Some of us remember growing up in homes where money was rarely discussed except in the context of frugality. Postwar Britain, with recent experiences of rationing, was in recovery during Paul's childhood, for example, and money was mostly discussed in the context of what the family could or could not afford. A philosophy of saving before spending and avoiding debt wherever possible was ingrained from an early age. This led to a strong belief that without careful money management, there would never be enough money. If you were born a decade or two later, your family experience with money might appear to have different beliefs such as viewing impulsive spending and credit card debt as the norm.

David Shriner-Cahn, host of *Smashing the Plateau* and *Going Solo* podcasts, told us, "I grew up in a family where money wasn't talked about. And so what I've learned about money, I've pretty much learned on my own, and yet, at the same time, there's some stigma associated with the money that I still hear in my head from my childhood. When I'm working with other people it doesn't play out, but when it's my own money, it's very interesting how those issues are still around. I have often taken too long to take action and I was reluctant to charge enough."

Not worrying about money is not the same as not caring about money. Claude Morency was 84 years old when Paul first met him. He had spent 25 years sailing the South Seas on a 38-foot sailboat where his backyard was the ocean. He said, "Money is something I never worry about. I found out when I was very young that you should follow your spirit without hesitation, and the universe will always rearrange itself to accommodate your picture of reality. I have some investments and my pension. There is nothing I can think of that I could possibly need. I could have more money, but so what? I have enough." Married at 80, not for the first time, Claude described his life with his new wife as "the most beautiful thing that has happened to the both of us." Claude took care of his money, but his philosophy of life was "don't worry about the money."

Although Claude's story presents a view of a happy person not worrying about money, many of us are not like Claude, and we experience major money worries. We suggest speaking with a certified financial planner with fiduciary alignment to best assess and plan for optimal financial well-being. We're not advocating focusing so much attention on money that you miss out on other aspects of your life, but we know that *not* talking about money can limit us financially as well.

Limiting beliefs about money can prevent us from building new positive beliefs. Numerous phrases capture those limiting beliefs about money that can constrain our possibilities and our potential. Do these limiting beliefs sound familiar?

- You have to have money to make money.
- The rich get rich; the poor get poorer.
- Rich people are not happy.
- There is never enough money to go around.
- If I have more, others will have less.
- The more money you have, the more problems you have.
- Making money requires hard work.
- The love of money is the root of all evil.
- It's selfish to want a lot of money.

- I'm just not good with money; I should be better at this by now.
- If I make a lot of money I will be less spiritual.
- You can't get rich doing what you love.
- I'm too old to get rich.

How do these beliefs affect us as we move into midlife and beyond? What are our positive beliefs around money, and what possibilities stem from them? How can we transform some of the beliefs into a more positive money consciousness mindset?

Lion Goodman, creator of the Clear Your Beliefs program and the Belief Closet process, believes you can delete negative thoughts and limiting beliefs. An initial inquiry begins with three questions:

1. What do I want? (your destination)
2. How can I get it? (your path)
3. What's in my way? (your obstacles)

After addressing these questions, Goodman offers a three-step process to uncover your beliefs, understand your beliefs, and then create new beliefs.[3]

Another way to shift from limiting beliefs about money toward more positive beliefs is to change the narrative. Personal transformation expert Sonia Ricotti[4] suggests reprogramming our brains from limiting to positive beliefs like these:

Limiting Beliefs about Money	Positive Beliefs about Money
Money doesn't make me happy.	I choose to be happy with the money I have.
I'm not smart enough to be rich.	Within me I have everything it takes to be rich.
It's hard to make money.	It's easy for me to make money.
Money isn't important to me.	Money is a powerful tool that can help me.
It's too late for me to make money.	I can make money at any age.
I'll never be rich.	I can be as rich and abundant as I desire.
Money is the root of all evil.	Good things can be done with money.
Making money is out of my control.	I have complete control over my finances.
If I'm spiritual, I can't be rich.	I can be spiritual and have financial success.

The financial philosophy of T. Harv Eker, president of Harv Eker International, an online personal success training company, focuses on our inner work in relation to money. Here are some of his thought-provoking wealth principles:[5]

- Consciousness is observing your thoughts and actions so that you can live from true choice in the present moment rather than being run by programming from the past.

- If you want to change the fruits, you will first have to change the roots. If you want to change the visible, you must first change the invisible.

- If your motivation for acquiring money comes from nonsupportive roots such as fear, anger, or the need to prove yourself, your money will never bring you happiness.

- If your goal is to be comfortable, chances are you will never get rich. But if your goal is to be rich, chances are you'll end up mighty comfortable.

- Where attention goes, energy flows and results show.

- Thoughts lead to feelings, feelings lead to actions, actions lead to results.

There are numerous aphorisms and advice about money beliefs to be found (see the Resources section at the back of the book for more recommendations). Let's explore how they relate to our relationships with money in more detail.

RELATIONSHIPS WITH MONEY

Having the right relationship with money may help us as we think about money in the context of our transitions in midlife and beyond. Our relationships with money have been shaped by our life experiences, and those experiences influence our personal money characteristics, beliefs, and practices. How would you describe your own personal characteristics relating to money? Are you indulgent? Reckless? Guarded? Obsessive? Controlling? Indifferent? Nonchalant? Charitable? Generous? Chances are your relationship with money reflects some of these personal characteristics, and these characteristics may reflect your beliefs about money. Consciously exploring and nurturing our relationships with money can be a truly valuable process.

In her book *The Soul of Money*, Lynne Twist describes money as being like water flowing through our lives, sometimes like a rushing river and sometimes like a trickle, yet with the potential for purifying, cleansing, and nourishing our souls.[6] Accumulating wealth may be important during our years of full-time working, although without a clear purpose, our relationship with the accumulated wealth may not be so healthy. Our culture encourages us to measure our success in terms of how much money we have, yet we hope our success in life is measured by much more than our financial assets.

Having the right relationship with money is about managing the subtle inner tensions we carry about money. Deepening our relationship with money can create huge value shifts and not just in our financial net worth. Our relationship with money reflects and affects every area of our lives: our friendships, intimate relationships, self-worth, career, health, and spirituality.

So what is your relationship with money, and what is your money story? How do your beliefs about money show up in your life? What do you tell yourself about money? Step back in time. What messages did you receive about money as a child? Did you consider your family to be poor, rich, middle class, or something else? Have you had any major money moments in your life—big successes, painful events, struggles, or breakthroughs? Becoming conscious and aware of our money stories is an important first step in understanding our relationship with money and, if necessary, beginning to change our money stories going forward.

Our direct relationship with money is changing. Bank notes and coins, although still necessary, are being increasingly replaced by credit and debit cards, electronic wallets, and bank-to-bank transfers. Unless we consciously keep track, we may have no idea if we are spending more than we should. Some of us keep careful track of our spending, but it's easy to miss something and find an unexpected debit at the end of the month. Paying for goods and services online does not always feel like spending "real" money, so we need to be aware of our habits.

Having explored how we can consciously shift our beliefs about money from limiting beliefs to more positive beliefs and also the importance of having the right relationships with money, let's explore the age-old question of how much is enough?

HOW MUCH IS ENOUGH?

One way to answer the question "How much is enough?" is with the shoulder-shrugging response, "How much do you want?"[7] There may be many things we think we want—the latest sports car, a luxury cruise, a second home, or expensive jewelry—but can we afford them? Do we really need them? Even if we can afford them, having more than enough can bring difficult choices.

So what does enough mean to you? Perhaps it means enough time to do the important things, enough work (paid or unpaid) to feel valued, enough community or camaraderie to feel nourished, enough love to feel warm inside, and enough money to spend on the necessities of life with some left over to make a difference in the lives of others. The question is, can we recognize when we have enough? This is an important query to use for reflection, particularly for those among us who are collectors. For example, for many years Paul collected paperweights, many of them made in Scotland by Caithness. Some he bought himself; others were gifts. The variety of sizes, shapes, colors, and patterns of the pieces in his display case represents beauty, imagination, and creativity. He recognizes that he has enough of them, but when he sees a new design he is often tempted to buy just one more. Maybe you collect jewelry, tools, technology, kitchen items, books, or something else you love. As we get older, we have the opportunity to rethink what having enough really means for us. As the saying goes, "Enough is a decision, not an amount."

Before we move on to the more practical issues around having enough money in midlife and beyond, let's explore the concept of scarcity and its relationship with abundance and sufficiency. Lynne Twist has described many positive reflections on how money can serve as a vehicle for fulfillment of our life's purpose and how a sufficiency mindset is more powerful than a scarcity mindset or even an abundance mindset.[8] Here are some differences between a scarcity mindset and a sufficiency mindset:

- **Scarcity mindset:** never enough, emptiness, fear, mistrust, envy, greed, hoarding, competition, fragmentation, separateness, judgment, striving, control, busy, survival, *outer riches*

- **Sufficiency mindset:** gratitude, fulfillment, love, trust, respect, faith, compassion, integration, wholeness, commitment, acceptance, partnership, responsibility, resilience, *inner riches*

See the difference? While the fear of scarcity is understandable, shifting to a sufficiency mindset frees up energy for us to make a difference in the world with what we have. Take a moment to reflect on what a sufficiency mindset means for you.

CONSCIOUS MONEY PRACTICES

The inner work of your relationship with money may reveal your desired lifestyle in the second half of life. Perhaps you want to reduce the time you spend working for a living or maybe start a new entrepreneurial venture. Or maybe you want to remodel your home or downsize by moving elsewhere. Perhaps your desired lifestyle includes travel or new hobbies. Converting these dreams into reality will require a degree of financial planning. Understanding the cost of these dreams is critical as you figure out how to transition from a full-time career to whatever you hope will come next. Will you have enough money to turn your dreams into reality?

If you don't have a clear and accurate picture of your spending habits, now is the time to start. Make a list of all of your significant assets: home, savings accounts, pension funds, anything that has a significant financial value. Find a spreadsheet template online or create your own spreadsheet listing all of your assets with their current value. At the beginning, monitoring these assets quarterly can help identify trends: which assets are appreciating; which are depreciating? Conduct an end-of-year review, estimating and recording end-of-year values. Once you have enough data, you can compare trends based on end-of-year values over previous years.

Tracking expenditures may be more difficult, although the principles are the same. List the main spending categories: mortgage or rent, property taxes, utility bills, transportation, insurance, groceries, vacations, family gifts, and a miscellaneous category. List the main categories and subcategories as needed on paper or in the first column of a spreadsheet. Create columns for each month, and monitor your monthly expenditures for a year. What do you notice? Once you know what you currently spend, you can begin to look at possible changes as life unfolds.

The final piece of the puzzle is income. As an entrepreneur, you may have multiple streams of income, or, if you are an employee, a regular paycheck. Monthly income may be consistent or highly variable, but either way, track your income along with your expenditure and keep a record of annual income. Consider how your income may change in the future as your lifestyle changes.

Tracking income and expenditures and projecting into the future can give insights into what is possible. Of course, there are no guarantees, so give some thought to the risks: health issues, relationship changes, and other family matters. Avoid simply relying on the 80 percent rule, which assumes post-retirement expenses to be 80 percent of preretirement expenses. Retirement is not what it was. Your income may be higher or lower. Your cash flow may be impacted significantly by changes in health and healthcare costs, changes in retirement income, and how the lifestyle you hoped for eventually materializes. Map out your retirement cash flow based on multiple scenarios to gain confidence in your perspective of how much will be enough.

Now let's examine conscious money practices in more detail: from making money and funding retirement, to managing your money and becoming debt-free, and spending your savings after you eventually stop working for a living.

MAKING MONEY

By the time we get to midlife, we have likely learned how money flows into our lives. We may be working hard, devoting long hours to paid employment. We may have advanced degrees or special skills or personalities that have resulted in high-paying occupations. We may be entrepreneurial, creating financially successful businesses with multiple income streams. We may have inherited wealth from relatives who have passed on. Pause for a moment and consider how money has been flowing into your life.

Although money may be flowing into our lives, money is also flowing out. The challenge in the early days of the second half of life is increasing the net inflow and building a nest egg to support a long and happy life. Maybe you started early and are well on your way to financial freedom, or maybe, due to a range of legitimate reasons, you have no financial assets on which to build. Maybe you're well past midlife and realize you haven't saved enough. Whatever your current situation, getting clear about your goals and intentions around making money is essential.

Let's look more deeply at goals and intentions for making money and achieving financial freedom. Our money goals should be very specific and clearly stated. Our intentions around money are more about our philosophy of money and how we show up as we raise our money consciousness. Most of us aspire to financial freedom: a state where we have no money worries, where we have enough to see us through and are confident that we won't outlive our money. Let's pause and think about your specific money goals.

Visualize yourself at a time in the future when you have realized your dream of financial freedom. You are living the good life, doing the things you dreamed of doing. You are not worried about the money. You have financial freedom. What does your life look like? Now think about where you are now. How can you get from where you are now to the financial freedom you dream about? What specific goals are important to you? These goals might be longer-term goals focused on the transition from a full-time career to whatever you want to come next. You may also define goals for the short term that are essential to pave the way for working on those long-term goals. For example, your goals might include

- To be able to retire from full-time work in ten years with no loss of spending power
- To be debt-free by the time I am 60 years old
- To ensure that my partner is financially secure if I should die first or encounter a major health issue
- To go on a world cruise on a milestone birthday or anniversary
- To support my children through college.

You can make your goals more specific by adding monetary and time-bound targets. Take a moment and write down three money goals that are important to you. Be as specific as you can.

Next, let's explore some practical ways to shift toward more positive money consciousness that will lead to financial freedom.

Jack Canfield, a pioneer and legend in the field of personal development and peak performance and founder of the billion-dollar Chicken

Soup for the Soul publishing empire, is another inspiring teacher. One of his 67 success principles is *pay yourself first*.[9] What does this really mean? Canfield recommends investing at least 10 percent of what we earn and making that investment inaccessible for expenses. Paying yourself first requires the financial discipline to save at least 10 percent of what you earn, investing wisely, and not spending the accumulating nest egg unless your income declines below your expenditures. If you can save more, that's great—but 10 percent is a good place to start.

In simple terms, building wealth requires you to do two things: 1) increase the difference between your income and expenses, and 2) save that difference and grow it exponentially over time with careful investment. That, of course, may be easier said than done. The question to ponder is, what is your fastest path to more money?

Here are some possible strategies to consider:

- **Increasing income:** seek out higher income streams, find a higher-paying job, improve education and skills, take on additional side hustles, start your own business

- **Reducing expenditures:** eliminate high-interest debt, stop spending on unnecessary luxuries, mercilessly cut spending on things that don't serve you, avoid impulse shopping

- **Growing investment:** pay yourself first, increase monthly savings, develop investment strategies, diversify investments, hire an independent certified financial planner, track investments rigorously

If making money is a high priority for you now, take action to increase income if possible and reduce unnecessary expenditure. Plan to save a percentage of your income with a focus on saving enough to support your desired lifestyle in later years. Let's look specifically at saving for retirement.

FUNDING RETIREMENT

Retirement is perhaps the largest purchase of our lives, yet most of us find ourselves underprepared. Regardless of your age, you may have significant concerns about funding your retirement as you transition from a full-time career into whatever comes next. You are not alone! The average cost of retirement has been estimated as being about 2.5 times that of the average house. It's truly the purchase of a lifetime. Three major forces are transforming the challenge of funding retirement: the massive baby boomer retirement wave that continues to dramatically increase the retiree population, increasing longevity, and dramatic shifts in the retirement funding formula.[10]

What if you're approaching or are already past your planned retirement age and realize you haven't saved enough? What can you do? One strategy is to keep working, but that may not be so easy. A recent report from the Transamerica Center for Retirement Studies[11] found that more than half of retirees (56 percent) in America retired sooner than they had anticipated because of job loss, ill health, and family responsibilities, among other reasons. The coronavirus pandemic may also have caused people to consider transitioning out of the workplace sooner than planned. Working longer can be a smart strategy to bridge gaps in retirement savings, but it cannot be relied on as the only strategy. In addition to the wealth-building strategies described earlier in this chapter, you might need to seriously consider downsizing. Even if you have paid off your mortgage, the costs of home ownership—particularly property taxes, utility costs, housing association fees, and maintenance—can be a sizeable drain on your retirement income. You may be enticed by the numerous equity release plans or reverse mortgage offers you see, but before taking that step, research the implications and talk to a trusted financial advisor and family members about the risks and rewards of this approach.

If you are able to continue working, income generation may be a priority. See the ideas and strategies offered in the next chapter, "Working for a Living," including entrepreneurial endeavors and multiple streams of income.

Now let's explore some money management strategies.

MANAGING MONEY

Perhaps one of the most important differences between financial success and financial failure is how we manage our money. Making money requires a growth mindset with strategies that create wealth. Managing money builds on this moneymaking mindset but requires more specific money management practices. We can set up daily, weekly, monthly, and yearly practices to engage with our income and expenditure figures. Managing our finances requires a more conscious approach to budgeting, earning, spending, and saving. The goal is to do it all in ways that are personally meaningful, aligned with our values and beliefs, and with awareness of our relationships. At the same time, we need to keep the increasing life expectancy in mind and consider that retirees will need to fund more years in retirement.

Managing money requires us to manage our cash flow. We must build on our wealth-creation strategies as our lifestyles change. As we age, we are likely to have more ability to manage our spending than to control our income. How conscious are you about your spending practices? Conscious spending is not about frugality; it is about awareness and choice. It is also about eliminating wasteful spending practices that no longer serve you. Review your expenditure tracking analysis we explored earlier in this chapter. What stands out in your analysis? How much money are you wasting?

We all view wasteful spending differently, and one person's waste may be another's necessity. Here are some common ways we waste money:

- Luxury purchases sometimes exemplify Thorstein Veblen's concept of conspicuous consumption.[12] If you stop trying to impress others, think how much you will save!

- Making minimum credit card payments when you could afford to pay more and avoid the interest payments

- Buying expensive beverages at the coffee shop on the way to work rather than making your own coffee at home

- Paying for memberships and subscriptions you no longer need

- Replacing household items before they are worn out

- Having someone do the work around the house that you could easily do yourself

What would you add to this list? How do you waste money?

BECOMING DEBT-FREE

Debt can feel like a heavy burden. Every month you may have to pay the mortgage or rent, the car loan, and worst of all, accumulated credit card debt. Debt is not always bad, but paying interest is a waste. Getting control of your debt, paying it down, and becoming debt-free is an essential part of managing your money. Here are seven steps to become debt-free:

1. Stop incurring debt. Cut up some of those credit cards and spend only the money you already have.

2. Know what you owe, itemizing all current debts with their interest rates.

3. Set a debt-free target date that is both realistic and challenging.

4. Create a debt elimination plan with attention on wasteful spending and disciplined debt consolidation and repayment.

5. Begin reducing debt by paying off loans with high interest first.

6. Monitor debt reduction progress monthly.

7. Celebrate progress toward becoming debt-free.

We may encounter family or health crisis situations where there is no alternative but to borrow money. Don't let these life events curb your desire to be debt-free. When these crises occur, take time to consider the best loan strategy. Look for the lowest cost of the money you need. Talk to your financial advisor, your bank, and even family members. Maybe someone in the family will help out so long as you commit to a repayment plan. Borrowing against your pension may be possible, but if you take this route, plan to pay back this loan as soon as you can. Be aware that taking money out of retirement accounts too early may incur penalties. Keep your eye on the goal of being debt-free.

SPENDING YOUR SAVINGS

At some stage, we may find ourselves transitioning from earning a living to spending in retirement. This can be a frightening financial transition from saving *for* retirement to spending *in* retirement. Government pensions, referred to as Social Security in the United States, will be one source of income. You may have a company-sponsored pension, or you may have saved well using pretax income. Conversations with your financial advisor will be essential as you explore the financial issues surrounding the topic of spending in retirement. Even if you have sufficient funds to support a comfortable transition away from the regular paycheck, this can be a psychologically stressful period. In addition to your financial advisor, a life transitions coach may help prepare you for impending lifestyle changes.

MONEY IN RELATIONSHIPS

We've explored our personal relationships with money, but what about the way money influences our relationships with others? Money can be a major source of tension and stress in our relationships with family, friends, and business associates. Couples may have different beliefs about money: one may be a spender, the other a saver. Financial contributions to household budgets may be uneven. Life partnerships take different forms these days, adding to the complexity of money in relationships, and with such high separation and divorce rates, disentangling can be treacherous.

In long-term relationships, couples may have developed practices to deal with issues around money, finding ways of sharing income and spending responsibilities through conscious conversations or by simply falling into unconscious money management practices. In some relationships, one person takes care of the money with varying degrees of involvement from the other. Some create a joint account, while others keep money totally separated. No one way meets the needs of everyone, and many couples find it hard to talk about money. Even worse, according to Olivia Mellan, author of *Money Harmony*, "Money is a primary cause of marital discontent and discord."[13] Talking about money is essential for the well-being of a relationship and for being confident that, should the relationship end for any reason, money would not be a source of concern.

A recent coaching session highlighted the importance of couples setting aside time to discuss financial matters. Mateo and his partner had been together for over 22 years, but a recent house move had resulted in a significant capital gains tax liability that highlighted some deep-rooted yet unspoken concerns for both him and his husband. Although individual incomes were now about the same, this hadn't always been the case, and contributions to major purchases had varied over the years.

They had both funded a joint account for monthly expenses, but one of them contributed significantly more for the new house purchase and arbitrarily stopped funding the joint account. The immediate question was how the capital gain tax liability was to be apportioned and where the money was going to come from.

One of them had cash available to pay the entire tax bill; the other had company shares that could be sold, with some timing constraints. In the past, the one with the cash had brushed aside discussions about payment, saying it could be sorted out later. The lack of specific conversation around the principles of agreed financial responsibility and a fundamental belief in equity and fairness left much unspoken and a feeling of tension in the relationship. This was compounded by tentative plans to leave full-time careers and transition into more relaxed, purpose-driven lifestyles.

Ultimately, a candid conversation about the payment of the capital gain tax and about long-term financial contribution arrangements cleared the air and created an even stronger foundation for an ongoing meaningful relationship without fears about unspoken financial worries. But many couples fail to plan for changes in the relationship and the effect of breakups, divorce, new relationships, blended families, or the death of one. Who's managing the money in your relationship? Have you been hoping for the best or planning for the worst? What is one small step you can take to learn more about money management?

Conscious conversations about money are essential for couples early in a relationship, especially when planning for transitions in the second half of life. Couples manage money in different ways; some have joint accounts for everything, others maintain separate accounts, and some have both separate and joint accounts. Each approach has advantages and disadvantages, and it is often difficult to make major changes later in the relationship. Money can be a difficult topic to discuss even in the most committed relationships, but having conversations about our individual philosophy and intentions around money is essential to the well-being of both partners.

> "My husband took care of the money. I was not interested in it, so when he died, I had to learn from scratch. An accountant helped me, and that is one thing that I passed on to my kids—how to manage money! So learn how money works and how to manage it." **—Betty McDowall,** a social justice advocate

How confident are you that if something happened to your partner, you would be able to manage your finances? Or if something happened to you, how would your partner cope? Higher life expectancy means that women in relationships are more likely to become widowed and at an age earlier than men. Although same-sex couples may have less significant differences in life expectancy, the challenges of losing a partner are similar. What is one small step you can take to learn what is needed to handle your finances in light of an unforeseen loss of a partner? It's best to start sooner rather than later. If you're a couple preparing for midlife and beyond, we recommend this checklist:

- Take an inventory of respective responsibilities, some of which may be taken for granted.
- Review bills and payment schedules.
- Assess how income and expenses may change.
- Communicate locations of important documents such as wills, bank account information, and passwords.
- Create a physical container for copies of important documents.
- Talk to your adult children about your financial arrangements and the locations of important documents and valuable assets.

- If you experience the loss of a partner, avoid making important financial decisions too quickly during an emotional time.

Whatever stage you're at in the second half of life, have some conscious money conversations. Review where the money is coming from and what might change if your partner passes on. You may already have a joint bank account for day-to-day expenses. If you don't have a joint account, open one and make sure you both have access at the bank and online. Agree on the funding of the joint account and maintain the account balance at a level that can sustain a surviving partner for an agreed period of time.

FAMILY ISSUES

Beyond our relationships with partners, many of us have other family members to consider. By the time we reach this stage of life, our family relationships may have become intertwined. Blended families and relationship changes later in life may bring added tensions. Again, take time to have essential conversations about money. Hold family meetings to share individual and joint philosophies about money, and share your intentions for how you would like to see your wishes interpreted. Where there are potential conflicts, encourage open dialogue, surface possible disagreements, and find common ground.

Think carefully about potential life-changing events that could affect the financial aspects of the relationship. What if a family member desperately needed financial support? What if one of you became unable to earn an income or if one of you passed away? Have conversations with each other and trusted family members. Consider drafting a financial togetherness agreement that documents current assets and agreed actions should life-changing events occur. These may not be easy conversations but may be a priority for many people.

LEAVING MONEY BEHIND

If your financial situation is such that you will have enough to leave some behind, estate planning is another essential conscious money practice. This is what Lynne Twist, in her book *The Soul of Money*, calls the "legacy of money consciousness."[14] With a legacy of sufficiency, we may have accumulated wealth that we can leave to our family and the causes we are passionate about. If you have wealth that may incur inheritance tax, estate planning may help ensure that the government takes no more than its fair share.

Planning for leaving money behind may be as simple as writing a will that directs how your money should be distributed. We want to be responsible for those we love, but with the complexities of many family relationships, you may also wish to consider setting up a trust that allows money to be managed on your behalf after you've gone. For example, money can be set aside to support your spouse while they are alive and then distributed according to your wishes when their life comes to an end.

If you have more complex family situations or a high net worth, comprehensive estate planning may be needed. In addition to your last will and testament, consider revocable living trusts, advance healthcare directives, and a financial power of attorney. This is a complex area for which we advise seeking the advice of specialists, such as a trusted estate planning attorney.

PRACTICAL ADVICE

Consciously considering your relationship with money can help open up discussions with your partner or other family members. As we've noted, you may also want to engage the services of professionals who can help—so in this section, we offer some practical advice.

SELECTING A FINANCIAL ADVISOR

Consciously selecting a financial advisor you can trust is an important step in managing your money. Recommendations from friends and family can be a good place to start, but also take the time to learn more about the different financial planning services available to you before contacting a financial advisor.

Some financial advisors make money from sales commissions from third parties offering financial products such as insurance plans, investments, and annuities. Others are described as independent fee-only financial advisors who earn money from the fees you pay for their services. These fees may be charged as a flat fee, an hourly rate, or as a percentage of the assets they manage for you. Some do both, deriving part of their income from third-party commissions and part from direct fees. In the United States, fee-only financial advisors usually describe themselves as fiduciaries and are bound by fiduciary duty, meaning that they are legally required to always act in the best interests of their clients and to place clients' best interests before their own. Advisors who earn third-party sales commissions on the financial products they sell to you are not bound by this fiduciary duty. If you choose to work with a financial advisor who earns sales commissions, you need to take extra care. Here are some questions you might want answered before selecting a financial advisor:

1. How do you get paid?
2. If fees are charged, how are the fees determined, and what am I getting for the fee?
3. What are your qualifications and experience as a financial advisor?
4. Who are your typical clients?
5. What is your investment philosophy?
6. What happens if for any reason you are not available when I need you?

If you're not quite ready to work with a financial advisor (or don't have it in your budget to do so), you can consider "robo-advisors" or digital advisors to help you achieve your financial investment goals. Robo-advisors provide an online, low-cost investing platform that uses software algorithms to create and manage investment portfolios via the internet without direct human interaction. Financial professionals typically design the investing strategies employed by robo-advisors. The ongoing day-to-day management of the portfolios is handled by computers. With relatively low minimum investment thresholds, online robo-advisors can be a great place to experiment with small-scale investing without the need to engage with an expert financial advisor. But be cautious, as some robo advice models may not meet regulatory and anti–money laundering requirements.

TRUSTED RESOURCES

These days, access to your financial accounts and other essential documents is increasingly through rapidly advancing technology on our digital devices. Remembering passwords and being able to reset them when necessary is challenging while we are in the best of health, but what if you or a close family member is incapacitated or has passed away? Is there someone who has access to your financial accounts and other essential documents? As a minimum, print out a list of the accounts and store it in a safe place. Select and brief a designated family member about where to find everything and your wishes for managing your money. Consider appointing a power of attorney who can legally act on your behalf if you are unable to take action on your own.

Educating ourselves about the financial matters described in this chapter is important. Local and online classes, free financial counseling, and numerous books and video programs from trusted sources all provide valuable information to support your financial journey through the second half of life. Visit the Resources section at the end of this book for more information.

Living consciously requires us to become more conscious about money. In this chapter we have explored our inner beliefs around our relationship with money and considered the question of how much is enough. We have also explored our outer work around money and provided some conscious money practices about making money, managing money, and leaving money behind. Conscious conversations about money with partners and family members as we journey through the second half of life are important. We invite you to further reflect on your relationship with money with the following questions.

CONSCIOUS LIVING PRACTICES

Questions for Reflection

- What are your beliefs about money?
- What does a sufficiency mindset mean to you?
- What are your financial goals?
- Which money practices require increased attention?
- What do you need to do to prepare for managing your finances in later life?

Try This

- Dialogue with yourself. In service of self-discovery, open your journal and have a conversation between two opposing characters that are part of your inner voice, for example, sufficiency and scarcity, courage and fear, the saver and the spender, and so on. You may begin with the dialogue already in your head, that negative inner voice or gremlin conversation, and then move to the desired dialogue, the conversations you want to have. Write out the script in your journal or, if you have a good friend, act it out with a vocal dialogue. Then begin to tame those gremlins, those negative inner voices.

- Document all income, expenditure, and asset information for yourself while you are alive and for your family after your death.

- Explore trusted resources to support your financial future.

Living
Well

Bouncing
Forward

Appreciating
Money

Living with
Technology

Working
for a Living

Exploring
Purposefully

Helping
Humanity

Working for
Fulfillment

Minding
Relationships

Savoring
the World

Living Life
Creatively

CHAPTER 4

WORKING FOR A LIVING

I don't live to work; I work to live.
—NOEL GALLAGHER

During our early careers we work to earn enough money to support ourselves and our families. At times it may feel as if work is all there is and that we're just living to work: working because we have to, not because we want to. As we journey into the second half of life, our feelings about work may change. Although we may still have to work for a living, we may find we have more choices about our work life. In this chapter and the next, we explore the differences between working for a living and working for fulfillment—and how we might begin consciously examining the kind of balance we want to find as we move into the second half of life. We focus on work reimagined, working longer, reskilling, recareering, rebranding, and moving to entrepreneurial options.

THE MEANING OF WORK

The word "work" conjures up different images and definitions for each of us. We may think about work as purely transactional: a job where we give our time and energy in return for money that we use to pay the bills. This is why we often hear people talk about work in terms of stress, drudgery, or "the daily grind." If this is our mindset, then it's no wonder that we all want to work hard so we can leave the daily grind and find a life of less stress and freedom.

As we approach midlife and beyond, the meaning of work and what it brings us may begin to change. Maybe it is time for a mindset shift, where work becomes more than just a paycheck. For some the workplace is a sanctuary, where friends gather together for a common goal and a place to commune with others. For others it may be an opportunity to use enjoyable skills that are in alignment with our values and beliefs. Whatever work represents for you, the definition is evolving. The good news for many is that work is becoming less about a job and more about a sense of self, identity, and purpose. The impact that our work has on our customers, our communities, and the world gives us a reason for being. We want to feel as though our work has meaning.

It is an exciting perspective that there is no one-size-fits-all approach when it comes to decisions about career and working later in life. Some may be ready for a career intermission to figure out what's next, while others may not have the luxury to take time off and to fulfill their dreams. Earning a living may be a necessity, so staying in your current job may make the most sense. It's important to look at what work means to you. There is a continuum of working for a living from a primary source of income; to where you go to learn, use your skills, develop new ones, and share knowledge with others; to infusing your purpose in the work you do. Where do you fall on the continuum?

Work certainly isn't drudgery for everyone. Theoretical physicist Stephen Hawking once said, "Work gives you meaning and purpose, and life is empty without it."[1] Hawking achieved scientific greatness despite a severe physical disability, all while displaying a zest for life that seemed quite miraculous under the circumstances. Work can be an opportunity to provide value to others and the community, and it gives you something to do with your intellectual and physical energy. If we love our work, why would we want to retire? However you feel about your work, we are living in a world of possibilities and conscious choices. How will you look at what you do for a living in new ways with fresh perspectives?

CHANGING PERCEPTIONS OF WORK

As we travel into the second half of life or start thinking about what's next, there is often a sense of endings and beginnings. There may be a letting go of the old to embrace new opportunities. According to Marc Miller, founder of Career Pivot, "Growing up in the '60s and '70s, someone who was 60 was really old. There was no thought of a career in the second half of life. Period."[2] Much has changed, and today we're all generally working longer. Work has become part of who we are, our identity.

According to Bob Buford, author of *Half Time: Moving from Success to Significance*, "The first half of life has to do with achieving and gaining, learning and earning. For the second half of life to be better than the first, you must make the choice to step outside of the safety of living on autopilot."[3] This may be the key to a successful and significant second half of life.

That might involve holding on to our present positions, embarking on a completely new career, or maybe a combination of the two. Our priorities may change, and our purpose may start to have a greater influence on our life and career. We may want to shift from making a living to making a life.

Do you feel like you have been on autopilot just getting through your days? We have talked to many who felt this way. We may be going through our normal routines unconsciously, completing our work and home tasks without giving them much thought. In many cases we have perfected these routines, but unconscious living can lead to stress and impact our emotional well-being. Moving from living unconsciously to living consciously can help change our perceptions of work.

Steve Jacobs described how one can burn out from loving the fast train and the people on it too much. His career has spanned church ministry to university life. During his ministry years, he worked in service to people and loved it. His work with a dynamic congregation became his life, being available 24/7 and moving on a fast train with few refueling stops along the way. "Successful ministry wasn't a narcotic, but it fed me because I loved it; yet there were times when I was moving too fast and being fed in unhealthy ways. Fortunately I saw burnout coming and walked out rather than blew out." Retiring from ministry, Steve found the work-life balance he needed in university life.

Many of us will experience a pivotal time in our work when we decide it is time to change it up and discover who we will be next. Sandy experienced this after her granddaughter was born across the country. For two weeks she could not get enough of her new granddaughter. It was also a time to reflect and reorder priorities, starting with envisioning more family time and refocusing her business vision to align with her lifestyle. These awakenings are valuable—but we believe that we all need to reassess our personal and professional goals on a regular basis.

Do we work to live or live to work? Many of us—especially if you are over the age of 50—were taught that to be successful in life and work you had to get a good education, which would lead to a good job, and that after working 30 to 40 years we would be rewarded with retirement—a life of leisure. That paradigm is outdated, and now we have a fantastic opportunity to reevaluate what has been and envision what could be. There are so many things we want to do. This becomes a period of imagining what's possible.

Working later in life can pay off in more than just income. Benefits such as mental stimulation and social engagement are associated with being well, wise, and whole. Early in our lives, we learn the significance of hard work. This translates into work ethic and how it is valued in our culture. The value of a strong work ethic is reinforced throughout our lives. We start our careers fresh, excited, and ready to conquer the world. As we move into the second half of life, many of us are interested in bringing back the feeling we once had.

WORK REIMAGINED

Time has a way of passing quickly. Sometimes it seems that life is like a toilet roll: the closer we get to the end, the faster it goes. We spend a great deal of time at our jobs, and if the job is not providing meaning or fulfillment, we start to get stagnant. We wonder if it's too late to make a change and reinvent ourselves. When we were children we were asked what we wanted to be when we grew up. Fast-forward to now: are our current jobs or careers related to our childhood dream? While our dreams may have changed since we were children, it's worth tapping into that time to see whether what we do truly aligns with what's important to us. Reimagining work with a fresh mindset can get us closer to living a balanced life with purpose and meaning. Those we interviewed shared their wisdom and experience around reimagining work in the second half of life:

> "Find what you love and do that. Experiment. We don't
> know what we like until we try different things. This
> self-development goes on until we die. It does not stop at a
> certain age. We have the opportunity to grow in different
> directions."—**Candy Spitz,** career transition coach

"I stepped away from a successful senior executive position in the financial services industry to pursue a compelling call into art and creativity."—**Fred Mandell,** author, life transition expert

"The most important factor is mindset—move to an opportunity or entrepreneur mindset whether you are working for yourself or for someone else."—**Marc Miller,** author, founder of Career Pivot

In *Work Reimagined*, authors Richard Leider and David Shapiro write, "Uncover your calling and you will never have to work again."[4] What they mean is that when we are following our calling or purpose, work doesn't feel like work anymore. People who think of their work only as *jobs* are often focused on the financial benefits of working. On the other hand, those who view their work as a *career* have a deeper investment in their work. In addition to earning a living, they are interested in developing mastery, achievement, and advancement in something that drives them.

We learned from our conversation with Amy LaBelle, cofounder and owner of LaBelle Winery, that after spending years as a successful lawyer, one day that all changed. "Owning a winery began as a dream of mine—a dream that happened as I visited a small winery in Nova Scotia, Canada," she says. "The moment I walked into that winery, I had a lightning bolt moment, and I knew that I was meant to make wine. After many days of hard work and perseverance, we opened the doors of LaBelle Winery in 2012. With that dream was born a vision of a place where community could gather and enjoy excellent food, wine, and culture." Amy had always loved to read about wine, but she never had a thought about making it until that moment when she visited Nova Scotia. She listened to that strong voice telling her *You need to do this*, and that is where her new adventure began. "Wine is my reason to be," she says. Despite her success as a lawyer, she'd found her calling—and she has never looked back.[5]

Uncovering our purpose in life is valuable in navigating the changes we will inevitably experience in our work lives. Paying attention and listening to that inner voice is part of living and working consciously. What changes or shifts might be in your work future? Give yourself the gift of time and space to reflect on how you might reimagine work. Whether you make big or small changes, thinking about the differences between a job, career, or calling can lead you to find meaning and fulfillment in addition to a paycheck.

WORKING LONGER

Many people are working longer. "Seven in ten Baby Boomer workers in the United States [expected] to work past age 65, are already doing so or do not plan to retire."[6] The labor force participation rate of workers 65-plus has risen to levels not seen since the 1950s. In the last decade or so, older workers have accounted for virtually all workforce growth, and those 65-plus continue to be the fastest-growing segment. Here are some reasons why:

1. **Longevity and increasing life expectancy.** Because we're living longer and healthier and have more active lifestyles, this may mean working longer too. According to Marc Freedman, "Retirement as we have known it is in the midst of being displaced as the central institution of the second half of life."[7]

2. **Elimination of defined benefit or final salary pensions.** According to the United States Bureau of Labor Statistics, "There is a decline in defined benefit pensions, which now cover 18 percent of private-sector workers, down from 35 percent in the early 1990s."[8] This shift from employer to employee

retirement funding puts the onus squarely on the individual to support themselves after working for a living becomes difficult.

3. **Sandwich generation challenges.** Today's middle-aged adults are taking care of both parents and kids at the same time and juggling with many family responsibilities. Statistics show costs of supporting multiple generations financially are increasing. About one in seven adult families are financially assisting both their parents and one or more children.[9]

4. **Economic or life uncertainty.** The coronavirus pandemic and recent financial recessions, as well as life changes such as health challenges, divorce, or the death of a spouse, all contribute to the need for working longer and changing life plans. Those in midlife or later are responding in different ways, with the central focus being one of reassessment, asking questions about what is most important and meaningful in the years ahead.

5. **Re-envisioning later life.** Generation Xers and boomers are reinventing their lives and work. They value purpose, vitality, stimulation, connection, and fulfillment, and want to receive it from work as well.

Implications of older people in the workplace are significant for both employers and employees, and employers may need to push the reset button to create more age-friendly workplace environments.

READY, SET, RESET

Maybe it is time to press the reset button on your own work life. This reset begins with our inner voice: our thinking and our mindset. It is time to expand our imagination and think creatively. Slowing down and evaluating our priorities and what we want may provide some useful clues as we reimagine what our work lives might look like. Maybe you are able to consider a sabbatical, an intentional pause, that will allow time for this inner work or for learning new skills.

> "If you stop learning, you die. Every day I intentionally seek to learn and grow in some way. Every day I learn something new and that truly energizes me." —**Dawn Pratt,** founder of Tech Up for Women

In Sandy's work as a seasoned career coach, she sees many in the second half of life wanting something new and more meaningful, but the reality is that they also need to earn a good paycheck. For many there is no choice, and experienced workers are forced to work longer. On the flip side, other opportunities either in or outside of a current organization are available, and consciously examining what we truly want is the first step in this ongoing journey. Sandy has found it valuable for clients to frame this period as "what's now" and "what's next." For example:

What's Now	What's Next
senior VP of sales	adjunct professor
director of veterinary hospital	leadership coaching
school nurse	health advocacy entrepreneur

Beginning the process of moving to something new starts with self-awareness and letting go of what is not currently working. Knowing what changes you want to make is key. For instance, if you want more flexibility in your life, your career or business options need to align with that. It's about reordering priorities. Building on the previous "what's now" and "what's next" examples, here are some questions to ask yourself:

- What are my strengths?
- What lessons am I learning right now?
- What new skills do I need to develop?
- What do I need to do now as I think about future work that lights me up?

The lessons you learn from reflecting on these questions now will be valuable when you are ready to move on. Perhaps there are changes you can make to pivot within your current organization. Be creative, curious, and open to new possibilities. How might you reimagine your work life? Is there a career change in your future or perhaps a change of your perspective?

Before pressing the reset button, let's explore some of the options for working for a living in midlife and beyond.

WORKING FOR A LIVING

Depending on our financial goals explored in the previous chapter, working later in life may not be optional. For many who need to continue working and may not have saved enough to let go of the regular paycheck, working a few extra years, even at a reduced salary, could make a significant difference in the quality of life in those later years. We may be working because we have to more than because we want to, but *how* we work and what we do for work can become more conscious choices. Even if you are a decade or so away from ending your full-time career, setting intentions for future directions cannot be started too soon. As you consider working for a living in midlife and beyond, broad categories might include growing in your existing career, switching careers, becoming an entrepreneur, exploring multiple streams of income, and personal branding. We explore each of these options here.

GROWING IN YOUR EXISTING CAREER

Continuing to work at the same job may be sufficient to meet your financial goals and satisfy your need for fun and fulfillment. However, your financial goals might also include increasing your earning potential. Sometimes we get in our own way, stuck in the daily grind, and may overlook proactive steps to consciously move forward in our existing career. Consider increased training to level up your skills and value leading to higher pay or a promotion. Or perhaps you want to seek out a mentor or coach to help assess where you are and find the best ways to optimize and maximize your potential with your existing employer.

SWITCHING CAREERS

Many of us spend time looking beyond our existing work environment, envisioning greener pastures in different organizations. Maybe you're burnt out on what you've been doing, or growth with your current employer may feel impossible.

Making any change from the familiar is scary, and so often we think about it but don't take action. The place to start is to identify what you really want to create and achieve in your next chapter. Some questions to ask yourself are:

- What skills and talents do I want to utilize?
- What business outcomes do I want to support?
- What type of people, environments, and cultures do I thrive best in?

- Which values, standards of integrity, and needs must be supported through this work?
- What types of challenges do I want to face in my work?
- What financial compensation and benefits are non-negotiable for me?

Once you've defined the essence of what you want, then it is time to discover the type of work that fits you, your lifestyle, and your needs. Once a few career options have been identified, it is helpful to talk to those in your network to learn more about options. Do research and exploration and dig as deeply as you can to determine what you really want from this career change.

> "After working for organizations, I knew I could make more of an impact by starting my own training and event company. I was able to create new ideas, innovate, and collaborate with so many. Through one of my clients, I created a program to advance women in technology. Seeing this need, I was inspired to start Tech Up for Women. This has led to 358 speakers on our stages, and the business continues to grow worldwide. I am making an impact!"
> —**Dawn Pratt,** from corporate training to entrepreneur

> "Being a business owner for 35 years, I was ready to sell and discover my next adventure. I knew I wanted to work for someone else, be challenged and engaged yet not be married to a business. Through self-assessment, collaborative conversations, and reflection, I am now employed at a bank as a sales associate." —**Mark Dartnell,** from business owner to bank sales

"I am a professional career changer. I went from a computer
programmer, running a tech company, to sales and more. I
was able to shift gears with the mindset that there is always
another opportunity. That led me to my most important
role as entrepreneur, author, and founder of Career Pivot,
creating a community of those looking to make a pivot
or change midcareer and beyond." —**Marc Miller,** from
technology career to author and entrepreneur

If you want a career change, keep in mind that it is a process, and
it will take time. You owe it to yourself to find out. Address your life
and career change with eyes wide open, and with seriousness, rigor, and
intention. Commit to the process—you deserve to discover what your
next career will be.

BECOMING AN ENTREPRENEUR

As we reimagine how we work, it may sound appealing to go off on our
own—especially at the midpoint in life, when we have several working
years and experience behind us. Entrepreneurship is on the rise, and it's
not hard to see why; being your own boss can come with many perks.
Even despite the economic downturn due to COVID-19, many individuals are embarking on an opportunity to start new business ventures
and meet the new, post-pandemic demands of consumers. In the US
as well as in many other countries, people are starting businesses at the
fastest rate in over a decade.[10]

An entrepreneurial direction may have emerged from your exploration of purpose in chapter 1. For many it is appealing and exciting to
think of being our own boss and creating a business idea. And as it
turns out, the evidence shows that entrepreneurial ventures are well

suited to midlife. "Entrepreneurs in their 50s are 2.8 times more likely to start a successful company than a 25-year-old founder."[11]

Kerry Hannon, author of *Never Too Old to Get Rich: The Entrepreneur's Guide to Starting a Business Mid-Life*, shares that the midlife and beyond entrepreneur has untapped resources to launch a business:

- A well-built social network formed from decades of engagement in school, work, and community that can help with information, contacts, opportunities, and more.
- Financial capital built from years of work with benefits, assets, investments as well as a possible partner that can help offset expenses.
- A cornucopia of experience, knowledge, skills, and wisdom.
- Resilience, grit, and a strong work ethic.[12]

Of course, there are some risks to be aware of as you consider starting a business. Without a financial safety net to fall back on, it could be a challenge. The motivation or reason for starting a business is also an important clue. Many people have wanted to work for themselves for years and see midlife as the golden opportunity to invest their time, energy, and money now—because if not now, when? Others feel pushed into this option because they have lost their jobs or are experiencing ageism. The first three to five years of starting a small business can be challenging, and about half end up closing within five years. If you're retired, or close to that stage, there is less time to make up for losses.

Starting your own business means that you have the freedom to set your own hours, to decide on your business model, and choose what services or goods you will offer and who you want to serve. But this is not for everyone, and working independently requires discipline. Before you take the leap, do your research and reach out to other small-business owners who might be helpful in terms of learning what is involved. You can also look into advice from small-business development centers in your area.

Many leave a job working for someone else for more flexibility and freedom and soon find out they are working more—at least in the beginning. Also keep in mind that there will most likely be a lag in earnings as you start a business, so it is wise to consider a side hustle or gig while you're getting your business established. Testing the waters before making an all-in commitment will provide important information as to whether this is the path forward.

Being independent and in charge are clear advantages to working for yourself. However, it can also be lonely at times. You may want to find a community or network to explore—or perhaps you can create your own. Fellow entrepreneurs can become a community or family, sharing their own understanding of the joys and challenges of running a business. Or maybe you don't want to do it entirely alone: perhaps starting a new venture with a partner is an option, or explore buying a franchise for more structure and support.

Perhaps you already have your own business, and you're considering selling or handing over the reins to someone else. Similar to other career transitions, it is a time of letting go. It is the ending of something that you put your heart and soul into for a long period of time, and it can be a very emotional time. Many entrepreneurs thrive on being in charge, and they don't always think about the issues that might arise when they consider selling their business. What happens when this control goes away? It can be challenging, but as with other transitions, it presents an opportunity to create a new reality—one that takes you beyond your business to new possibilities of freedom and a fresh new beginning.

Starting your own business is a conscious choice and one that requires reflection, research, and resetting your mindset to one of opportunity and self-motivation. If you have a passion and a call to start a business, we will take a deeper dive in the next chapter, including encore careers and volunteering.

MULTIPLE STREAMS OF INCOME

As we transition from full-time careers with some focus on earning a living, we may have the opportunity to consider multiple streams of income. Paul, for example, transitioned from a full-time consulting career into part-time consulting, leadership and life transitions coaching, teaching at the doctoral level for an online university, and writing. These multiple streams of income, while inconsistent and much lower than the full-time career, provided a degree of financial support and the flexibility to engage in both working for a living and contributing to social and environmental causes and not-for-profit endeavors.

Another term for combining work in this way is *portfolio career*. According to Caroline Castrillon, "A portfolio career is a working style where you combine multiple streams of income—often creating a mix of full- or part-time employment, freelancing, or working as a consultant."[13] Portfolio careers offer flexibility, variety, and freedom. They're also a good option for those who have diverse interests and skills but don't want to focus them in one particular area. Having multiple streams of income can alleviate the stress of choosing one option that may not be quite the right choice. Today more than ever, workers are prioritizing freedom and flexibility over the security of a corporate job.

Though there are many positives to a portfolio career, there are challenges to be aware of. Gig workers, freelancers, and part-time workers may have few if any benefits like health insurance and paid time off. While flexibility and freedom are reasons to pursue a portfolio career, every day may be unbalanced. Depending on your current set of jobs, you may find yourself working more than you would like. Step back and think carefully about all angles of portfolio careers. Understand your why in pursuing a portfolio career. Perhaps it is temporary while looking for a full-time job, or maybe more flexibility or balance is the goal. Carefully evaluate what you want as you chart this path with your eyes wide open.

YOUR PERSONAL BRAND

Wherever your next chapter takes you in working for a living, your personal brand will show the world what value you bring to your work role. Think of your personal brand as a way of conveying the purpose and identity we explored in chapter 1. Wendy Marx, a marketing and branding expert, defined seven foundational principles for self-reinvention and branding in her book *Thriving at 50+: The 7 Principles to Reinvent* and *Rebrand Yourself*.[14] These principles were distilled from the extensive interviews Wendy undertook during her research for her book:

- **Having a growth mindset:** People who reinvent themselves are adept at trying something new and are unafraid of failing. They imbibe a growth mindset.

- **Being uncomfortable:** To reinvent yourself you need to embrace the paradox of being comfortable enough with being uncomfortable to take risks.

- **Willingness to learn:** The path of reinvention is often stocked with zigs and zags as you try new things. You'll need to make mistakes to learn and grow.

- **Finding your purpose:** To find your purpose you must claim your own life, which often gets lost in the day-to-day shuffle. Your life purpose is about finding what's most important to you.

- **Storytelling:** Stories are a lifeline during your reinvention process, providing emotional ballast to support you. They reassure you that your plans make sense. Similarly, they are a narrative of your life you share with others.

- **Personal branding:** Think of personal branding as subtraction and addition. First you scrape away the excess—what's no longer relevant or what's holding you back.

- **Mentoring and social media:** The keys to getting reinventions to fly are catalysts, such as social media and mentoring. Think of them as the propellor to your reinvention—what helps it soar.

As we move to new jobs, careers, or roles, rebranding brings focus and clarity to what we do. Without a clear brand, we may come across scattered whether we work for ourselves or someone else. Being proactive with rebranding will put us in the driver seat of how others perceive us. We have all seen signs of ageism, so owning our brand will demonstrate value and what we bring to the world of work. Being conscious of how we show up and are seen will increase our confidence as we make shifts in the second half of life.

ORGANIZATIONAL PERSPECTIVES

There are numerous resources for business owners and executives to use for organizational planning, far more information than we can cover here. Whether you are in a managerial role or not, it is helpful to have some idea of the challenges today's multigenerational organizations face—and how they may affect you as an older worker. In this section we explore issues surrounding ageism and generational issues in the workplace.

THE MULTIGENERATIONAL WORKFORCE

Today's workforce includes up to five distinct generations, ranging from Gen Z, who are at the beginning of their careers, to millennials and Gen Xers, to the baby boomers and the traditionalists (or Silent Generation), many of whom are nearing the end of their working lives. Each generation brings different perspectives, expectations, work patterns, and communication styles, and working together in a multi-generational workforce brings both challenges and rewards.

In the movie *The Intern*, a 70-year-old widower takes the role of senior intern who becomes popular with his younger coworkers, including the young founder and CEO. The film inspired Sally Susman, a vice president at Pfizer, to experiment with intergenerational learning. Sally thought of a man she knew named Paul Critchlow. Paul had a wealth of experience—the kind that, while not inevitable among the older set, is only possible with age. He'd been a college football star, a decorated Vietnam veteran, a journalist, a press secretary, a corporate communications director, and a vice chairman of Merrill Lynch Bank of America. Paul was 70 years old and retired, but Susman had a hunch he wasn't enjoying retirement all that much.[15] The idea was for Paul to share his experiences and learn how millennials view and approach their careers and lives.

The intern experiment resulted in a consulting job and turned out to be a win-win for both Paul and the company. What if this experiment could be brought to life with many organizations? Looking beyond generation and age to focus on experience, wisdom, and learning would erase some of the misconceptions and assumptions we all have at one time or another.

A multigenerational workplace can provide many assets. No one knows this better than Chip Conley, the former hotelier who served as global head of hospitality and strategy at Airbnb, where the CEO was decades younger. In fact, most of the team he worked with was much younger. He felt like a senior intern in many ways and coined the term "mentern."[16] A mentern combines the roles of a mentor and an intern, and they are often experienced professionals looking to share their knowledge with a younger workforce while learning additional skills from different age groups of peers and partners. This is an example of reverse mentoring, where Chip shared his business and leadership wisdom, and younger workers at Airbnb shared their fresh ideas and technological knowledge.

Maintaining connections and utilizing the experience of multiple generations in the workplace is likely to increase the connections we already have thanks to the internet, media devices, and social media; and perhaps in other ways, we are moving closer together in our shared expectations and experiences. "Perennials" is a term coined by internet entrepreneur Gina Pell: "People who transcend the entire concept of generations by remaining current and timeless." Perennials are "ever-blooming relevant people of all ages who live in the present time, know what's happening in the world, stay current with technology, and have friends of all ages."[17] The concept of perennials celebrates inclusivity and an enduring mindset. It is a hopeful new way of looking at how sharing generational knowledge and experiences can enhance our experiences in the workplace and help older workers stay relevant—and staying relevant is a top concern for those who are older than 50.

A perennial mindset may also help with the issue of ageism in the workplace. In Sandy's work as a career coach, she sees older workers challenged with finding new jobs, and having a perennial mindset does make a difference. One of Sandy's clients came to her a few years ago and was in shock after a job interview when she was asked, "Do you think you'll have enough energy to do this job?" Many older workers are asking themselves, "Am I too old to learn these new skills? Do I have the energy to do this job or start this business?" This uncertainty can rattle our confidence. Take the time to review all you've done over the past years, and think about how your skills are transferable for today's employers. Those years of experience are part of your success story! Along with the willingness to learn new skills with enthusiasm, reframing your experience with a perennial mindset can help make you feel relevant as you reenter the workforce or shift your goals.

It's important to realize that age discriminations may be systemic or quite subtle in organizations. When we don't see obvious signs, we think it doesn't exist. To evaluate your organization, take stock of who the learning opportunities are offered to, who is being given the challenging assignments, and who is being passed over or left out of meetings or activities. Take note of microaggressions too, such as jokes about being over the hill. Sometimes they seem innocent, but they can add to our culture of ageism. If you're in a leadership role in the workplace, how are you actively changing the narrative of older workers? Look for more on ageism and workplace discrimination in chapter 9, Helping Humanity.

WHO'S IN CHARGE OF YOUR CAREER?

Ultimately, we are all the directors of our jobs and careers. As we go off to work, how will we show up, and what mindset will we have? We have a career story that is important. Our career speaks to our experience, background, and personal journey, and will take us to where we want to go next. How will our story of unique traits and background create satisfaction and fulfillment in our current role and next adventure? What actions can you take today to identify and seek that next position, whether it's within your current organization, your own business, or another field entirely? It's up to you to do the internal and external work in creating your story today and in the future.

Whether we are working because we want to or because we have to, we often don't pay attention to the benefits of working for a living beyond the financial compensation. It's important to remember that beyond that, work can provide social connection, engagement, learning, and community—all important aspects of living consciously in midlife and beyond. Being socially connected and engaged is a key factor in aging well.

If you are transitioning from full-time working or preparing for the transition, we hope that you will consciously chart your course with thoughtful planning. If you need or want to work longer, embrace the journey with thoughtful and inspired action and consider all the options open to you.

In this chapter we explored the many facets of working for a living. Our work journey is not a straight line but one with twists and turns, and we can make conscious choices to pivot or adjust our work roles, new careers, or entrepreneurial options. We can take advantage of the multigenerational aspect of today's workforce to feel connected and relevant. Directing our careers and stepping up to new challenges, priorities, and roles is part of our journey. Let's show up with confidence and know our value as we continue on our path with openness to what can be.

CONSCIOUS LIVING PRACTICES

Questions for Reflection

- Where are you on the working-for-a-living journey?
- How will your financial health influence your decisions about working for a living?
- What are you being called to do?
- What is possible in the short term and in the longer term?
- What is most important to include in your rebranding?

Try This

- List your past jobs or positions and reflect on what skills energized you and those that drained you.
- Jump-start this brand-building exercise: respond to the following questions as you start crafting your branding statement:
  - What's the one word that describes you best?
  - What strengths do people admire most about you (including your boss, instructors, coworkers, colleagues, friends, family members, etc.)?
  - How do you operate differently from your colleagues to get things done?
  - What strengths do you want employers to perceive in you?

Living
Well

Appreciating
Money

Bouncing
Forward

Living with
Technology

Working
for a Living

Exploring
Purposefully

Working for
Fulfillment

Helping
Humanity

Savoring
the World

Minding
Relationships

Living Life
Creatively

CHAPTER 5

WORKING FOR FULFILLMENT

Our first half is about how to make a living, and our second
half has the promise of being about how to make a life.

–BOB BUFORD

We spend the first half of our life working because we have to,
but what if in the second half of life we work because we
want to? What if our work life brought us more fun and joy,
and greater meaning and fulfillment? As we move into the second half
of life we can consciously think about how we want to work, engaging
in experiments and rethinking what's next with awe and wonder. This
is a time to look inward to what excites us, what moves us, listening
to that inner voice about what we are called to do next. In this chapter
we explore the many possibilities and work options in part-time work,
encore careers, business and social entrepreneurial options, and volunteering and philanthropy. Our hope is that you will be enlightened and

inspired to follow your own path and use your internal compass as you transition from full-time career to what comes next.

For many of us, our work life and our social life have been quite separate, but what if we could bring together working for a living and working for fulfillment? As Robert Frost put it in his poem "Two Tramps in Mud Time," "My object in living is to unite my avocation and my vocation as my two eyes make one in sight." As we approach our next phase, bringing together avocation and vocation may provide a foundation for creating more meaning, purpose, and fun in our work. In chapter 1 we explored discovering purpose, and now is the time to rethink work and how to infuse purpose into our work as we merge vocation and avocation. Our Conscious Living journey continues with mindfulness and thoughtfulness as we step into a place that may warm our heart and soul.

SOMEDAY ISLAND

Many of us spend way too much time marooned on what we call "Someday Island." *Someday* I will find a fulfilling career or start a business. *Someday* I will give back more. *Someday* I will have a great adventure. *Someday* I will be happy. In her book *Someday Is Not a Day in the Week*, Sam Horn tells the story of her father, who had a dream of visiting all the national parks when he retired. As director of vocational agricultural education for the state of California, he spent five or six days a week driving hundreds of miles to high schools and county fairs to advise students on their projects. He felt an obligation to make a difference, and he did. But that dedication came with a cost. "Dad finally took off on his long-delayed dream a week after he retired," Sam writes. "A week after that, he had a stroke in a hotel bathroom. Dad never got to do what he had dreamed of his whole life."[1]

This is not an uncommon story; we all delay doing things we dream about. But we also have the opportunity to get off Someday Island and start living our dream. We explore where to go in our next chapter on savoring the world, but let's first consider disentangling ourselves from the notion of "someday" as we consider uniting our vocation and our avocation.

What if you cleared your mental clutter to start thinking about implementing that brilliant business idea? What if you have the freedom from financial worry and are now free to pursue work based on what energizes you or holds meaning to you? What if you finally said *yes* to doing what you really love? Now is the time to tap into your imagination and get those creative juices flowing to think about what's next.

Often our dream is so far on the back burner that we forget what it is—or we think it's too late. Whether you're 40 or 80, you still have time ahead of you to live. We often hear the word *reinvention*. What gets in the way? Limiting thoughts we commonly subscribe to include

- I don't know where to start.
- I am too old.
- It's too late.
- What if it doesn't work?
- I'm not smart enough or tough enough, or I'm just not ready.

It's all too easy to let these thoughts limit us, and we forget that "the path of purposeful aging is a choice to wake up every day with the intention to grow and give."[2] Making conscious choices is important in creating our identity and assuming new roles. To remind yourself of what really matters to you, we suggest investigating some of the self-assessment tools we note in the Resources section at the back of the book—anything to inspire you to get off Someday Island and get closer to making your work your passion. Let's look a little closer at how meaning and money intertwine.

MONEY OR MEANING

As we navigate our next stage toward working for fun and fulfillment, the reality is that for some, earning an income is still a necessity, and how much we need to earn will be different for each of us. Ask yourself: How much does it cost to be me?

The trend of many experienced workers navigating their next chapter is to channel their workaholic status into discovering a new or renewed sense of purpose while still earning an income. We learned through our interview with Nancy Collamer, author of *Second Act Careers*, that she and her husband may end up being in semiretirement. "The emphasis will no longer be on earning income; it will be more on blending work and play. If we want to take a year and spend that volunteering, then we'll have the flexibility to do that." She continues by saying that "once you remove income from the equation, it frees you up to pursue things that speak to you." Like Nancy, many of us reaching traditional retirement age are redefining our work priorities.

Semiretirement is on the rise, with workers looking for flexibility, part-time work, and a healthy blend of other activities to optimize their time and talents. The Bureau of Labor Statistics estimates that 13 million Americans aged 65 and older will be in the workforce by 2024.[3] For many, the idea of a new career based on a passion or hobby is a strong motivator, so we see this trend continuing in many creative ways for those midcareer and beyond.

As we enter or travel through our second half of life, fulfillment becomes increasingly important, and it is natural to take stock of our lives and look ahead to determine priorities for the next chapter. With each year we gain more knowledge, life experience, and expertise that can be shared. This is a prime time to dabble in a side gig or business or bring your talents to a cause that you are passionate about. Those in retirement may choose to work less or in different ways, moving away from full-time work. Encore careers, entrepreneurial options, and volunteer work all provide opportunities to live a fulfilled second half of life.

ENCORE CAREERS

Many in the second half of life are making conscious choices to invent an entirely new stage of life—the encore years. When Sandy asked people how they defined an encore career, she heard answers ranging from "doing volunteer work" to "your last hurrah job" to "making an impact." What exactly is an encore career? The term was coined by thought leader and author Marc Freedman in his book *Encore: Finding Work That Matters in the Second Half of Life*. Marc defines an encore career as "work in the second half of life that combines continued income, greater personal meaning, and social impact . . . an encore career is often pursued for social purpose, sense of fulfillment and financial reasons. Many of these jobs are paid positions in public interest fields including education, health, environmental, government, and social services."[4]

Encore careers include many types of work. Our encore careers may be working in organizations on our own terms, with impact, and giving back to the community. Does this resonate with you? Maybe an encore career can align with your values and purpose. Perhaps you have always wanted to work with children, for example, or in the healthcare field, or with some other cause that holds special meaning for you. Now may be the right time to consider these possibilities.

Many of us in the second half of life are craving purpose-driven work and are ready to become the architect of our next chapter. This next age and stage may be characterized by new priorities, new perspectives, and the capacity to do something with those hard-earned insights—not just to leave a legacy but to live one. Millions are trading the old dream of freedom *from* work to new possibilities and the freedom *to* work.

Perhaps it's time to retire from a long-held position and set ourselves free to pursue something new with meaning.[5]

In the *Pathways to Encore Purpose Project*, researchers at Stanford University found among other things that:[6]

- The majority of older adults exhibit high levels of prosocial values and behaviors, such as helping and caring for others, caring for nature and the environment, endorsing equal treatment for all, and seeking to understand people who are different from them.

- Purpose is an equal-opportunity pursuit. The prevalence of purposeful living does not vary significantly across income, health status, or geography. The one meaningful difference is that the prevalence of purpose was higher among people of color than among whites. Overall, however, what stands out is that purpose is available to all.

- People who are purposeful have a positive outlook on life. The great majority (94 percent) of those interviewed who were unambiguously purposeful share a trait we call "positivity," which refers to joy, hopefulness, optimism, and other related emotions. Though many people in this group were dealing with serious life problems—such as poverty, poor health, family difficulties, and bereavement—they emphasized the joy and satisfaction they experience in their lives, especially in their beyond-the-self engagements.

While some career changes occur due to circumstances beyond our control such as layoffs, being forced to leave a job, an empty nest, loss of a partner, or illness, others may be initiated by consciously seeking an encore career bringing new challenges and excitement. This is a time for imagining new possibilities and opening ourselves up to the unknown.

MORE TO GIVE AND DO

As we move along life's journey, we find ourselves early on focused on learning and then move on to a focus of finding a mate, a job and creating a family. The next period is often referred to as the third life stage or act and is focused on gathering wisdom, embracing one's true self and giving back. Many are embracing the encore years and choose to work and contribute as they are seeking purpose and meaning.

> **Dorothy Keenan** developed the GrandInvolve program, bringing together her love of people, intergenerational collaboration, service, and building community. Her mission is "changing the world, one child at a time." She brings together caring adults to volunteer to connect the community to local schools to help teachers so that vulnerable students can achieve and maintain grade level skills. She spent time getting intentional about what activities she wanted to do to make life worth living.

We can all make a difference in our lives, community, and world—both large and small. And it's important to recognize that we may all navigate an encore career differently based on our style, interests, and motivation. If you tend to plan things out, research possibilities, prioritize, then develop a concrete goal. Perhaps you're waiting for the right time—when you become an empty nester or when you can take early retirement from your company. Need new skills or degrees? Consider what will benefit you most. Others may have such intense passion or energy around a specific cause or career that they just take the plunge and learn as they go. Either way, thinking consciously about what you want your encore to look like and what it will bring you is important.

Here are some considerations to keep in mind as you transition to an encore career:[7]

- A path to an encore career may look quite different to each person on this path. Midlife is a long period of time, and each of us is at a different point. Your abilities, interests, and circumstances may influence your life choices.

- Some will plan for years; others will transition very quickly into encore careers. Some will settle into new work that may last fifteen to twenty years, while others will mix it up every few years. Do what's best for you.

- Encore work involves trade-offs. You may trade money for meaning and flexibility. You may trade power and influence for the opportunity to work more closely with people you can help.

Keep in mind that this is a journey for you to embrace and enjoy. As you begin to think about starting an encore career, it is helpful to talk to others who have done so. Not only will you learn, but you'll likely be inspired by their stories.

One such story is that of Mark Barden. His encore career was born from personal tragedy. After his nine-year-old son Daniel was taken from him in the tragic school shooting at Sandy Hook Elementary School in Newtown, Connecticut, in 2012, he was called to take action. He cofounded the organization Sandy Hook Promise to honor his son and protect other children. "More than 2 million youth and adults have been trained with their Know the Signs programs. The programs include Start with Hello and Say Something, which encourages students to engage with those who seem isolated," Mark said.[8] His encore path was not planned but propelled by tragedy, as was his passion and motivation to develop new skills to create a successful organization with his love for Daniel at the core.

What is calling you? Whatever it is, perhaps now is the time to start your exploration. Is there a cause or experience that is speaking to you? Start with one small step and see how it evolves. That step may be experimenting or meeting with others who have built an encore career to give you inspiration.

Another example speaks to interest and setting goals to bring action. Through our interview with Elizabeth Mahler, she enlightened us with her encore story. She spent the earlier part of her career in a variety of educational endeavors, and she channeled her love for education to her encore path. Creating a message of awareness to people in midlife and beyond that we have the gift of time was at the core of her encore. The question is how will we make the most of the years ahead. She believes we have time to do something different, creative, or to stay with what we love. We can choose. This started her quest to redefine what an encore path could be.

It begins with interest, intertwined with purpose, and then creating a goal. Her goal was twofold: to bring awareness of the gift of time, and the second part is working with towns, cities, or counties to open up opportunities in a way that is appealing and attracts those in midlife and beyond.

Elizabeth enjoyed speaking and took her passion to all different groups, and this created a buzz. She researched and found that giving back was one motivator of an encore, but the many other reasons included learning, gaining new skills, going back to school, building a new career, doing something completely different, meeting new people, and more. Though some want to volunteer and give back, others want to make money in their encore. She expanded the definition of an encore career to one that opens up possibilities and engages more expansive thinking to whatever we want to do. There is not just one direction. Her education and inspiration of creating an encore path was contagious. Her goal evolved to wanting every person in their forties and fifties to understand the term "encore" as their opportunity to start thinking about their future in a different way: one with fulfillment, engagement, and starting anew.

For Elizabeth, finding what she enjoyed brought value to herself and to others. When we create purpose-driven work, it brings great joy and energy to our lives and those around us. Our interests are often the impetus to our encore path, so notice what lights you up and how you might translate that interest into your path. Reflecting on what is most meaningful and creating goals is an ideal place to start.

ENTREPRENEURIAL VENTURES

In chapter 4, we discussed entrepreneurial options in the context of earning a living. Here, let's explore it as an option for finding more fulfillment and meaning in our work.

If making a difference and using your creativity and innovation appeals to you, midlife is a great time to bring all of your experience to bear in an entrepreneurial venture. According to Chris Farrell, author of *Purpose and a Paycheck*, "Many adults in the second half of life will start their own business or keep working well into the traditional retirement years. An impressive body of scholarly research suggests that, given the opportunity, people in the second half of life can be as creative, innovative, and entrepreneurial as their younger peers."[9] Many experienced workers want to stay in the game and are staying connected to the economy by optimizing their skills, life experiences, and connections by starting a business.

Is an entrepreneurial encore in your future? Perhaps there is a problem you would like to solve or a passion you have to bring more fulfillment to your life. There are many reasons for starting a business. Maybe you've had an idea for years, and now is the time to try it out. Or perhaps as you leave your full-time career you want to bring your skills to a different business endeavor, one of your own. Whatever the reason, learning all that we can to make a conscious choice about this potential path forward is important.

SOCIAL ENTREPRENEURSHIP

For some, starting a business is a way to improve the quality of their life, and some have a strong desire to work for themselves and see an opportunity in the market they can't resist. For others, the desire to start a business is a means of creating positive change. This is social entrepreneurship. While the main objective for a business entrepreneurship may be making a profit, for a social entrepreneur the main objective may be to contribute to helping humanity solve a social issue. Social entrepreneurship is about starting a business for a philanthropic cause and with a commitment to give back.

Although the motivation of a social entrepreneur has a more philanthropic focus, making money may still be part of the picture (and any business needs to be financially successful to survive). It's possible to be successful as a business owner and do good at the same time. It may also be harder to measure success for social entrepreneurship. It is always easier to measure profit, but it's more challenging to measure impact on people or the planet.

Often a strong belief sparks a desire to do good and become a social entrepreneur. Through our conversation with Shawn Perry, we learned how he started his mission-driven work to help seniors. He explains that for the first half of his life he worked hard, learning and developing skills. At some point, his work no longer brought him joy and fulfillment. This became a time of reflection and introspection. He wanted to bring value to seniors to enhance their lives. He was strongly motivated by his past experiences being in service in the military and providing health insurance to seniors. Shawn attributes his dedication to older adults to his late grandmother, Rosa Perry, who instilled a profound sense of empathy for the vulnerable, frail, and elderly.

As a way of giving back, Shawn founded *The Senior Zone*, a weekly radio program focused on serving the needs of seniors in the community. Being service oriented and a retired military officer, he made his first broadcast in November 2012 on Veterans Day. Shawn says, "The more I give, I get much more back in return."

Like many entrepreneurs, Shawn's idea started with a dream—for a radio station to support seniors. If you are wondering if he had radio experience, the answer is no. He took a leap of faith. He feared moving into something new and different. He took one step at a time and moved outside of his comfort zone. Taking a risk and learning as he progressed was the key to the growth of *The Senior Zone* and to his fulfillment.

Often when we have a mission and move outside of ourselves, we find true meaning and what truly matters. Do you have a mission or cause that is calling you? Perhaps it is time to say yes and start building your social entrepreneurial venture.

There are different ways to adopt a business model that puts mission at the center of the business. As part of our Conscious Living mindset, you may want to explore what causes ignite you and see whether social entrepreneurialism is a potential path for you. Here are a few questions to get you started:

- If you had a million dollars to invest, in what two types of business ventures would you invest?

- If you were to produce a documentary film, what subjects would it be about?

- What problems or issues in your community interest you?

- If you could attend a conference on any subject, what would it be?[10]

As you review your answers, look for common themes or clues that may help you learn more about what you want and what causes are speaking to you.

CONNECTING WITH OTHER ENTREPRENEURS

For any entrepreneurial pursuit, it's a good idea to continue your exploration by talking to entrepreneurs about their journey and how they got started.

There are also many free resources to take advantage of, including small-business development centers in your area and Service Corps of Retired Executives (SCORE), a partner of the Small Business Administration, which provides free business mentoring and training to get you started. Your community may have other resources, so start with your local Chamber of Commerce. You can also look for Rotary Clubs, shared workspaces, business incubators, or Business Networking International.

MINDFUL VOLUNTEERING

Volunteering and contributing to your community are fantastic ways to expand your horizons and gain a greater sense of purpose. In addition to work, at this point in your life you may find yourself wanting to give back by volunteering. So how can you ensure that your volunteering time is meaningful? Psychologist Abraham Maslow gave us the term "self-actualization." He called it the desire for fulfillment, "to become everything that one is capable of becoming."[11] For many of us, the road to self-actualization is through our work. But many of us also look forward to having more time to do the things that didn't fit in when we were working full time and raising families.

"I have relationships with so many organizations; at some point I want to do something to benefit humanity—the key is to find the one that drives you to make the difference." —**Michael Stuart,** legacy and estate planner

"I believe that volunteering is educational, rewarding, and necessary. I think every person should be in service at some point of life, and [it] is payback for the incredible privilege for being American." —**Susan O'Neil,** business owner and writer

"Volunteering has many benefits: connection, engagement, meaning, self-esteem, camaraderie, fun, and the realization that the world is more than just yourself. Volunteering can be a public type of activity or within one's family or community. It can be a variety of different contributions that you care about." —**Dorian Mintzer,** therapist, author, and coach

Finding the right fit in volunteering can help you not only deepen a sense of purpose but also renew your sense of identity. Finding your cause and what is most important is the key to meaningful volunteering. And the nature of volunteering is changing, just as we change in the second half of life.

NEW WAYS OF VOLUNTEERING

Volunteering is evolving, changing how many are volunteering their time in meaningful ways. An AARP survey reports a disconnect between how we define volunteerism and the true level of generosity that we share within our communities and neighborhoods.[12] Roughly half of adults participate in "informal volunteering," consisting of activities like cooking a meal for someone, driving a sick neighbor to an appointment, or lending some kind of unpaid help without coordination of an overarching organization.[13] We can also learn and reimagine ways to volunteer by leveraging technology and creating more flexibility for those who want to give back. Limited time can be a barrier to volunteering, and part of the evolution of volunteerism is to get creative in helping busy adults find the time and opportunity to do so.

Finding meaning and fit involves a self-assessment of personal and professional goals. One woman recalls her father, who had recently retired. She explained how her dad was a "volunteer on overload." As he panicked about losing his identity and self-worth that came from his long-term career, he started volunteering at four or five organizations with the goal of staying occupied. Though his intentions were good, there was no fulfillment or purpose. He was running from one thing to the next. What was missing was a connection to the mission and intentionally using the skills he most wanted to use or develop.

Sandy and her husband Russ have an idea to merge their two interests volunteering in their community. Russ enjoys gardening and Sandy loves to cook. Bringing both interests to teach children at a local elementary school about gardening and how to cook a meal with fresh vegetables is their focus. Teaching children and healthy eating are meaningful to both of them. Perhaps you can get creative and discover what a new way of volunteering looks like to you. There is no limit to the number of volunteer options. Whether you create your own way or want to explore nonprofit organizations, volunteering is alive and well.

CHOOSING THE RIGHT ORGANIZATION AND ROLE

It's important to choose the right organization to volunteer for. Consider some of the organizations in your area. What causes speak to you? If you can answer by saying, "I need to do something about that," then that might be the right organization for you.

It is also important to find the right role. What are the skills you most enjoy using? You might consider taking on a role very similar to the role you had when employed—but that could also be a mistake. Those may be strong skills, but they might also be the reason you retired. What are adjacent skills or skills you haven't used but are of great interest? Developing new skills may be a way to get outside of your comfort zone, which can inspire learning and growth. You may discover something new that you truly enjoy.

Here are some questions to ask yourself when you consider volunteering:

- Why do I want to volunteer?
- What causes are most important to me?
- Who do I want to help?
- Which skills do I want to use? What skills do I want to learn?
- Do I miss what I did and desire something similar?
- Or, do I crave something new and different?
- What do I want to get out of volunteering?

The answers to these questions will help you determine which organizations and volunteer roles will best suit you. Discovering what energizes you will create a more meaningful experience. You should also consider what type of time commitment is right for you. For example, do you want to find an opportunity with a regular schedule, or would you prefer to commit to a term or project with a specific endpoint? There are many options, depending on the needs of different organizations. Many organizations list specific volunteering opportunities on their websites—and you can also reach out and ask. Search in your community for volunteer match programs, like VolunteerMatch, Retired and Senior Volunteer Program (RSVP), and faith-based communities, or start asking others in your community about their volunteer experiences. Let the exploration begin!

CHARITABLE DONATIONS

Another option is to donate money to a charity. You want your donations to count, so it's important to do some research before giving to a charity. Here are some things the Federal Trade Commission suggest you can do to learn more about a charity and avoid donating to a scam:

- If you are not familiar with an organization you want to support, search online for a cause that you care about. Once you find a specific charity, search its name plus "review," "fraud," or "scam." This will help you to discover if there are bad reviews before you donate.

- Check out the charity's website: Does it give you details about the programs you want to support? How much of your donation will go directly to support programs you care about? If you can't find detailed information about a charity's mission or programs, you may want to reconsider donating to them.

- Check if the donation may be tax deductible: If this is important to you, confirm that the organization you're donating to is registered as a tax-exempt organization.[14]

Once you have determined that the charity is legitimate and one that holds importance to you, here are ways to donate:

- **Monetary:** It's best to make financial donations by check or credit card, as these payment methods will be a record of your donations, protecting you from scams.

- **Goods and personal property:** Some charities accept non-cash donations, such as clothing and household items. Keep a list of the items for your taxes and ask for a receipt (which most organizations will provide).

Whether you volunteer your time or donate money or goods, both options are compassionate acts. When we are generous, we feel compassion for others and learn more about the needs of our community and the world. Every hour spent volunteering and every dollar helps. With so many missions in need of support, seek out nonprofits that speak to the concerns that matter most to you. Over time, you can grow with the organization and see how your gifts are making an impact.

In this chapter we took a dive into discovering work that matters. We want to know that our lives and work matter, so this new stage of life is an important time for thinking and assessing. We explored the significance of getting off Someday Island and bringing our dreams to center stage to live a more fulfilled life as we move to our next chapter. Paths to encore careers, entrepreneurial options—both business and social—and mindful volunteering all lead to greater purpose, fulfillment, and meaning. Our hope is that you will look ahead at what could be next with imagination, curiosity, and anticipation for those wonders that are over the horizon. Be inspired to start living your "somedays" today!

CONSCIOUS LIVING PRACTICES

Questions for Reflection

- What are the dreams that will get you off Someday Island?
- What are possible encore options you want to test out?
- What's your wildest, most creative entrepreneurial fantasy?
- What community and global issues would you like to be involved in?
- What might be a new way of volunteering for you?

Try This

- To identify aspects of your personality that will inspire working for fulfillment, interview your friends, family, and colleagues! Ask questions like the following: What do you think is my greatest strength? My biggest weakness? What do you see as my special talent, ability, or gift? What do I do naturally and effortlessly that is special? If I were on the cover of a magazine, what magazine would it be, and what would the article be about?
- Brainstorm what comes up for you from your heart, not your head. What brings you joy? What activity are you doing where you completely lose track of time? What energizes you?

Living
Well

Bouncing
Forward

Appreciating
Money

Living with
Technology

Working
for a Living

Exploring
Purposefully

Helping
Humanity

Working for
Fulfillment

Minding
Relationships

Savoring
the World

Living Life
Creatively

CHAPTER 6

SAVORING THE WORLD

The way to develop the habit of savoring is to pause when
something is beautiful and good and catches our attention—
the sound of rain, the look of the night sky, the glow in a
child's eyes, or when we witness some kindness. Pause . . .
then totally immerse in the experience of savoring it.

–TARA BRACH

L iving consciously includes an increasing awareness of this beautiful
planet we call home, appreciating what is within and beyond our
world, grateful for what we have and yet dreaming of possibilities
beyond our imagination. Savoring may be thought of as pausing and
stepping outside of our experience to review and appreciate different
elements of our beautiful world. Savoring can help intensify the positive emotions that come with being somewhere or doing something we
love. In this chapter, we explore savoring the places we live and the
places we visit.

Where we live and where we go are choices we can make more consciously as we progress through the second half of life. Some of us grow up on the move, going wherever our parents take us, which is especially true for military families; some parents stay put and we grow up in a single location. Our extended families may be mostly in one geographic location or may be distributed around the world. Where do you want to live? Where do you want to go? These are important questions explored in this chapter on savoring the world. We will begin with an exploration of possibilities for where we might choose to live in midlife and beyond and then consider possibilities for travel as more time and opportunities become available in the second half of life.

WHERE TO LIVE

Work opportunities and family responsibilities often determine where we're living as we approach the second half of life. We may have moved around a lot or a little, with maybe only limited control of where we ended up living. With the global nature of our world, people today often live somewhere different from where they were born or grew up. People may have moved to different towns, different regions, and even different countries. Many of these moves may have been reactive, responding to new opportunities or specific demands. We may now be able to shift to a more proactive approach.

Choosing where to live may be a no-brainer for you, yet, when it comes to the second half of life, new possibilities may emerge that were not evident before. In any case, moving or staying is a huge decision facing many people, and the final choice may be difficult. Here are some questions to consider and then discuss with a partner or with close family members or friends:

- **Which country?** Do I want to stay in the country where I have been living or move to another country?

- **Which environment?** Do I want to live in a city center or a rural location, beach or mountains, house or apartment? What are the most important features of my dream home?

- **What about work?** What work opportunities, paid or volunteer, am I looking for?

- **What activities are available?** What recreational activities and communities are important to me?

Wherever you are living now, take a moment to consider the ideal place to live. Maybe you are already there, or maybe you dream of living somewhere else. Think about your life purpose, your health, your relationships, your finances, your work. As you age, where in the world do you see yourself living? Which country, which region, which city or town? What sort of home? What would your dream home look like? Let's explore some of the options.

WHICH COUNTRY?

In the future, we may be able to consider on which planet we might want to live, especially in light of Elon Musk's imaginative ideas with SpaceX. For most of us that may be unlikely, so let's begin at the country level. Wherever you are currently living, which country would you most like to call home in the second half of your life? Do you want to stay in the country you are living in now, or do you have aspirations to live in another country, maybe returning to your country of origin or somewhere completely different?

In Europe, people seeking warmer climates often choose to move south, to the Mediterranean coasts of Spain, Portugal, France, or Italy.

In North America, popular destinations include Arizona, Florida, and North Carolina. Farther south, Mexico, Costa Rica, and Ecuador are increasingly popular. Those who can afford to may choose to own a second home in these regions of the world, while others may sell their primary residence and relocate permanently to these warmer climes.

During the research interviews for this book, we found many people who had moved or are considering moving to another country.

Marc Miller, professional career changer and founder of Career Pivot, had traveled the world for business and was living in Texas. Because of the high cost of health insurance in the United States, Marc and his wife considered moving to another country. He began "dating" different countries, visiting Mexico and Ecuador, among others. In 2018, still in his early sixties and while still working, Marc decided together with his wife to move across the border to Ajijic, a mountain location near Guadalajara, Mexico. Becoming an expat is not for everyone, but leasing rather than purchasing a home gave Marc and his wife initial flexibility, and they are only a short flight or a long drive away from friends and family in Texas.

As the only American in his family, David Treece, a financial advisor living with his husband in Miami, had a choice: stay in Florida or move to another country. With family in Argentina, Brazil, and Spain and friends in the United States, David had to choose whether to move abroad or remain in the United States. Moving abroad brings many different challenges, but your money can go a lot further, depending on where you choose to go. Expatriate communities in places like Mexico, Costa Rica, Panama, or Ecuador were attractive to David and his husband. Another attractive option was Argentina, where he already owned a beautiful ranch. The final choice was yet to be made as we completed this book.

Glenys and Brian Davison moved from southern England to the island of Madeira, an autonomous region of Portugal, off the northwest coast of Africa. Having been married for 27 years and retiring from careers in the UK's National Health Service, they started looking for a more relaxed way of life, enhanced standard of living, and a more stable, warmer climate. On a holiday and fact-finding visit to Madeira, they fell in love with a wonderful property with scenic landscapes overlooking the Atlantic Ocean. They returned to England and began a due diligence process with careful examination of government websites and interaction with local English-speaking groups on the island. Their offer on the property they fell in love with was accepted. Within a few months, they had sold their home in England and moved with their furniture and their animals to Madeira.

They felt welcomed, made many island friends, and settled in quickly. The relaxed, go-with-the-flow philosophy suited them, and the gloriously warm weather exceeded their expectations. They took language classes to learn Portuguese. Madeira proved to be a wonderful island. They were living the life they imagined. Family and friends came to visit, and although it tugged at their heartstrings when they left to go home, they were enjoying life.

After six or seven years, with the looming prospect of Brexit where the UK would leave the Euro Zone and the likely changes to residency rules and taxation, they seriously considered returning to England. They were getting older, family was back in England, medical care was better there, and the potential isolation of living on an island off the coast of Africa all became more important factors for consideration. They decided to return to England, but selling their property turned out to be a protracted experience. Sadly, the value of the property had declined due to the reduced demand for homes on the island, and it took nearly three years to find a buyer. Eventually they returned to England, but the financial losses made finding a new home quite difficult, and reintegration took time. With family help, they managed to reestablish themselves.

Looking back, if they knew then what they know now, would they have gone? Probably not. They said they would also have rented a property rather than bought a home, which would have provided more flexibility in decision-making and not resulted in a protracted period before being able to return to England.

Moving to another country may sound exciting and adventurous—but it's also important to remember that it requires conscious choices, and there are big consequences in moving far from what you know. If you decide to move, be sure to not only do your research in advance, but have a backup plan in case you decide to move back.

Before You Make the Move

- Do some soul-searching. Be completely realistic in what you are doing; think with your head as well as your heart.
- Do your research: visit in advance, talk to locals, seek out others who have made the move and ask their advice.
- Rent, at least for a while, before committing to buy a property.
- Consider financial issues: the cost of living, taxation, and any implications for your pension, and the cost of traveling back and forth between your new home and your home country.
- Research the healthcare options and be sure they meet your needs both in terms of cost and accessibility.
- Consider the proximity of family and friends. Is it easy for them to visit?
- Learn the language! This will help you befriend locals and be part of your new community.
- Take the opportunity to experience a different way of life and fully embrace it.
- Be prepared for unanticipated challenges.
- Have a contingency plan for returning or moving on.
- Consider end-of-life issues such as estate planning and where you want to be buried or have your ashes scattered.

It's also worth considering whether you see yourself in this new location for the long term, including the end of your life. In any case, if you are considering moving to another country, consider all the implications carefully and talk to people who made that choice. Consider "dating" places in different countries to explore what you like and don't like about the location.

WHICH ENVIRONMENT?

Having decided on the country, consider the local environment where you would like to live. You may have lived most of your life in big cities and have a desire to move to a more rural location. In the US, you may want to move to a college town where open spaces and cultural amenities are close by. You may be thinking about downsizing, moving from a big house to a smaller home or an apartment, or "rightsizing" to allow for family visits and long-term care. You may be dreaming of greater luxury or, on the other hand, a minimalistic lifestyle with less stuff. You may imagine yourself living by the beach or in the mountains. You may want to move closer to or farther away from family. You may be looking for community living or long-term care facilities. There's so much to consider! Pause for a moment and consciously consider your preferences.

To imagine your new environment, you may wish to create or revisit your vision board, sometimes referred to as a collage or a Map of Life: a physical or virtual board where you arrange photographs, images, and words that represent your hopes and dreams for the future. John Assaraf, one of the leading high-performance success coaches in the world, tells the story of how he bought the actual dream home pictured on his vision board without even realizing it. The vision board process can include a physical board with cutouts from magazines arranged and pinned or glued to the board, or if you are tech savvy, you can use a program like PowerPoint, Canva, or Pinterest. Look online for real estate listings, pictures of cities or towns, and pictures of natural environments to create your vision of your desired future on the screen.

As we journey through the second half of life, our hopes, needs, and desires for the home we live in may change. Our health, finances, and relationships all play a part in determining our preferences, possibilities, and choices for where we would like to live. We may choose to stay in familiar surroundings or in a long-time family home, or we might decide that this new phase in life is a great time to downsize or move to a more maintenance-free apartment. We might consider options of renting or buying. We might also consider community living.

Depending on our age and stage of life, communities with on-site assistance and care services may be a priority. We may be considering aging in place in a smart home (see more in chapter 10, Living with Technology). We may wish to consider multigenerational living and co-housing options. Choosing the best environment for living in the second half of life requires a conscious evaluation of the possibilities open to us.

OUR COMMUNITIES

Consciously thinking about our communities is an important element of choosing where to live in midlife and beyond. Depending on where we live, day-to-day activities might include spending time with someone inside or outside; playing golf, tennis, or pickleball; or being there to support a partner or friend with meals or driving to and from appointments. There is a lot to be said about being there for others and others being there for you.

Even if you're living independently in a house or apartment, you may want to seek out others in your community who share your interests. Your local community center may have ways for residents to connect, and you can look for information about other community initiatives with your chamber of commerce, public library, or college or university.

If you're considering a home in a 55-plus community or retirement village, you'll have the opportunity to live among contemporaries and like-minded people offering shared interests in activities and events. Today's active 55-plus communities are also realizing that members want greater diversity with intergenerational activities beyond their immediate family. Lifestyle is an essential factor when considering where to live. You may be seeking a community offering lifestyle practices that support healthy living and spiritual growth with interconnections and interdependence and also continuing care facilities for later life challenges. Blue Zones regions and cities such as Southwest Florida; Loma Linda, California; Sardinia, Italy;[1] and eco-towns and villages[2] such as in Elmsbrook, England, and Yucatan, Mexico, are examples of regenerative communities promoting longevity and quality of life and offering healthy living, education, activism, and community. No matter where we choose to live, we need to think about practices and activities that support health and well-being.

Our relationships often influence our choices about where to live. Are you living with a partner or living alone? If you do have a partner, think about your community and what would happen if you or your partner were to be left living alone. Would you still have the support you need? We also explore solo living in Minding Relationships (chapter 8).

For the gay community, choosing where to live presents additional challenges. When openly gay author and round-the-world sailor Larry Jacobson talks about the gay community, he includes the entire community of LGBTQ+ people. During our conversation, Larry talked about the specific challenges of the gay community in thinking about where to live particularly when living alone, and he said: "Gay men and single women have a lot in common: we still experience prejudice in different aspects of our lives such as in renting homes, visiting people in hospital, and in moving into assisted living and nursing homes." We have come a long way in reducing long-held prejudices, but more education is needed.

While some people prefer living alone, others like the companionship of living with someone else. Multigenerational housing and co-generational living are becoming increasingly popular, sometimes with family members but also with nonfamily members. You may wish to consider offering free or low-cost accommodation in exchange for work around the home. Finding a compatible housemate may not be easy, but local resources are available as well as online resources for your area.

Whether you choose to live in an urban or rural environment, you'll also want to consider the proximity of your community to family and friends, transportation centers such as airports and railway stations, or local entertainment, sports, and recreational activities. What's important to you, and what do you envision needing now and in the future? Take some time to reflect on the possibilities, your hopes and dreams, and the importance of each of the different factors.

HOME SITTING AND HOUSE SWAPPING

Something else to consider—especially if you haven't yet decided on the community where you want to live—is home sitting or house swapping. In other words, living the good life rent-free.

Perhaps you want to explore a new place for weeks or months without paying for a hotel, and you don't like the idea of an exchange where you have strangers living in your house. Consider a position as a property caretaker or house sitter, which allows you to stay in someone's home for free in return for providing services such as pet care, gardening, or property management. In addition to free housing, some caretaker positions offer a stipend, while others may even include a salary and benefits.

Caretaking can offer more exotic surroundings than typical tourist fare. A recent issue of *The Caretaker Gazette* advertised a salaried position for a retired couple to maintain a private lodge in the wilderness of southwest Alaska—though you'd need some experience with small motors and cutting firewood! Another gig—three months in Sedona, Arizona, looking after three cats and a garden. Does a five-week house-sit in Hawaii, on a property bordered by rain forests, sound appealing? You must be willing to care for a cat, six dogs, and fish tanks, and to water young plants.[3]

Another option is a house exchange or home swap, where you exchange your home with another homeowner for a few days or weeks. You get to choose your ideal home and location from thousands of beautiful homes in countries around the world. Joining a home swap membership site provides access to these opportunities.[4]

Choosing where to live may represent a huge decision for you. Take the time to explore possibilities and make conscious choices about the future.

WHERE TO GO

As you make transitions in the second half of life, you might also find that you have more free time and more disposable income, which presents opportunities to travel and explore the world. The question then becomes, where to go? What travel ideas fit with your lifestyle? Do you want to visit friends and family and the places around where they live or try out something entirely new? There are so many possibilities and places in the world to visit.

Here's what we heard during some of our interviews:

Travel Inspiration

Different countries: "We love to go to different countries to see different people, different food, you know, arts and crafts and things. That's what we enjoy." —**Monty Patch,** author and AARP volunteer

The people: "When we travel, it's important to learn about the people that live there, not just the beautiful sights." —**Dorothy Keenan,** GrandInvolve Founder and positive aging advocate

Travel blogger: "You name it, we probably want to go there. We feel like for the next 10 years, we want to do as much traveling as possible, while we can. I write a travel blog when we travel; I like to think of myself as a travel writer." —**Mike Bernhardt,** writer and grief support volunteer

Road warrior: "You can't buy happiness, but you can buy an RV, and that's kind of sort of the same thing." —**Gregory Peters,** artist and author

Climate impact: "For ecological reasons, I'm very conscious of the miles I travel at high altitude, knowing that it's quite impactful on global warming. So I travel virtually now." —**Alain Gauthier,** member of the Leadership Council, Elders Action Network

One of Paul's coaching clients was ready to travel but could not get agreement with his long-time life partner about where to go. Paul invited them each to make a list of the top ten destinations around the world they would like to visit and then reduce each list to the top five destinations, ranked in priority order. After comparing their lists, they were able to identify destinations they both wanted to visit and also places where one of them really wanted to visit and the other was happy to go along.

If you simply have a wanderlust, you could try coddiwompling, which may be thought of as traveling purposefully and pleasurably but without a specific destination in mind. Maybe you are someone who is consciously or unconsciously coddiwompling through life. If you know you want to travel to well-known places but are unsure about where to go, consider the seven wonders of the world or locations of cultural significance such as the UNESCO World Heritage sites, or learning adventures offered by organizations like Road Scholar and Explore! Read travel blogs available online. Think about what you want to experience or learn more about. If you are concerned about the environmental impact of traveling the world, consider more conscious travel options.

CONSCIOUS TRAVEL

Sustainable travel, regenerative travel, and mindful travel are among the new terminology being used in the tourism industry. Conscious travel embraces this new terminology. Most of us consider conscious travel from the perspective of the traveler—but it's also important to consider other perspectives through the lens of the tourism industry, such as the impact on particular destinations and the supply chain relating to the travel and tourism industry.

A sustainable tourism industry is a laudable aspiration. Jonathon Day, author of the book *An Introduction to Sustainable Tourism and Responsible Travel*, set out to make tourism the most sustainable industry on the planet while enriching our cultural experience and helping us to understand and appreciate our environment. He is committed to helping tourism be a force for good in the world. Jonathon leads the Travel Care Code initiative, a group of researchers and marketing executives committed to helping travel organizations and their clients travel more responsibly. The mission of the Travel Care Code is to ensure that every traveler contributes to the sustainability of the planet—supporting local economies, protecting the environment, celebrating local culture, and promoting social justice. The code includes being a good guest, being a fuel-efficient traveler, and making informed decisions, or what we might call conscious choices.[5]

Sustainable travel is about being aware of the environmental impact of travel, not making a mess of the environment, slowing down the degradation, and leaving places no worse than before you were there. Regenerative travel goes a step further, challenging travelers to leave the places they visit *better* than how they found them by improving the quality of life of the people who live there and upgrading the health of the local ecosystems. Restoring and regenerating the ecosystem of the places we visit can help build new positive relationships between the traveler and the local environment. Regenerative travel may be thought of as more of a supply-side concept, but as world tourism recovers from the coronavirus crisis, it will be up to both the tourism industry organizations and individual conscious travelers to take responsibility for our sustainable future. As conscious travelers, we can make more considerate choices about where we go and how we impact the environments we visit.

Playa Viva: An Example of Regenerative Travel

Looking beyond sustainability, Regenesis, a world leader in the field of regenerative development, worked on developing Playa Viva, a sustainable resort and residence community south of Zihuatanejo on Mexico's Pacific Coast. The development of the 200-acre property embraced the entire ecological system of the site along with the needs of the inhabitants of the local village. Adopting a biomimetic framework of gradual, adaptive expansion based on functions that work like nature, the development of Playa Viva included an organic agricultural system, sustainability education programs, and local hiring practices that benefited both the property and local residents. The small town of Juluchuca became the gateway to the property, and a 2 percent fee added to any stay funds a trust that invests in community development.

At the core of all of this work, the Playa Viva project was able to uncover a rich and amazing history that had largely been forgotten in the area. Through public education regarding this history and the place's potential, Playa Viva has enabled members of the community to feel, rightfully, that they have a say in how their community should evolve in the future.[6] Playa Viva is one of a select few resorts belonging to Regenerative Travel, a community of independently owned hotels dedicated to creating regenerative impact through travel, creating positive social and environmental impact, and restoring, repairing, and regenerating local communities and ecosystems.[7]

Don't let the climate crisis stop you from traveling, but as you consciously consider where to go, think about the impact of your trip and how you can mitigate that impact. Ask yourself, "What can I do to offset the impact of my travel?" Things to consider might include calculating the carbon footprint for your travel using one of the online tracking tools, selecting destinations with a focus on sustainability, choosing an airline that is proactively working on reducing reliance on fossil fuels, or hiring a car from rental companies that offer a carbon offset. Alternatively, look for places closer to home or explore virtual holiday tours online.

SOLO TRAVEL

Many of us plan our travel experiences with others, yet traveling solo is also popular and well worth considering. Maybe you don't have a travel partner, or maybe you want to go somewhere your partner has no interest in going. For many reasons, you might be faced with the choice of traveling alone or not traveling at all. Don't let the lack of a travel companion stop you from enjoying amazing travel experiences!

Traveling solo can give you complete freedom and control to go wherever you want and do whatever you want, whenever you want. And, if you choose and are even a little outgoing, there's a good chance you will meet new people on your travels. Numerous resources for the solo traveler are available on the internet, including accommodation-sharing plans to avoid single occupancy supplement charges. There are many possibilities, including themed cruises, in-depth or multicity tours, and retreats in locations close to nature.

Traveling alone is not without its challenges, but consciously choosing where to go and which travel organization to partner with, along with an awareness of the potential risks you may face, can help overcome any potential hazards. With solo travel, you are likely to have new experiences in new places and find new friends that you would never have found by staying home alone.

SPIRITUAL OR INNER JOURNEYS

In addition to physical journeys, many of us explore spiritual or inner journeys. For more than 25 years, *The Power of Purpose* author and executive coach Richard Leider organized "inventure" expeditions to East Africa. These inventures combined the adventure of a walking safari with an inner journey of discovery. Paul joined one of these inventures in 2009 (as was noted in chapter 1).[8]

An Inventure in Africa

"My inventure in East Africa was a fifteen-day walking safari across the Serengeti, sleeping in tents erected by a support team and unplugged from all electronic devices. Conversations around campfires and during long treks across the plains, personal reflections during quiet periods of solitude, and daily journaling provided opportunities to get back to the rhythm in the place where the original people on earth emerged. I set no specific goals and embraced this inventure as a learning opportunity: learning about the region, the animals, and the way of life of the people of the Hadza and Maasai tribes; learning about my fellow travelers and Richard Leider's power of purpose; and, perhaps most importantly, learning about me and my own life's journey. The inner transformations that began during that inventure continue today." **—Paul Ward**

Spiritual journeys often combine the solitude of personal transformations with intimate group conversations. An internet search for spiritual journeys reveals a multitude of different types of spiritual explorations. You might consider the Shamanic Journeys and vision quests offered by Sparrow Hart at Circles of Air & Stone[9] or Journeys of the Spirit offered by Sheri Rosenthal.[10] The profound experience of learning from the Hadza—the "original people"—with Dorobo Safaris[11] in Tanzania, East Africa, has shifted many people's view of the world and themselves. Alternatively, consider companies creating immersive and powerful experiences such as The Explorers Passage,[12] which partners with organizations such as Jane Goodall's youth-oriented program Roots and Shoots[13] and Robert Swan's 2041 Foundation with expeditions to Antarctica.[14] You may wish to consider an extended hiking trip along trails such as the Appalachian Trail in the United States, Camino de Santiago in Spain, or the Trans Pennine Trail in Northern England, all of which are favorites of those seeking to add a spiritual aspect to a physical journey. Consider looking at the world from different perspectives or through the eyes of different people. You might even take a ride in Paul's hot air balloon or Richard Branson's Virgin Galactica trips to the edge of space.

In this chapter on savoring the world, we have explored the conscious choices relating to the places we live and the places we visit. Beyond our focus on where to be and where to go, we encourage you to pause at any time to savor what you find in the world around you: the people, including the very young, the very old, and everyone in between; the natural world, the animals and the birds, the plants, the trees, the land, the seas, and the sky; the moment-to-moment experiences that bring joy and laughter, sorrow and tears. Whether being in the present moment, remembering an experience from the past, or planning for future conscious travel experiences, savoring these positive thoughts and images can bring greater joy and happiness into our lives. Despite the challenges we face, it is still a beautiful world.

CONSCIOUS LIVING PRACTICES

Questions for Reflection

- Where would you choose to live?
- What type of home do you want?
- What are your community needs?
- Where would you choose to go for travel and adventure?
- What do you need to begin savoring your world?

Try This

- Select one experience to truly savor each day in your world or your community, such as a walk in nature, quiet time in your favorite armchair, or a conversation with friends.
- Make a list of the places you dream of living.
- Name all the places you dream of visiting.

Living
Well

Bouncing
Forward

Appreciating
Money

Living with
Technology

Working
for a Living

Exploring
Purposefully

Helping
Humanity

Working for
Fulfillment

Minding
Relationships

Savoring
the World

Living Life
Creatively

CHAPTER 7

LIVING LIFE CREATIVELY

The creative process is defined not only in the approach to the
arts, but also how it relates to living each day with the kind
of creative thought that leads to a more fulfilling lifestyle.

–JILL BADONSKY

Creativity is the door to a fun, flavorful, and fulfilling life. You are
the one who can open the door to let the magic in. Where in
your life might you like more sparkle and engaged enthusiasm?

In this chapter we explore creativity and the link to imagination,
examining themes of creative living and creative aging. We look at the
soil, seeds, and sunlight required for living life creatively, and present
ideas for getting in touch with your creative side so you can integrate it
into your lives for maximizing joy, fulfillment, health, and well-being.
You'll discover mindsets, practices, and plans for living more creatively
in midlife and beyond.

We often use the words "imagination" and "creativity" interchange-ably, but they have different meanings. Imagination is something that exists or happens only in our minds. It can be thought of as a picture of something that may or may not be real, and maybe something we have never seen or experienced before. Famed astronomer and planetary scientist Carl Sagan said that "imagination will often carry us to worlds that never were. But without it, we go nowhere."[1] Imagination may be considered to be where creativity begins.

Creativity is a process of using your imagination to bring something new into existence, such as an idea, a process, or a product. Creativity represents potential, promise, and hope. It provides us with an abun-dance of health and well-being benefits, making us feel energized, alive, and happy. Creativity stimulates the brain and adds to our cognitive health. It helps relieve stress and lends balance to our lives. It allows us to uniquely express ourselves to bring meaning to our lives. Creativity has practical applications too, as it can save us time, money, and diffi-culty with new ideas to streamline and make a product or process more effective and efficient. It provides for social connections, friendships, and building community—all of which become even more important in midlife and beyond. Creativity provides inherent rewards, especially if we consciously decide to approach it as an adventure and explore the possibilities. Perhaps most importantly, creativity grants us the freedom to be fine with not knowing the answers of what we want to do immediately in the second half of our lives.

There is an art to cultivating and living a creative life. Whether it comes naturally or not, we can always learn more fun tips and tricks for enhancing our lives. Curiosity about responding to challenges are catalysts that get our imagination going, our ideas flowing, and our creativity ignited into new and exciting possibilities. Surely it is an ideal time to reimagine and reinvent ourselves and how we want to live our lives.

CREATIVE AGING AND CREATIVE LIVING

Perhaps you've heard the term *creative aging*. But what does it really mean?

Creative aging, in its broad scope, is all about the possibilities, lifelong learning, and the fun of its expression. It is about creative generativity, which are the creative ways we contribute to the next generation as we age. It is about the joy in the journey of the creative process and all the tangibles and intangibles that come along with the journey. It is about finding new and different ways to be, do, have, and give as we age. In its more specific scope, creative aging refers to the enrichment of the lives of older adults through professionally run art education programs.[2] These programs are widely offered and based on Gene Cohen's creativity and aging study with their significant health and well-being benefits.[3]

We prefer the term *creative living*, because it encompasses an expansive lifestyle approach of activating our brains for fun and fulfillment, addressing the challenges and opportunities that can show up in the second half of life. It aligns well with our emphasis on living consciously. It is an approach for everyone.

Elizabeth Gilbert, author of the best-selling book *Big Magic: Creative Living Beyond Fear*, says that when she is talking about creative living, she is speaking more broadly about living a life that is driven more strongly by curiosity than by fear. She writes, "And while the paths and outcomes of creative living will vary wildly from person to person, I can guarantee you this: A creative life *is* an amplified life. It's a bigger life, a happier life, an expanded life, and a hell of a lot more interesting life. Living in this manner—continually and stubbornly bringing forth the jewels that are hidden within you—is a fine art, in and of itself. Because creative living is where Big Magic will always abide."[4]

We use the phrase "living life creatively" to emphasize the active creative engagement of living life consciously with imagination, curiosity, courage, and cheer as an attitude and a way of life.

SOIL, SEEDS, AND SUNLIGHT

Like a beautiful garden, midlife offers the perfect medium of events and experiences to grow and flourish. We need soil, seeds, and sunlight for living life creatively.

Our full and rich experiences during the first half of life may have provided the soil for our creativity. The periods of growing up, going to school, getting a job, building relationships, owning a home, and having children may have included enriching experiences that fertilized our imagination and prepared the ground for the second half. Abraham Maslow,[5] the acclaimed psychologist for his hierarchy of needs theory, believed that once all basic needs are satisfied, people can then move on to the higher levels of optimizing their potential and achieving self-actualization.

During our life and travel experiences, seeds may have been planted in our imagination. We may have harbored secret desires to write, draw, paint, photograph, cook, perform, or embark on other creative endeavors. Maybe these seeds have already been watered, resulting in significant accomplishment—or maybe they're lying just below the surface, ready to burst into life. This may be the time for exploring and discovering your creative passions and paying attention to the seeds of your imagination. What are your seeds of imagination?

With water and sunlight, these seeds can begin to germinate and grow. You may need to learn new skills or take classes; you might want to share your creative ideas with others. Check out your local art or recreational centers, museums, and adult education centers for new ideas and offerings. For specific areas of interest such as culinary, design, or fashion, look for offerings at meetup groups or specialized centers in your area. Take the time to seek out like-minded creative thinkers. It is time to let the sun shine on your imagination and allow your creativity to emerge.

THE JOY FACTOR

Joyful experiences can be found as we immerse ourselves in the creative process—simply the joy of creating! When we're doing something we love and are in a flow state, our sense of time is freed from our mind.

The concept of creative flow comes from Mihaly Csikszentmihalyi, psychologist and author of *Flow: The Psychology of Optimal Experiences*[6] and *Creativity: The Psychology of Discovery and Invention.*[7] When we're totally immersed in a creative activity, time seems to fly. That's flow. Being in a flow state is credited with providing us with happiness, enjoyment, and fulfillment. What experiences have you had where your sense of time evaporated while you were completely immersed in a joyful activity? Making the decision to rediscover creative activities or find new ones adds to the purposeful core of our Conscious Living Wheel of being intentional with our lives.

Perhaps you had a hobby or interest that inspired you but you gave it up to pursue education, work, or family. You may have wondered if you would ever get back to it. Midlife is often the catalyst for seeking to rekindle our past interests and pursue new ones, because now we may have more time. Do you have a creative pursuit you'd like to take up again?

Also, think broadly in terms of creativity! You don't have to be a concert pianist or accomplished painter to be considered "creative." Writer Ann McKerrow says that "creativity is being open-minded to creative approaches. You do not necessarily need to have a product to show as a badge of your creativity, although some may desire that." For her, it is more about creative approaches to living our lives. Here's how some of the people we interviewed find their creative flow:

A Range of Creative Activities

- **Candy Spitz** (career transition coach) knits legacy afghans for family and friends, makes jewelry, devises exciting travel itineraries, and designs Zen places in her garden.
- **Donna Kraus** (business owner and yoga instructor) sings, teaches yoga, and noodles around with solutions to challenges in her business.
- **Monty Patch** (author and AARP volunteer) is retired. As an AARP volunteer, he gives lectures to senior groups and participates in community activities. He published an e-book entitled *SparkE the Sparrow*.
- **Susan O'Neil** (business owner and writer) has written since she was a teen and now enjoys the freedom to write what she wants and attend her writing clubs.
- **Kathy McEvoy** (retired executive, entrepreneur, lifelong volunteer) finds joy simply in the creative integration of her roles of being a wife, parent, and engaged community member.

We encourage you to look back on your life for clues as to what has interested and excited you. Now is the time to draw upon your imagination for new ways of thinking about how you can experience creative flow with joyful activities.

SPONTANEOUS SPARKS

Midlife and beyond is especially abundant for ideas because of the mileage in our years, our vast experiences, and new challenges. We begin connecting the dots in new and different ways. Simply asking ourselves questions taps into our curiosity, stimulating our imagination about what we want for our next life chapter—and serves as sparks to get our creative juices flowing.

With curiosity and courage, pause and consider these questions:

- What energizes and excites you?
- What do you like to talk about?
- What activities cause you to lose track of time?
- What type of books, podcasts, or videos interest you?

Once our interest in something is sparked, we tend to ask ourselves, "Now what?" As Steve Jobs said, "Creativity is just connecting things,"[8] so we start to connect the dots. Conversations with others are abundant sources for connecting ideas, sparking courage and creativity, acquiring wisdom, and building community. Like a bee in cross-pollination, the more diverse the people we engage with in our creative pursuits, the more diverse the viewpoints and the more creative potential exists for creative living and blooming in midlife and beyond. Spontaneous creative ideas emerge and evolve as we share ideas, thoughts, and musings. Sharing our experiences and life lessons brings new and different ways of thinking, doing, being, giving, and receiving. All are powerful sparks for creativity and wisdom.

So how do we do this? To get your creative juices flowing, you might take an improv class where creativity, collaboration, communication, and critical thinking are nurtured in a fun, judgment-free environment. You might also take a creativity class. For example, Eileen teaches one called Explore, Experience, and Expand Your Creativity, where attendees explore creative expression in writing memoirs, speaking, photography, and more. In another class called Creative Life Design, her participants explore creative expression to include approaches to midlife challenges and opportunities. One person decided to paint and stencil her old unwanted furniture in bright colors to give away or sell, and another person transformed broken family jewelry into unique framed art. These types of opportunities are widely available both online and offline. Improv classes are offered by theater companies, comedy clubs, and colleges, often with drop-in classes so you can get a taste of a class before committing. Creativity classes can be found at adult education centers, art studios, and some museums. You can also look for classes or workshops that specifically focus on midlife and beyond creativity, such as those that use Julia Cameron's book *It's Never Too Late to Begin Again: Discovering Creativity and Meaning at Midlife and Beyond* as their class base. Meetup groups, faith-based communities, and professionals offering coaching can be another place to connect with others, spark ideas, and connect those creative dots.

Another way to connect to others is through what we call *Conscious Living conversation circles*. What do we mean by that? In a Conscious Living conversation circle, participants engage in a facilitated group discussion on a wide variety of specific themes of intentional engaged living such as re-careering, staying healthy, and building up your support network. Some topics have guest speakers. Participants gain insights and inspiration for creative or enhanced ways of living and develop fellowship with other attendees in the process. Participants can suggest topics of interest. (Refer to the Resources section at the end of the book for more info.)

Chip Conley, founder of the first global midlife wisdom school, the Modern Elder Academy,[9] of which Eileen and Sandy are alums, firmly believes that wisdom is not taught; it is shared. The academy offers extensive programs online and in person and fosters connections among participants to share experiences and wisdom. Programs include classes, workshops, sabbatical sessions, group activities, diverse guest speakers, media presentations, and the development of supportive fellowship to help you venture forward on your midlife path.

Significant wisdom and life lessons arise from any life stage or age. We advocate sharing experiences and wisdom to include multigenerational perspectives—so talk about creativity not only with your peers but also with your children, your parents, or the fifth-grader who lives down the block from you! If you join a group, look for one that invites people of diverse ages and backgrounds. Sharing ideas and life lessons with a wide range of people makes our communities strong, vibrant, and alive. It also helps us realize that we're not alone and gives us hope.

Here are some thoughts on life lessons and shared wisdom from our interviews that may inspire your own creativity:

Life Lessons and Creative Wisdom

- **Jill Badonsky** (creativity expert and author), a fully active creative guru whose whole life is focused on creativity, says that creativity *bridges the age gap* and connects the generations. She relays that there is no age differentiation in creative pursuits like Toastmasters or Open Mic nights because everyone is on the same plane and platform just sharing their creative work. It is something to keep in mind in connecting with other age groups and the sense of vitality and being alive. Following your curiosity and interests keeps you healthy and feeling young. In fact, she speaks of creativity as a healing channel to help process your feelings and thoughts.

- **Bruce Frankel** (author, president of the Life Planning Network) knows quite a bit on creative lives from his work interviewing people for *What Should I Do with the Rest of My Life?* "People, generally, are more creative than we think, and express their creativity in various, often unheralded ways. *Creativity is the ability to translate ideas and thoughts into an expressed reality.* Musical notes on a page are translated to sound, emotions can be translated into dance, imagined tastes into a meal." Creative possibilities abound for all of us, he says, citing the philosophy of MacArthur "Genius Grant" choreographer Liz Lerman, founder of the Dance Exchange, who has a vision of dance in which everybody can dance, from trained professionals to older adults—no matter their body type, ability, age, or training. Bruce's book is an example of storytelling as creativity. We acquire wisdom and build community by sharing our stories.

continued

> - **Candy Spitz** (career transition coach) tells us that through her work she has noted that a thread that runs through many women's lives is that it is particularly nice to have something else to create after raising a family.

When we share what sparks our interest and our wisdom with others, we are exposed to new and different ways of thinking that amplify our creativity as well as our understanding of different experiences that connect us to our humanity.

DEVELOPING OUR CREATIVE POTENTIAL FOR LIVING LIFE CREATIVELY

Creativity is like a muscle that can be built up with practice. In this section we present tips to help you nourish the seeds and soil of creativity so that it blooms in your life in new and different ways and leads to the benefits that make living vibrant and fulfilling.

Having the desire to live creatively is not enough. We need tools to develop that muscle. Read on to discover conscious creativity practices designed to enhance your creativity mindset. We'll introduce you to practices and mindsets to get you started, a process and skills to develop, and a guide to developing your pathways and plans for living creatively.

MINDSETS AND PRACTICES

Some of us already have a creative mindset—but some of us may think we lack this ability. We believe we can all be creative. Adopting this belief is key to a creative mindset, along with a curiosity to ask questions that generate ideas and possibilities. Many practices can be used to enhance our creativity and build a creative mindset. We hope the following practices will inspire you to develop greater confidence and begin cultivating and nurturing your creativity mindset.

Creating Space

New ideas often come to us out of the blue: maybe in the shower, during sleep time, surfing the internet, on a long walk, or in conversations with others. Consciously creating space for creativity can help provide room for creative ideas to flow. Take time to relax and clear your head of all distractions. Go for a walk in nature, along the beach or through a forest or a field, and up hills or through valleys. If you live in a city, find a quiet space in a local park. Even short spans of time offer real possibilities for resting, dreaming, and for our subconscious to be gently awakened for inspiration and ideas. Allow those creative juices the time and space to flow. If you consciously set aside time to do this, what ideas pop into your mind?

Fueling Our Imagination

Having created the physical and mental space, we can begin gently fueling our imagination by inviting in some sensory activities of our choice. Whether it is walking in nature, listening to music, doodling, surfing the internet, smelling a rose, golfing, visiting new places, or trying a new restaurant, consciously notice what is going on around you. Be curious. Set an intention to actively observe, really noticing what is there. How often do we go somewhere familiar yet see something that was there all along for the very first time?

Julia Cameron, creativity catalyst and author of more than forty books on creativity, has written two especially inspiring and fun books with activities to spur and fuel our imagination and spark our creativity:

the well-known *The Artist's Way*[10] already in its 25th edition and the follow-up *It's Never Too Late to Begin Again: Discovering Creativity and Meaning at Midlife and Beyond.*[11] Julia suggests the practice of going on "artist dates," which are little solo trips of exploration and discovery. It could be a trip to a bookstore or a gardening center, a yoga studio, a museum, or to watch a local woodworker in action. She also suggests "solo walks" to clear and calm our mind, and "morning pages" where you write daily, private, stream-of-consciousness thoughts with the goal of clearing the mind and providing a clear focus for starting the day. She insists that we are all creative beings, and that cultivating our own creativity helps us redefine, re-create, and navigate the new life terrain ahead.

Engaging in practices like this leads to creative ideas—and the more ideas we have, the more connections, options, and choices we have. Think of ideas as doors that can open new possibilities. Initial ideas—even if they seem strange or unformed—can lead to other ideas that resonate. Allow yourself to be free of judgment and see what evolves. Don't let your inner critic douse the flames of imagination.

Collecting Ideas

How often do you have an idea but later can't remember it? Capturing ideas is essential. Think of it like an old-fashioned piggy bank or glass jar: Each evening we would drop some coins and maybe paper money into it so we didn't lose it. We encourage you to start a creative idea jar—which could be an actual jar but could also be a stack of colored sticky notes, a special journal, your mobile device, or a Word file on your computer. You could also try a vision board for your ideas (described in the previous chapter). Whatever you do, capture and collect your creative ideas so they're there for you whenever you want them.

Being Courageous

A truly creative mindset requires us to be curious, adventurous, and courageous. In addition to sparking your curiosity and sense of adventure, practices like those described previously will grow your courage. Being curious by asking questions about topics of interest and being adventurous by going beyond the confines of immediate surroundings and exploring new possibilities enhance our creative mindset. Going all in—persevering and accepting mistakes and imperfections as part of creative thinking—allows you to courageously go further than you may have imagined. Be courageous with your creativity.

Creating with Others

Many of our ideas are personal relating to individual projects, but collaboration and co-creation can help enhance our creative thinking. The book you are reading would not have been created without the co-creation and collaboration of the authors. Cultivating shared space with people with similar aspirations yet diverse perspectives can help with nurturing our creativity. Creative conversations with others can help inspire imagination and develop ideas. Bring to mind one of your creative ideas. Who could be a valuable co-creator for this project?

Co-creating with others does not have to be a big project. It can be discovering that your neighbor likes to garden like you do, and you both co-create a vegetable garden together. It could evolve to learning together how to cook vegetables in a variety of flavorful ways. It could also be helping the neighborhood children build a small book box for the community or working with friends to develop a themed dinner. You can find your co-creator in your neighborhood, faith community, local yoga studio or woodworking center, or any place where you gather with others. Co-creating also adds to the courage component.

A creative mindset with enhancing practices goes hand in hand as the foundation—to inspire and support living life creatively. We now look at the larger creative process and specific skills that allow for ideas to bubble up and start moving forward.

PROCESS AND SKILLS

A creative process is the movement of ideas from inspirational sparks to new approaches, new activities, or newly created items. Although the process moves along, it is often not an immediate shot to a finish line because creativity takes time to incubate, nurture, and expand ideas. The fun is in the process, and creatives often say the process is the destination.

The Creative Process

Someone who deliberately works to create a more fulfilling life by adopting a broad view of creativity and finding ways to bring it into all aspects of their lives is what life transition expert Fred Mandell refers to as a "Life Change Artist." We will share his wisdom on moving from the start of the creative process to the point where we're able to integrate it and really use it.

Fred Mandell and Kathleen Jordan introduced the "creative dilemma" as the start of the creative process of exploring, discovering, and integrating in their book *Becoming a Life Change Artist: 7 Creative Skills to Reinvent Yourself at Any Stage of Life.*[12] Their model is built upon research of the great creative master artists and more than 100 interviews of individuals going through a variety of life changes. The creative processes and skills the master artists used apply not only to the arts but also to practical challenges: in other words, to life changes and transitions and to living creatively.

The process begins with awareness that there is a gap between our current state of life and a sense that it could be better. This poses a creative dilemma to act on it or not. A creative dilemma can arise in any area of our Conscious Living Wheel: It can involve where we live, work, learn, play, and more. For example, it could be seen in our physical health, such as the desire to be more active; or it could be seen in the area of work, as to whether to re-career or retire; or the area of purpose, in terms of how to live the rest of your life with new purpose and meaning.

Once we decide to act on the creative dilemma, we move into exploring possibilities, then discovering the best path forward and integrating the discoveries into new ways of thinking and being. To address expectations, note that the process is fluid, which means it involves some twists and turns, as with art; it also involves adding and subtracting, rethinking and tweaking as you go along. Here's an example:

The Fluid Creative Process

Creative Dilemma → Explore ←→ Discover ←→ Integrate

Sarah recognizes her *creative dilemma* is she no longer has energy or interest for her current job. She *explores* retiring by researching the topic. She finds it a bit overwhelming, so she puts on some music to relax and goes on nature walks during the week. After percolating on the possibilities, she *discovers* her "aha moment"—she will retire. She *integrates* her thinking and decision by implementing an action plan.

As the time to file retirement papers draws near, a new, exciting job is offered to her. New information is available. She wants to *explore* this option in person, so she excitingly cancels her retirement plans and takes the job. She tries out this new path only to *discover* that once in it, it does not fulfill her. Stepping back from her life canvas to see the big picture, she reviews her decisions and does a deeper dive into *exploring* options again. After further percolation on the possibilities, a new clear path is illuminated and she *discovers* that becoming an entrepreneur in her field will provide the fulfillment and fuel her energy. The "aha moment" has become much clearer to her.

She *integrates* her new learning, overcomes some barriers and a learning curve, and finally arrives at a fulfilling sweet spot in the entrepreneurial field she desires.

The Seven Creative Skills

Mandell and Jordan's approach to life's creative dilemmas entails employing some of the same effective skills that artists use to create their work, whether that's a painting, a book, an opera, or a piece of pottery. They identify seven creative skills within the creative process for being a successful life change artist.[13] Which ones are you already using, and which ones might you want to develop further?

- Preparation
- Seeing
- Using context
- Embracing uncertainty
- Risk-taking
- Collaboration
- Discipline

Preparation involves deliberately engaging in activities that predispose you to creative insights. The purpose is to relax and release you from the pressure of expectations so that ideas flow easily, as well as expose you to different stimuli so they act as catalysts for new ideas. There is a plethora of simple preparatory activities you could choose from such as doodling, juggling, gardening, biking, going to a new restaurant, walking the dog, raking leaves, and showering. Discover the activities when ideas pop up for you. Try new ones too.

Seeing involves discerning new possibilities, new connections, and fresh perspectives. This is a gateway skill to your creativity! One way to see is to "step away from the canvas," which refers to stepping outside of your usual perspectives. For example, stepping out of your office or home from your usual time demands gives you fresh perspective. Another way to see is to look beyond what seems obvious and notice what is missing. For example, you may be extremely successful at work and notice that free time to have fun or be creative is missing. Additionally, seeing can involve discovering connections that might not initially relate. For example, having fun and being creative may not initially feel related to your work, yet you connect the two and decide to gather interest at work for some new approaches. Looking at opposing thoughts can provide fertile ground for new insights. What might you notice with fresh eyes?

Using context entails awareness of how various environments and contexts such as where we live and work influence our thoughts and behaviors—and using that knowledge to create a life change. We can use the Conscious Living Wheel and select a context such as work, technology, or helping humanity, and then examine the roles we play and the trends in these areas. For example, you may not have had an active role in helping humanity, and now with more time you would like to help a local school build wooden theater props or sew costumes, or be active with an environmental trend in the community such as building beehives.

Embracing uncertainty is about acting on opportunities (sometimes hidden) presented by change. This skill is necessary for gaining new information and self-insight in navigating change. Accept the fact that answers or solutions may not be immediately apparent. Take your time. Live in the creative dilemma for a while, as it can be a source of creative insights. Activate patience and let your mind incubate on the ideas and information you gathered to allow your subconscious mind to connect the dots. For example, being let go from a joyless job may give new direction or possibilities that were not apparent before, such as creating your own consulting business or seeking out an alternative position that would allow you to feel energized.

Risk-taking is the taking-action skill without any certainty of outcome. Even if risk-taking makes us uncomfortable, you can start small! For example, you can set up an informational interview or shadow someone in an encore career you are interested in, rather than signing on to a new job. You can clarify your risks involved, such as staying in a joyless career versus learning about a new venture as an easy small step. Practicing this skill with small steps grows your confidence, and the small steps add up. Risk-taking applies to all areas of the Conscious Living Wheel. The information you learn from risk-taking will provide clarity for next steps.

Collaboration is engaging with others to help you make desired changes. This skill helps diminish risk-taking fears and provides built-in support and accountability. It can apply to any area. For example, say you want to do something beneficial and creative in the community but are not sure what, so you take a risk and host a BBQ to those interested in this idea. A few folks gather, and together the group decides to set up a plant-sharing day with a master gardener neighbor as a speaker, followed by a celebratory luncheon. You can develop your own collaborative group from family members, neighbors, faith-based groups, and other kindred individuals with special interests.

Discipline entails acting consistently, whether you're feeling motivated or not. It will help in putting forth the energy and effort to proceed intentionally when the spirit may not move you at the time. Self-renewal activities, goal setting with accountability partners, and self-determined rewards are some examples to build your discipline muscle. A creative mantra is another way to help motivate action. Fred Mandell shared his energizing mantra with us, which is "create, integrate, make a difference." Every morning he asks himself how he will create, integrate, and make a difference, and at the day's end he asks how he lived his mantra. If he did not fully meet his goal, he simply recommits to stay on track.

Remember that these skills take time to develop—this is why it's referred to as the creative *process*. Once you start practicing the skills, they will all elegantly combine to help you develop further awareness and intentionality for conscious creative living.

PATHWAYS AND PLANS

We've explored how mindsets and creative practices can spark your imagination, and using some of the skills within the creative process can move you to action and make your creative ideas happen. To truly open up the second half of your life creatively, you'll also want to envision pathways and plans to keep you moving forward.

As you immerse yourself in the creative process using the creative skills to address your creative dilemma, new insights and useful information emerge that help you discern your unique path of how you want to live creatively in one area or many.

"There are many paths up the mountain" is a familiar proverb, and this is also true for the pathways to your envisioned future. You can use the context of the Conscious Living Wheel to help you view, organize, and choose from possible paths. For example, you may specify the dimension of "Savoring the World" or "Living Well" or "Work" as your path to explore living life creatively. We suggest you prioritize the path-life dimension that speaks the loudest to you in terms of your values, what energizes you, and the sense of it enriching your life.

After choosing a pathway or a life dimension or two, the next step is the planning. Another creativity concept that can be useful here in your planning is that of the "big C" and "the little c."[14] The big C refers to extraordinary accomplishments, such as Einstein's theory of relativity and inventions. The little c refers to creativity as it relates to everyday living. You can decide whether you will focus on the big C or little c or something in between. Many choose to consciously nurture, engage, and enhance their lives with a little c focus—which can still make a big difference in our own lives.

This concept can help you specify if you want to go all in or just somewhat. For example, would you want to go the big C route in the Technology or Helping Humanity pathway with an invention? The concept can also help you plan how much energy you want to invest.

If you choose the "Savoring the World" path, do you want to go on a month-long visit to Italy to learn about the culture and how to cook there, or would you just like to visit a local Little Italy community, visit a museum, and take a cooking class there?

Let's consider little c creativity as it relates to the dimensions of our Conscious Living Wheel. For example, in terms of our health and well-being, little c creativity might include figuring out fun ways to get exercise without going to a gym, such as finding new places in the neighborhood to walk and explore or creating beautiful topical art designs for baking focaccia bread. It could be finding an activity that adds meaning and purpose, like using woodworking skills to make desks for home-schooled students. For relationships, perhaps you enjoy meeting others in a community garden or taking classes or joining garden clubs. You could build a wooden beehive for the neighborhood, which is not only creatively satisfying but also builds community and supports the environment.

You can also combine or piggyback little c creative elements in multiple life dimensions of the Conscious Living Wheel, such as themed Zoom meetings with friends (technology and relationships) or facilitating virtual workshops (technology, work, and money). Eileen's homeowner association combines multiple interests into a monthly Friday Fellowship Food Day. Each month a specialty food truck is selected to come into the neighborhood for neighbors to try new foods, socialize, and build community. Little c ideas are infinite!

Add your little c ideas into your decision and action points. In planning your path ahead, consider potential obstacles to your progress and possible solutions, all the while maintaining a possibility mindset. Avoid high-risk shortcuts, but don't necessarily take the most chal-lenging route. Add fun and flexibility into the mix. With the pathway chosen and plans mapped with alternatives in place, you can develop more detailed plans toward living a creative life. If you are starting early enough, these plans may cover years.

Kathy McEvoy, a retired executive and volunteer, is a great example. She allocated five years to develop a post-employment life of moving to a warmer geographical area that also offered activities with others. It was a lot of work: searching for an ideal new community, clearing and selling the house, and finding new doctors and other significant contacts in the community. All the planning paid off. Kathy suggests keeping a binder to organize the work, saying, "Be sure to keep the big picture and small picture in mind to cover what matters to you."

If you find yourself with a bit of resistance or overwhelmed at times, know that this is common. In his book *The War of Art: Break Through the Blocks and Win Your Inner Creative Battles*,[15] Steven Pressfield suggests simply acknowledging that resistance exists, being patient, and showing up for your creativity in small ways. Jill Badonsky, creativity expert and author of *The Muse Is In: An Owner's Manual to Your Creativity*,[16] suggests asking yourself, "How can I make this fun?" This key question can be enough to get you happily back to your creative muse. Whether your creative endeavors result in a concrete product or an activity, the important part is connecting to what brings you joy and fulfillment.

Keep the vision, energy, and excitement of your next life chapter consciously in your mind, all the while remembering that the creative process involves implementation—the doing. This is what pathways and plans are for. We encourage you to establish some milestones and create your creative plan for implementation. Then, when you step back from the canvas of life, you will see the integration of your creative process of how you moved from your creative dilemma, to exploring interests, to discovering fresh insights, to choosing a path, to implementing a plan, to ultimately living life creatively.

In this chapter we explored imagination and creativity and how midlife and beyond is a prime time for our creativity to develop. We described creative aging and creative living and how the joy factor and spontaneous sparks lead to creative ideas. We introduced practices and mindsets for cultivating and nurturing creativity, a process and skills for building a creative life, and pathways and plans for fully integrating creativity into your life. Living life creatively is a work of art—always in progress, to sculpt as we wish. We invite you to begin living life more creatively as you navigate midlife and beyond.

CONSCIOUS LIVING PRACTICES

Questions for Reflection

- What are the creative dilemmas you are facing?
- What practices for cultivating and nurturing a creativity mindset do you want to develop?
- What do you need to learn to become more creative?
- What could you use to collect your ideas (journal, sticky notes, idea jar, Word doc, etc.)?
- What benefits are you discovering as you bring more creative touches into living a creative life?

Try This

- Write down activities you wish to try for sparking creativity.
- Visit a bookstore and see what books you are drawn to for ideas and interest.
- Select one of the seven skills and practice for a week. See what you discover.

Living
Well

Bouncing
Forward

Appreciating
Money

Living with
Technology

Working
for a Living

Exploring
Purposefully

Helping
Humanity

Working for
Fulfillment

Minding
Relationships

Savoring
the World

Living Life
Creatively

CHAPTER 8

MINDING
RELATIONSHIPS

Treasure your relationships, not your possessions.

–ANTHONY J. D'ANGELO

R elationships can be wonderful, beautiful, and fun. They can also be complicated, messy, and frustrating, yet mutually caring relationships are essential for enhancing our health and well-being. Moving into the second half of life, we can consciously focus on things and people that matter. As we change and go through different life stages and circumstances, so do our relationships. Some deepen, and some wane. There is growing evidence that loneliness and isolation increase with age, so being aware of how we are connecting with those important to us will be instrumental as we transition to new chapters and adventures.

In this chapter we explore the challenges, joys, and rewards of relationships. We address the significance of connection that each of us navigates, beginning internally with our relationships with ourselves and moving externally to our partners, family, friends, and community. We examine loss through separation, divorce, and death and how to move forward with a fresh perspective and inspiration. Relationships are the foundation for a meaningful life. Our relationships with a spouse or life partner, family, close friends, and community all matter in how we age and our level of happiness. Tending to your relationships has a big impact on your health and well-being. According to Robert Waldinger, current director of the Harvard Study of Adult Development, which is considered one of the longest studies of adult life, "The surprising finding is that our relationships and how happy we are in our relationships has a powerful influence on our health."[1]

During our interviews, we heard reflections and wisdom on relationships that we want to share as you begin your own reflection:

"It's only till you begin to know who you are that those greater friendships and stronger relationships manifest."
—**Shawn Perry,** founder of *The Senior Zone* radio show

"People were not together 24 hours, and now all of a sudden he's home all day—wait a minute, we got to do something."
—**David Treece,** business owner, financial planning company

"I learned from my grandfather the power of asking questions and engaging with all ages. I believe it kept him young, and he lived to 105." —**Dawn Pratt,** founder of Tech Up for Women

"The best way to maintain relationships is to be intentional; I spend time with people who matter to me. Also, I've learned to force myself to reach out to people more in my network."
—**Nancy Collamer,** author and semi-retirement coach

RELATIONSHIPS IN TRANSITION

Our relationships are always in transition. As we go through the second half of life we may find our relationships anywhere along a continuum of beginning, emerging, expanding, strengthening, maintaining, declining, and maybe ultimately ending. This can create mixed feelings. You may be recently retired, for example, with a shift in your identity and the loss of structure and relationships that your job once provided. Or maybe you have been a primary caretaker for children or aging parents. As we become empty nesters or retired from full-time work, we may now suddenly be spending more time with a spouse or partner at home who wants attention. With both of you at home 24/7, there are challenges and changes that you have not experienced up until this point of your relationship.

Even if times of change upset the status quo, they also offer an opportunity for growth and for building even more meaningful relationships with the people in your life. Whether with your spouse, family members, or friends, a deeper level of closeness and intimacy is now more possible.

It's never too late to decide how you want to live and connect with others. Sandy fondly remembers a couple years ago spending a weekend at a beautiful inn in Vermont, where one night at dinner she sat next to a geriatric doctor. She asked her, "What is the most important step to age well?" She responded that hands down, it was staying socially connected and being engaged. There is a direct connection between having a flourishing and healthy life and your relationships with family, friends, and community.

KNOW THYSELF—AND OTHERS

At the heart of meaningful relationships is learning to connect with ourselves so that we can more easily connect with others. This can be more challenging than it may seem. You've been with yourself since before you took your first breath—surely you know who you are! But according to physician Vivek Murthy, "The truth is no one is born with self-knowledge and it takes time to acquire it. It is not as easy as you may think. The challenge is that knowledge requires a degree of objectivity, which is difficult to summon when we are the subject. We also constantly change and our identity changes over time."[2]

To begin to know ourselves better, we need to step away and give ourselves permission to think about questions that reveal what we value and why we respond to others the way we do. This is a time of self-discovery. Take a moment to think about these questions: What matters most to you? What do you love doing and why? What do you yearn for? If we can listen to ourselves, we really listen to others. If we can be authentic with ourselves, then we're likely to be authentic with the people we know. If we can accept ourselves in a loving, compassionate way, this too can be mirrored back to us from others. The better we know and love ourselves, the stronger and more fulfilling our relationships can be.

When exploring self-knowledge, the goal is to gain insight and self-acceptance through examination and reflection. When we look inward for the answers, we may find our path and direction. We've already recommended some in-depth personality tests (see the Resources section at the back of the book). Personality tests and assessments may be an ideal place to start.

It's also important to reflect on your relationships. Take some time for self-reflection and answer these questions about the relationships in your life—your spouse or partner, family, friends, and new relationships:

- What am I getting from my relationships?
- What am I giving to my relationships?
- Am I neglecting any of my own needs because of this relationship?

- Do I feel my contributions and communications are heard and noticed?

- Do I feel my values align with this relationship as it is today? Am I trying to shape this relationship to fit my values?

- Have I changed for the better because of this relationship?

- Am I happy with this relationship as it is today?

- How much work would it take for me to be happy with this relationship? Is that work I want to do?

Asking ourselves these thoughtful questions helps us to gauge the quality of our relationships and where we need to focus our attention in this area. The second half of life is an excellent time to take stock and decide how you want to conduct your relationships going forward. Let's explore the different types of relationships in our lives in more detail.

RELATIONSHIPS WITH YOUR PARTNER OR SPOUSE

One of our most meaningful relationships is with our spouse or life partner. Our relationship with our partner may be loving, joyful, and harmonious, or it may be challenging, frustrating, or antagonistic. Couples develop routines for division of labor, for ways to spend leisure time, and for how to make decisions in everyday life as well as bigger life choices. For couples thinking about possible retirement, as well as other transitions in midlife and beyond, different perspectives and priorities may come into play.

While many couples embrace employment and life changes in later life together with open arms, others find the transition confronting and difficult. Suddenly, your spouse who spent hours every day at the office is home constantly, and you may not have the distraction of work to keep you busy. For many couples, years have been spent busily managing the house, careers, and raising children. Then children leave the home, and there's more time, space, and privacy for intimacy. When couples have nurtured their relationship over the years, midlife and beyond can be a time of renewal.

> "I love spending time with my wife. Not everybody can say that they love being at home with their partner. But I do, and she loves having me home." —**Mike Bernhardt,** writer and grief support volunteer

> "I've been married to my wife for 54 years. She is my best friend." —**Monty Patch,** author and AARP volunteer

But some couples find they have neglected their relationship, which results in disconnection and loneliness. This may be the right time to reflect on any changes you want to make in your relationship. What is the balance in your relationship? Does one partner want more or less than the other, or does one partner seem to control the relationship? Transitions in midlife can be difficult, but by adopting the idea of conscious loving with creativity, the transitions may become easier to navigate.

CONSCIOUS LOVING WITH CREATIVITY

In many marriages or partnerships, the years have been spent juggling snippets of quality time with each other with busy work schedules and family commitments—so what happens when all that's gone and it's just the two of you left? Our connection may have gotten smothered by lists and deadlines. Perhaps love has become routine. We can create more open and loving communication and honesty by moving away from the lists and routine to a more creative relationship, feeling awe about it each day. This renewed relationship comes from moments of choice, in which we choose to expand in love and transformation with our partner. What do you want your future of love in your life to look like? What choices will you make as you enter a new phase of life and love?

Let's look at ways to enhance and nurture our partner relationships. Kathlyn and Gay Hendricks, authors of *Conscious Loving Ever After*, encourage us to uncover our creative calling so that we can nurture and deepen our relationships with our creative essence.[3] Expanding upon the definitions for creativity we discussed in chapter 7, try thinking about creativity in connection with love. "Creativity is anything that opens awareness in new ways your body and mind can play," the Hendrickses remind us. "As you create and stretch your body and mind, you experience personal growth."[4] How are you opening up new possibilities within yourselves and with your partner? Connecting with your creative essence will open our eyes to new possibilities in your relationship.

Like any commitment, it takes work, and starting with small steps is always the key. Sandy and her husband, Russ, recently started their commitment to a daily 10-minute creativity practice. Sandy enjoys writing, and Russ, who is a task master and list maker, has started sketching houses and gardens. Starting the day with free-flowing creativity instead of checking emails and making lists has provided an opening to new possibilities for them. Their 10 minutes of sketching and journaling activity brought more creativity to the start of their day. They enjoyed sharing over their morning coffee and had stimulating conversation around new possibilities. Some of the possibilities were more short term as to how they could bring more connection and play into their week together, while others were more long-term envisioning where they might live next. After one of their conscious conversations of possibilities, they decided to play tennis, which they often do, and invited another couple to join them. This continued on to an adventure

back to their house with wine and a charcuterie board with a variety of
fun foods. They had lively conversation, lots of laughs, and connection
as a couple and with friends.

Conscious choices for our close relationships are likely to be the
result of deep soul-searching to explore the importance of the relationship. We may independently or jointly choose to go in separate
directions, or we may choose to go all in to achieve a more loving and
joyful relationship.

The coronavirus created new work options for remote working,
causing some couples to discover an unexpected trial period of what
might happen later in life—new rules of engagement. Many couples
have developed routines to enjoy time together as well as having time
to themselves. An important question to ask about this new phase is,
"Who are we now?" How will you move forward so that your close
relationship will thrive in this new phase of life?

For those empty nesters, you may be wondering and redefining
what your purpose is if your children don't need you in the same way.
And if you are a couple who did not have children, there are changes in
identity and focus on achievement in a different way. Both situations
will cause you to engage with your partner in new ways at this point in
life. It is sobering to recognize that retirement represents our last years
of life, our time to finally do whatever we want—health and resources
permitting. That freedom is a tremendous gift. With self-reflection,
good communication, and understanding, honesty, and creativity,
couples can choose to make the most of this new freedom and their
time together.

It's important to remember too that the ability to engage in your
relationship with your partner or spouse has powerful effects on health.
In the book *Growing Young*, author Marta Zaraska found that marriage
lowers mortality risk by 49 percent. "These findings brought to light
that in addition to healthy nutrition and physical activity, deepening

relationships, practicing empathy, and contemplating your purpose in life can improve your life span."[5] The quality of our relationships matters, and going about them consciously will help us thrive in the years ahead.

DRIFTING APART, SEPARATION, AND DIVORCE

However long you may have been with your partner or spouse, and however both of you have chosen to engage in the relationship, the reality is that not all marriages have a happy ending. Rates of divorce for those 50 and up are on the rise. According to Susan Brown, author of *The Gray Divorce Revolution*, "This phenomenon, which refers to divorce among people 50 and older, doubled between 1990 and 2010, with the rate rising from 0.5 percent to 1 percent per year, and has since evened out at this new high."[6] When looking at the gray divorce revolution, there are many factors to consider including health, finances, the history of the relationship, and the evolving roles of men and women.

Although gray divorce may represent grief and loss, if it's been a marriage filled with conflict and poor communication, this may feel like more of a relief or liberation. In addition, with more women being financially independent, there is less of a stigma about divorce than there was in previous generations. Because midlife and beyond can be a time where individuals are searching for identity and questioning their life, it can result in infidelity or a slow process of growing or drifting apart. Decisions about future planning may cause stress and instability in the partnership or marriage.

Separation or divorce is often not a sudden decision but one that has been festering for quite some time. This puts couples at a crossroad with marriage, with divorce being part of the conversation. Many couples who divorce later in life often wait for children to leave the nest.

Divorce is certainly a loss, even if it was your choice to end the marriage. It's a highly stressful event, and having a strong support network is extremely important. This is an emotional time. Connecting and reconnecting with old friends and family members will be helpful as you reshuffle your priorities. It's common for our interests to take a back burner when going through separation—but maybe now is the time to pursue hobbies or interests that you haven't had time for or have always wanted to try. Fill your life with positive activities and take care of your emotional health. The identity shift from married to single requires getting in touch with yourself and tapping into your self-knowledge. Though this can be a scary time, it is also a time for self-reflection and actually serves as a time to reinvent your life for the better. Who do you want to be next? This reinvention may lead to cultivating new relationships that support your new life priorities.

NAVIGATING THE LOSS OF A PARTNER

In the blog post "How Death and Divorce Compare in Degrees of Loss and Stages of Grief," Sonyan White writes, "Death and divorce are two very different life-changing events, and every individual has their own unique experience of each, but when they both result in the loss of your spouse, the degree of impact and the stages of grief are often very much the same."[7] Losing your someone who represents your closest relationship can be devastating.

Many of us envision growing older with our partner. However, as we reach our fifties, sixties, and seventies, we have all experienced some loss—friends, siblings, or parents. It's inevitable that when couples grow old together, the marriage ends with the death of a spouse. According to the US Census Bureau, "Fifteen million Americans are currently widowed, and five million more have been widowed and then remarried. And over three-fourths of the currently widowed are women. That's because women have superior longevity and tend to be, on average, 2.5 years younger than their husbands. It's also because widowed men tend to remarry more than widowed women do. Among all Americans over age 65, 32 percent of women and 11 percent of men are widowed."[8]

Losing a spouse is a life-changing event and impacts every facet of living. Each person's way of coping with the loss of a spouse is as different as they are. It's common to feel numb, shocked, fearful, or paralyzed about what to do next. Sometimes the surviving partner feels guilty for still being alive. And at some point in this process we may feel angry at our partner for leaving us. In the AARP article "There Is No One Right Way to Be a Widow," Ann Brenoff shares, "Since my husband's death two years ago, I have run afoul of conventional wisdom about how a widow is supposed to feel and behave. I have been accused of not grieving long enough and been cautioned by finger-wagging friends that I can't outrun grief and that it will, one day, catch up with me."[9] As a new widow, she has found it hard to continue to maintain relationships with prior friends that are couples. She tries to be open and welcoming to new people but is not looking for a new life partner. Each person has to navigate this difficult journey on their own and within their own time frame.

When we find ourselves unexpectedly alone, we rely on friends and family for support. The overriding coping strategy for Donna Kraus, who lost her husband to cancer, was to stay connected. Each day she thought intentionally about who she would connect with and reach out to—one day at a time. Donna recently remarried and is moving forward in her new life with the support of her family. To conquer the impact of isolation and loneliness, it's important to be proactive in maintaining important social contacts and meaningful relationships as well as seeking out new ones. Donna understood this and worked hard to stay connected. Remember that we each have our own story and ways to work through grief, so follow your heart and intuition in this process.

Finding support and connecting with those experiencing grief and loss can be helpful. Resources are abundant and include widow and widower associations, local government groups, faith-based groups, meetups, and more. In the United States, there is the National Widowers' Organization, and internationally, GriefShare and Soaring Spirits International. Some groups are online and others in person. Doing some research to find what resonates with you is valuable. Others we have talked to started their own groups.

NEW RELATIONSHIPS

Finding love again after the loss of an intimate partner can be a joyous experience for those who are ready. There may also be some challenges around trust, intimacy, and communication. You might be wondering: How will I know if and when I am ready for this? Does this mean I am forgetting my former partner? Can I ever love again? How will this impact my children? How you answer these questions will be unique to each individual. Moving forward means you are making a choice and saying yes to experiencing love and joy.

Deciding on a future relationship requires deep thought, a level of readiness, and a conscious choice. Take the time to see if you are ready to open yourself up to a new mate. Be realistic and know that there is no perfect scenario. This process will take time and understanding both from yourself and from the person with whom you begin a new relationship. If you find you have concerns or questions that are difficult to answer, seek advice from a close relationship in your life or from a professional counselor.

Older adults are looking for and finding love. And remember that fresh rules of engagement apply to new relationships! Even if you're embarking upon a new relationship after a divorce or death of your partner, you don't have to model it in the same way. Maybe you have a new relationship but are not ready to move in with them or have them move in with you. "I want you. I need you. I just don't want to live with you," says Sharon Hyman, a filmmaker who is currently making a documentary about partners who live apart and who recently celebrated her 23rd anniversary with her partner, Davide Demetre.[10]

This is a new trend as couples in the second half of life are rethinking and rewriting the terms of their relationships. With greater longevity and increased divorce rate of people over 50, there is an alternative option for partners. Many older adults (especially women) fear that a romantic attachment later in life may lead to caregiving. They may have already done this and are not interested in repeating it. But they may still want to have a relationship. Some older single adults find that having a long-term partner without entangling finances and relationships with adult children is their preference. Sociologist Susan Brown found in a survey of 2,166 adults ages 50–65 years old that nearly one-third of those in an unmarried relationship are in a committed long-term relationship but living apart. Demographers call this type of relationship "living apart together."[11]

Having another option for how to be in a committed relationship is appealing for many couples later in life. There is a feeling of cherishing private space and financial independence but a sharing of life and love. This decision, like many others, is a big one and one that needs to be talked about to be sure that each partner is suited for this way of being in a committed relationship.

RELATIONSHIPS WITH YOUR FAMILY

We have addressed our close relationships with partners and spouses, but for better or worse, family relationships also play a strong role in shaping our lives. Families can be both rewarding and challenging, especially as we move through the second half of life and family relationships become more complicated. It is up to each of us to consciously choose how to connect, interact, and manage our relationships with family to make the most of our years ahead.

Our first relationships come from family and are often the foundation of how we relate to others. But in many families, getting along isn't a given. We may experience minor challenges at certain times or major ones that impact our long-term relationships with family members. Like all relationships, creating close bonds with family members takes work.

The people we call family are more diverse than ever before, as family unit definitions have been changing over the past few decades. More families than ever are comprised of children with different parents who live together with stepparents. There are also a wide variety of arrangements, such as children being raised by a single parent, by grandparents, or by their much older siblings. Families have always been a complex web of connections, and now with the increase in blended families, they are even more so.

OUR PARENTS

Our parents are most likely the first people we ever interacted with in our lives. They set the standard for everything, from what values we develop to what our interests are and especially what our relationships with others may look like. For many parent-child relationships at all stages, the journey is life-changing, identity-shifting, and expansive. In our Conscious Living journey, we often reflect on our life and how our parents have influenced and supported us. In many ways our parents were our first love. They were significant to our development in everything from our physical needs to our emotional well-being. What do you remember most about your parents that stands out? What lessons have you learned that are with you today?

Our relationships with our parents may be challenging as well as joyful because they continue to evolve and sometimes become more complicated as we marry, have children, and grow older. Increasing life spans means we may have our parents in our lives for much longer than previous generations. Living consciously may require an increasing awareness of our relationships with our parents and our roles in their lives as they age. We may find ourselves with the responsibility of caring for our parents or facing their end-of-life challenges. The roles change—often with a clear role reversal.

Paul's parents died within a few months of each other after sixty-six years of married life. His mother passed away quite suddenly, two months after he had last seen her. Their parting words of "see you next time" had a hollow ring. His father could not get used to the empty chair in the living room and declined quickly after that. With help from his daughter, Paul cared for his father and was grateful for the time they spent together during the final two weeks of his life.

Sandy had many wonderful years with her father. The last few years of his life he was living with dementia, which was a sad and long goodbye. On Father's Day in 2019 (which also happened to be Sandy's birthday), she went to visit her father. They shared some memories, and he read her sentimental card with the words "Daddy's Little Girl" on the front. This was the last time she saw him, but she felt happy that it was a special and memorable visit. Sandy's mother had to adapt to a new life after living with her husband for 64 years. Sandy and her two brothers now support their mother. Roles change, and we all make a choice as to how we will care for and be in a relationship with our aging parents.

As much as we want to give care effectively and with love, we need to step back and take inventory of our own well-being when we do so.

Acknowledging that this is too much for you to manage may sometimes be the best way forward. For many, this is a time to give back to our parents and can be a rewarding experience. Coming together as a family and asking for support can make all the difference.

For many, this can be a time of challenge. Perhaps there has been a strain in your relationship over the years that has increased during this time. Or maybe new challenges have arisen with your aging parent(s). During this time you may, as an adult child, experience conflicting thoughts, behaviors, and even power struggles around how to best support your parents while still allowing them to make decisions if they are capable. A good place to start is to acknowledge the changes in our parents, accept that aging is inevitable, and determine how to best support them. It may be helpful to focus on what matters most in this relationship for the remaining time with our parents.

Reflect for a moment on the relationship with your parents. Maybe they have already passed on or maybe they are living independently. Perhaps you are already caring for one or both of them. As you peek into the future, how might your relationships with your parents change? What role might you be asked to play? What do you need to do to strengthen the relationship with them?

OUR SIBLINGS

In addition to navigating changing roles with our parents, our relationships with our siblings are likely to change in midlife. Transitions such as leaving home, getting married, having kids, and dealing with the divorce or death of parents offer natural opportunities for siblings to reevaluate these relationships. Often siblings become closer and join together more as parents age and they require help. Managing aging parents requires dealing with their health issues and other responsibilities, and sharing the related emotions and tasks with siblings can provide needed support.

Not all siblings are close. Perhaps the relationship has always been strained, or maybe recent events have created challenges. Caregiving and decision-making for supporting parents at the end of their life may bring out differences with siblings. It is important to acknowledge the differences and reflect on how to best navigate this territory. The good news is that sibling relationships can improve with work. Boundary-building, understanding, and insight are all important. Pause and reflect on how your sibling relationships have evolved over time. What are you most grateful for? How might you enhance or reinvest in your relationships with your siblings?

OUR CHILDREN

For most of us, our relationships with our children are like no other—special, close, challenging, and evolving. When we embark on the journey of parenthood, we don't tend to think about what it will look like when our children leave the nest—until they do. An empty nest creates a multitude of emotions. Even if we retire, parenthood does not. And these days, many grown children are boomeranging back home due to career and financial changes. An increasing number of young adults move back home for summers or after college, or even for several years of their young adulthood. For those who launch quickly, the challenge can be how to remain close. How we each choose to maintain our relationships with our adult children is a conscious choice. Remaining connected and involved in their lives and close to children is a high priority for many.

Many parents, like Susan O'Neil, we learned from our interview, feel they get closer to their children at this stage of life, especially if there are grandchildren involved. Regular calls on FaceTime can help

us stay connected, as well as getting together and planning family vacations. Decisions around whether to move to be closer to children and
grandchildren is at the top of mind for many.

Does everything go according to plan? Of course not! We have to
expect curveballs and decide how to catch them. We interviewed Bob,
for example, who on the eve of his retirement was bubbling with excitement to implement plans that had evolved over years. Then came the
unexpected: news that his daughter was pregnant and single, with little
income and resources. "It was not easy news," he reports. "In fact, I
experienced a lot of private anger. Letting go of well-laid plans in my
later years was one of the hardest things I have had to do in my life. I
had to summon emotional, spiritual, and financial resources to do what
was simply needed—to love and support this little girl to have the best
life she can have." As is often true with the unexpected, Bob reports that
this child has become one of the greatest blessings in his life. Sandy also
has a few clients moving closer to family, and there is an assumption
with their grown children that they will be built-in babysitters. Families
can be complicated, and healthy conversations around boundaries may
be needed.

OUR GRANDCHILDREN

For many in the second half of life, we have invested time in raising
our children and are now at this point of life where we look forward to
having grandchildren. As Kathy Simpson says, "Becoming a grandparent
can be life changing—an adrenaline shot that restores your energy, optimism, youthfulness, and sense of purpose. Recent studies also show that
emotional closeness between grandparents and grandchildren can protect
against depression, boost brain function, and lead to a longer life."[12]

As you think about this new role, consider what kind of grandparent
you want to be. Perhaps you're the fun seeker, or maybe you imagine

imparting wisdom and lessons, or maybe your role is to be a surrogate parent. Your style, circumstances, and relationship with your children will determine what type of grandparent you will be.[13]

Let's dive into modern grandparenting. As longevity increases, grandparents will be in their grandchildren's lives for longer than ever before. We have a unique gift to be part of our grandchildren's lives. Many make the choice to get in better shape and improve their health to keep up with their grandchildren. How are you prioritizing your relationship with your grandchildren? What are your greatest joys in this role?

As with all relationships, talking about expectations is crucial. Being mindful of your children's expectations for your role is essential. What are those expectations? What type of involvement works for both of you? If you live close to your grandchildren, what kind of activities will you do together? Are you expected to be a built-in babysitter? What if you have more than one grandchild? If your proximity to your grandchildren is long distance, how will you keep in touch? Will there be regular visits? Talking mindfully with your children about their expectations and yours will go a long way toward keeping everyone happy.

Some grandparents may shoulder more responsibility. Sometimes life circumstances for your children—divorce, health issues, employment—may put you in the role of assuming full- or part-time care of your grandchildren. More than 1 in 10 grandparents have a grandchild living with them, according to AARP's 2018 Grandparents Today National Survey.[14] Taking the time to thoughtfully consider whether this is the right decision is worthwhile, rather than jumping into it too quickly. As rewarding as the opportunity to parent your grandchildren may be, it may also mean giving up on leisure time, opportunities for travel, and other activities that you have long looked forward to.

It may be helpful to seek out others raising grandchildren. Consider finding a support group or someone you can talk to as you work through your feelings and reach an acceptance of the situation. Consciously traveling on this path and reflecting on what is most meaningful in this evolving relationship is important. Consider how you are taking care of yourself and what you may need from other family members in this perhaps unexpected chapter. What changes and choices will you make in regard to your life or health to enhance your relationship with grandchildren?

What if you don't have grandchildren? Some of us made a conscious decision not to have children, or tried but were not successful. Many focused instead on careers or other priorities. Not being a parent or grandparent may bring up complicated emotions when friends and other family members are spending time with children or grandchildren.

Let's remember that there are many different types of families and many roles you can play. If you're an aunt or an uncle, you can play a significant role with nieces and nephews, for example. Or you may be close with the children of a good friend. You could also participate in a program like Big Brothers or Big Sisters, Foster Grandparent, or Adopt a Grandparent (see the Resources section). We all have ways to give love and support to a child if this is of interest.

SOLO LIVING

More and more people are living alone today: "As of 2021, 28 percent of Americans were living alone, more than twice the percentage it was sixty years before."[15] For some, this is a matter of choice. For others, it is a result of the loss of a partner or another life-changing event.

Some of us enjoy solitude and have gotten accustomed to solo living. Others have had to jump into this lifestyle after the loss of a partner or children leaving the nest. For those going through a loss, there is a big adjustment to living alone. Along with the loss there may also be a sense of freedom, which can be liberating. Perhaps this is a time to get to know yourself better and prioritize what is most important.

Whether you enjoy living solo or not, isolation and disconnection can be challenging. The key is to stay engaged and have a strong network. How will you do this? Will you go out to meet people or invite others over for dinner? Perhaps starting a book club or merging your interests with socializing is a way to enjoy solo living and also connect with others in a meaningful way.

Whether living alone or with others, aim to spend meaningful time with people you care about and who care about you. Reflect on what meaningful relationships you have. Or perhaps explore new relationships, activities, and ways to connect as you transition to new chapters.

WHO WILL TAKE CARE OF ME?

Perhaps the biggest challenge of solo living is wondering how you will deal with care as you age. Some of us never married or had a partner; some have no children; some live too far away from family to count on any help or are estranged from them. "Estimates are that 20 percent of baby boomers are childless and for older women, nearly ⅔ of women over 75 do not live with a spouse."[16] While you may have enjoyed solo life over the years, as you age you may have some concerns around who will take care of you and give you advice, especially when you are in a crisis or medical emergency. This is especially the case if you have no family safety net.

When those solo agers have maintained ties to a strong social network of friends, colleagues, and others with whom they enjoy recreational activities or social groups, additional support may be available when help is needed with transportation, a task, or simply for some companionship. The best way for solo agers to plan for emotional support in later life is to start early in cultivating strong relationships. Be intentional about creating a support community, and be open and curious, as you may find new connections in unexpected ways. Expand your circles by engaging in activities and groups that suit your interests.

Another benefit of a strong social network is in preventing loneliness and isolation. Leaving your full-time career with a built-in community of coworkers and colleagues can leave us feeling isolated and a risk for poor mental health later in life, and this may be more prevalent for solo agers. Even if you're leaving a full-time career, you may want to consider engaging in part-time work or volunteering as a means of making new connections. Make conscious choices about whom you want to connect and develop new relationships with.

A LITTLE HELP FROM YOUR FRIENDS

Our friends can make our lives rich, beautiful, and fun. For Sandy, talking to a good friend is like being wrapped in a warm blanket while sipping on a soothing cup of tea. C. S. Lewis may have been on to something when he wrote that "friendship is born at that moment when one person says to another: 'What! You too? I thought I was the only one.'"[17] Close friendships are built on trust, sharing, listening, and reciprocity. When friends support us, they remind us that we are worthy of their love, which makes us feel better about ourselves.

In midlife and beyond, friendships may become more challenging. Making new friends may be more difficult. Did you used to know all of your neighbors, or did you once have a large circle of friends who have dispersed? This is not uncommon. In the article "Making Friends in Retirement," Kathleen Coxwell writes, "According to the analysis of the US Bureau of Labor Statistics' American Time Use Survey, Americans spend less time with friends and more time alone. We tend to spend more time with friends earlier in our life."[18] By the time we reach our eighties, we may spend the majority of time alone. How will you nurture your long-term friendships and make new friends in the second half of life?

It is time to take stock of your friendships and ask yourself whether your current friends support you—and whether you're engaged in supporting them. What are you getting from your friendships, and what do you think is missing? It's also worth considering that there can be an expiration date on certain friendships—so we each need to step back and determine who we want to invest time in.

Focusing on meaningful relationships as we transition to new seasons of our life may need to be reprioritized. Make an effort to set up regular dates with friends or be intentional about picking up the phone to call them. Maintaining our friendships is important to our health and well-being, and our friends may be the ones who will be there for us as we age.

INTERGENERATIONAL RELATIONSHIPS

Engaging with people of all ages provides learning, growth, and connection with those who may have different perspectives and life experiences. Looking beyond your own bubble can only help to broaden your perspective and bring new friends into your world.[19]

From an early age, many of our significant relationships were intergenerational: parents, grandparents, cousins, and siblings. As we move through life we tend to build relationships with those who are similar to us, which can often result in having friends who are close to our own age. Developing relationships with people of different ages gives older adults a sense of purpose, and younger adults can find value in their friendships with older adults. Intergenerational relationships also keep stories and history alive.

Intergenerational relationships are positive for all involved. Younger friends can offer fresh energy and new ideas and help invigorate the lives of their older peers, while having older friends in our life means having access to the wisdom of those who have literally been there before. Consider how you might connect with younger and older generations. Part of the Conscious Living journey involves reflecting on where you are and where you want to be. Perhaps it's time to shift to a mindset of openness and discovery to build new relationships with those of different generations. Deepening relationships between older and younger individuals can positively enrich their well-being.

COMMUNITY INVOLVEMENT

As we move from the first half of life to the second, our sources of connection and community may change. For many years, one of our most important connection sources has been the workplace. But our network may be more extensive than we think, or maybe we haven't thought much about it. As we transition from our full-time career to what's next, coworkers and business contacts who were part of our active working life will likely fade in importance. After all, once we are removed from day-to-day work, we will begin to lose track of the latest specifics and perhaps even interest in office happenings. In order to thrive, we need new relationships.

There are a number of ways to meet new people and broaden our community. How will we connect? Friends and family are important, but many of us may live far away from family and want to create our own. You are the one who must determine who belongs in your community, and keeping a growth mindset is essential.

For example, maybe you would like to join a group. Consider exploring Meetup, a website for users to organize get-togethers with others who enjoy the same activities. Common examples include hiking or walking groups, book clubs, and language-learning groups. Look for groups in your area that suit the activity you're looking for, or create your own group to bring others to you. (See the following box for more ideas).

If you find you are out of practice in the art of developing and nurturing new relationships, remember that every relationship begins somewhere—so go ahead and take the first step! You're likely to find that others will appreciate the gesture.

Suggestions for Connecting

- Expand your social network before you leave your job: replace workmates with playmates.
- Volunteering is a great way to meet like-minded people. Find a cause that is important to you!
- There are thousands of Meetup groups occurring in communities every day. Go to meetup.com and start exploring.
- Go back to the beginning. Was there an activity or sport you used to love to play? Find a group in your community where you can reignite the passion.
- Engage your mind. There are courses for everything out there, so look for opportunities with the Osher Lifelong Learning Institute (OLLI), colleges and universities, and your local library or community center.
- Get back to work by taking on a part-time job for socializing and fun.

Minding our relationships in midlife and beyond requires awareness and conscious planning. We are wired to be in connection with others.

Whether they are with our partners, family, or friends, our relationships will change—and the good news is our relationships can heal, with time and attention. As we move to new life chapters, we have the amazing opportunity to consciously nurture and strengthen our relationships, or let go when needed. With a growth mindset, your community can be a garden of energy and an opportunity to engage, connect, and meet new people. Our hope is that you will be inspired to reach out to have conversations with your loved ones and friends to plant your flag in a place that brings you happiness and growth.

CONSCIOUS LIVING PRACTICES

Questions for Reflection

- What is the state of your relationship with yourself?

- How has your relationship with your life partner changed at this point in life?

- How would you describe your friendships along the relationship continuum?

- What do you think about living solo, whether by choice or circumstance?

- How are you connected in your community?

Try This

- Make a list of activities you enjoy doing in solitude and ones you enjoy doing with your life partner.

- If you are living alone, create a support network map including those who will be there in a time of need.

Living
Well

Bouncing
Forward

Appreciating
Money

Living with
Technology

Working
for a Living

Exploring
Purposefully

Helping
Humanity

Working for
Fulfillment

Minding
Relationships

Savoring
the World

Living Life
Creatively

CHAPTER 9

HELPING HUMANITY

I wake up in the morning asking myself,
what can I do today, how can I help the world today?
—JULIA BUTTERFLY HILL

The second half of our lives can provide opportunities for us to make a positive difference in the world. In chapter 1 we explored identity and purpose and asked the question, "Who do you choose to be?" In chapters 4 and 5 we explored how our work can be aligned with our purpose. With clarity about our identity, purpose, and work life, this may be a time to ask, "What is my contribution to helping humanity and saving the world?" We may not be able to change the world on our own, but we can all do something to make a difference.

In this chapter, we explore three broad categories where we can contribute to helping humanity: environmental sustainability of our planet, social responsibility for people, and leadership in governments and business. The purpose of describing some of the challenges relating to helping humanity and saving the world is not to explore every topic in detail but to increase awareness and inspire readers to set intentions and take responsible action. If you are looking to find your unique contribution to planetary wellness and helping humanity, read on for some insights into consciously helping humanity today and for those who come after us.

During our interviews, many people expressed genuine concerns about the future of our planet, and many are already taking action. Here is some of what we heard:

What Concerns You?

- "We must realize that we are all human beings, and it doesn't matter what country you live in. We only have one planet."
  —**Betty McDowall**, social justice advocate
- "I worry about climate change and the resulting damage to unique species and plants, from plastics in the ocean, increasing forest fires, and the destruction of habitats for the animals."
  —**Mary Ann Esfandiari**, retired NASA senior executive and Navy Commander
- "The widening gap between rich and poor is a concern."
  —**Steve Jacobs**, university administrator
- "I see the world teetering on a knife-edge between environmental and cultural collapse and transformation. Conscious, committed elders can make a big difference in determining the outcome."
  —**Ron Pevny**, founder of the Center for Conscious Eldering

Member countries of the United Nations General Assembly have adopted a set of 17 Sustainable Development Goals (SDGs) to end poverty, protect the planet, and ensure prosperity for all as part of the 2030 Agenda for Sustainable Development. These sustainability goals, along with the 2016 Paris Agreement on climate change, provide aspirational targets for governments around the world. The degree to which progress is achieved will depend on the willingness of governments to invest financially in programs that will deliver results and to what extent individuals and businesses take action to support these ideals.

Let's look at some of the issues of environmental sustainability and how we might help our planet.

ENVIRONMENTAL SUSTAINABILITY

We humans now consume at an estimated rate of 1.7 times what the earth's regenerative systems can sustain, according to the Global Footprint Network.[1] We are on an unsustainable path unless we, individually and collectively, make different choices compared to those who have already accepted the path to self-extinction. David Korten, author of many books including *Change the Story, Change the Future: A Living Economy for a Living Earth*, suggests that we can transition to an ecological civilization dedicated to restoring the health of living earth's regenerative systems while securing material sufficiency and spiritual abundance for all.[2] We'll begin the big topic of environmental sustainability with climate change and then delve deeper into some of the sustainability issues relating to earth, water, fire, and air.

CLIMATE CHANGE

Global warming and climate change are often linked to natural disasters such as tropical storms, forest fires, and droughts, along with frequent examples of high and low temperature records being broken in different parts of the world. The rising sea levels and shrinking ice caps also point to rising temperatures. The past eight years (2015–2022) were the hottest eight years on record, and July 2023 was the hottest month on record, according to Europe's Copernicus Climate Change Service[3] and the World Meteorological Organization.[4] The global average temperature during this period was more than 1°C above pre-industrial levels.

Microsoft founder Bill Gates, in his recent book *How to Avoid a Climate Disaster*, claims that the world adds 51 billion tons of greenhouse gases to the atmosphere every year and that, to stop global warming, we need to aim for zero greenhouse gases by 2050.[5] Scientists believe that if we don't get to zero, temperatures will continue to rise. Melting ice caps, rising ocean levels, floods, fires, and other natural disasters will accelerate. If we fail to take action on climate change, estimates suggest that by the end of the century we could see an average global temperature increase of five degrees Fahrenheit or three degrees Celsius, sea level rise of 18 inches or 500 millimeters, and an increase in ocean acidification of 150 percent.

Climate change often dominates explorations about saving the world, and this is because of the impact of greenhouse gas emissions, in particular cardon dioxide, on global warming, but environmental sustainability embraces much more than just hot air. Let's take a closer look at how climate change affects earth, water, fire, and air, and some ways we can contribute to environmental sustainability.

Earth

The earth is eroding naturally, with coastal areas falling into the sea and topsoil wearing away by the natural physical forces of water and wind, but humans are creating much greater devastation through forces associated with farming and extraction. According to the World Wildlife Fund, planet earth has lost over 50 percent of its topsoil in the last 150 years.[6]

"The planet's soil continues to be in trouble. Each year we lose around 25 million acres of cropland to soil erosion worldwide. The loss is ten to forty times faster than the rate of soil formation, driving carbon into the atmosphere, and putting global security at risk," says soil steward and food sovereignty activist Leah Penniman, who also directs Soul Fire

Farm.[7] There, Afro-indigenous agroforestry, silvopasture, wildcrafting, polyculture, and spiritual farming practices have been used to regenerate 80 acres of mountainside land, producing fruits, plant medicine, pasture-raised livestock, honey, mushrooms, vegetables, and preserves for community provisioning. These ancestral farming practices increase topsoil depth, sequester soil carbon, and increase biodiversity.[8]

Most agricultural endeavors use fertilizer, which is controversial. Although fertilizers have been a key factor in agricultural development around the world, they are also responsible for adding more than two percent of the 51 billion tons of greenhouse gas added to the atmosphere each year.[9] We are trapped in a situation where our current food system cannot support our current population without the use of fossil fuel–based fertilizer, but the harm being done to the earth means we must stop using it or change how we make it.[10] How can you contribute to changing the use of fertilizers in your garden or local community?

Extraction is another concern. Much of what we use, particularly in construction and manufacturing industries but also in everyday life, requires vast quantities of natural materials. The cement used in concrete structures, the steel used for reinforcing those structures and in vehicles and domestic appliances, and glass and plastics used everywhere today all contain millions of tons of materials extracted from the earth. In addition to coal, natural resource extraction includes sand, gravel, rock, oil, natural gas, and other materials that are obtained by excavation, drilling, boring, or other methods.

Bill Gates, in his recent writings exploring how we make things and how to avoid a climate disaster, advocates electrifying every process possible: getting electricity from a power grid that's been decarbonized, using carbon capture to absorb the remaining emissions, and using materials more efficiently.[11] Even as we support the growth in electric vehicles, base materials such as lithium, nickel, and cobalt used in battery technology are being mined in different regions of the world, where the intersection of natural resource extraction and environmental justice represents significant sources of structural inequity.[12]

Water

We cannot live without water. A drop of rain, a glass of pure water, a river, a waterfall, an ocean, a cloud, or an iceberg: whatever the image of water that comes to you, it is a life-giving source. Eileen remembers being profoundly moved while standing on a slushy glacier in the Rocky Mountains, close to the border between Canada and the United States, realizing that parts of the Rockies supply water to three oceans (the Atlantic, the Arctic, and the Pacific) and that the glaciers were melting at an accelerated pace. She wondered if the next generation would be able to see this beauty and have water for their future needs. Protecting the water is protecting life itself.

Some of the water protection measures required for saving the world include healing our rivers, lakes, and oceans; water management, including conservation, purification, distribution, pollution, and the treatment of wastewater; and the efficient use of water in agriculture. How can our relationship with water benefit humanity rather than harm it?

The United Nations Sustainable Development Goals include two water-related goals: ensuring the availability and sustainable management of water and sanitation, and conserving and sustainably using the oceans, seas, and marine resources for sustainable development. This may not be enough.

Perhaps you feel called to be a water guardian for our world. One such person is Dee Kyne, an award-winning serial social entrepreneur and a supporter of the proposed World Water Law[13] who has spent many years "walking for water." Dee told us about her walking for water initiatives in Jamaica, from east to west and then around the edge of the island, and now in Portugal, where she is living. Her "One Water One Life" walk through Portugal to gather data and to capture the stories of the local inhabitants included visits to sites where the water is in danger of ecocide. Dee hopes that her 700-kilometer walk will be a story of connection with people and the environment. Water is life and we are life. We will not survive without good stewardship of water. This is what Dee believes and continues to work for.

Rising sea levels is one aspect of water that has captured Paul's interest. When in Florida, Paul lives on a barrier island at the edge of the Atlantic Ocean, and when in England he lives in an apartment overlooking the English Channel, where millions of pounds are being spent on coastal defenses. Walking along the beaches and around the harbors provides relentless reminders of the horrendous pollution of the oceans and rivers. Globally, more than one million plastic bottles are sold every minute.[14] Millions of tons of plastic waste end up in the oceans worldwide, much of it in giant garbage patches; a third of all plastics end up in ecosystems, while just 5 percent are successfully recycled. If current trends continue, plastic will outweigh fish in the world's oceans by 2050.[15] Recycling is increasing, and taking used bottles to the recycling centers is important, but reducing demand for single-use plastics remains a high priority.

Designers at a Dutch start-up company located in the north of Amsterdam have developed an innovative solution using air bubbles to intercept plastic products in rivers and canals before they reach the ocean. The Great Bubble Barrier creates a barrier of bubbles stopping plastics from flowing past, while at the same time allowing fish and ships to pass through the barrier unimpeded.[16] Much can be done by individuals actively supporting international initiatives such as World Ocean Day and local initiatives for reducing plastic pollution and restoring our water sources. For example, we can help with local cleanup activities and, perhaps more importantly, reduce our individual consumption of single-use plastics. We can also support intergenerational activities such as the Tide Turners Plastic Challenge, a Clean Seas initiative educating young people around the world about plastic pollution and giving them the tools to change their personal behavior, inspire their communities, and create a better future for our planet.[17]

Sustainable water management is another water issue. When we think of the availability of drinking water, our minds go first to the so-called developing countries, where millions of people still don't have easy access to safe drinking water. According to the World Health Organization, 785 million people out of a global population of 6.8 billion lack even a basic drinking water service, which is defined as an improved drinking water source within a round trip of 30 minutes to collect water, and at least two billion people use a drinking water source contaminated with feces.[18] You may already be supporting some of the drinking water initiatives such as the World Vision Clean Water program, the Global Wellness Institute Clean Water Initiative, and the many charities focused on providing clean water.

These issues may seem far away to many readers of this book, but with the effects of climate change, increasing population densities in some areas, and the irrigation demands of modern farming methods, water scarcity and droughts are on the increase in many regions of the world. The World Resources Institute says 17 countries, equivalent to one-quarter of the earth's population, are using their water resources too quickly.[19] Although most of these countries are in the Middle East and Africa, pockets of extreme water stress exist in many other countries. More than a billion people currently live in water-scarce regions, and by 2025 half of the world's population could be experiencing water scarcity! We all have a responsibility to stop wasting water.

The first step in water management is to conserve what we have. The

Project Drawdown Team[20] claims that the average American withdraws ninety-eight gallons of water every day with roughly 60 percent used indoors, primarily for toilets, clothes washers, showers, and faucets, and another 30 percent used outdoors, almost entirely for watering lawns, gardens, and plants. The remaining 10 percent is lost to leaks. The use of water-efficient appliances and low-flow fixtures can reduce water use within homes by 45 percent—a saving of 44 gallons a day in every home in the US. Water saving is an area where we can all take action.

Although water usage in agriculture and industry may be beyond the interest of the majority of readers of this book, the reuse of wastewater to recover water, nutrients, or energy is becoming an important strategy and is a significant contributor to water conservation. We can make a small contribution by harvesting rainwater for watering lawns and plants in our own gardens. We can also install low-volume water flow appliances and toilet flushes which can save money too.

The supply and distribution of our water is an essential utility. Reducing the energy used to move water from the source through water treatment plants and through pipes to our homes is an important function. Perhaps you may be inspired to help with water supply and distribution in developing countries. Access to clean water is essential to improving health and reducing poverty, hunger, and illiteracy. Not-for-profit organizations focused on addressing the world's water supply issues include Water Aid,[21] Water Is Life,[22] and Water.org.[23] You can donate to these organizations and volunteer to help with one of the many important water projects being implemented around the world.

Scott Harrison is someone who turned his life around and founded another one of these organizations: charity: water, a nonprofit organization bringing clean and safe drinking water to people in developing countries. Scott had a vision to reinvent and reimagine charity and promised that 100 percent of public donations would directly fund water projects, building a brand working through local partners. He created a brand built on hope and opportunity rather than on shame and guilt, restoring people's faith in generosity and giving. He inspired the idea of redemptive birthdays, where people pledge their birthdays to raising money for their favorite cause. His book *Thirst* describes how to build a better charity, a better business, and a better life—and demonstrates that it's never too late to make a change.[24] You may not be able to build an organization like charity: water, but you can make a difference. What are you inspired to do to improve accessibility to clean water?

Maybe replacing single-use plastic water bottles with reusable water bottles is a simple first step. Maybe we can stop using contaminating fertilizers for our lawns. These may seem like small steps, but collectively, they can have a big impact. If the subject of water is important to you, consider becoming a water protector or a water guardian in your own community.

Fire

Extreme heat blamed on rising global temperatures and prolonged drought in many regions is increasing the risk of devasting fires across the planet. Wildfires have always been part of the natural cycle and have a positive effect on the trees in these environments, but the loss of life and property can be devastating for people living in these areas.

Trees are also being lost due to deforestation. We need trees for a variety of reasons, not only for the products made from the trees we harvest but also because they absorb the carbon dioxide and heat-trapping greenhouse gases that cause climate change. According to the World Resources Institute, tropical tree cover could provide 23 percent of the cost-effective climate mitigation needed before 2030. Removing the trees not only takes away the absorption qualities, but when they are cut down and burned, the carbon dioxide stored in the trees and the soil is released into the atmosphere.

Planting new trees is one way to offset the effects of deforestation, but we may not be able to plant enough to counter the problems caused by burning fossil fuels. As Bill Gates suggests, maybe the most effective tree-related strategy is to stop cutting down so many of the trees we already have. Maybe we can take local action to make a difference.

Don Maruska, author of *Solve Climate Change Now* is one person who heeded the call to action. "People in our church wanted to take climate action and beautify the property with more trees," he says.[25] His church was a small congregation in Morro Bay, California, and they didn't have the money for the trees or for the irrigation that would be needed for them.

He went on to say that "a generous community member donated funds for the landscape planning to identify the location and types of trees, but with higher than expected estimates, people soon became discouraged. Instead of giving up, a group persevered. They found a state funding program for planting trees in response to local wildfires." The group attended a class at a local community college to learn about regenerative agriculture, and they discovered that nurturing naturally occurring fungi could make the soil more fertile—thus multiplying the ability of the trees and other plants to convert carbon dioxide into living carbon organisms that would stay in the ground. Despite further cost and labor hurdles, the group eventually planted the trees with an irrigation system in place to tend them.

Unless you live in a location threatened by fires, this may be a less important environmental issue for you—but planting trees is a good cause we can all support. As well as planting trees ourselves, we can support tree planting around the world and help with carbon offsetting.

Air

Many readers of this book will remember the 1970s hit song from the Hollies, "The Air That I Breathe." While air in earth's atmosphere is mostly gas, it also contains water vapor and many tiny particles called aerosols—a term we became all too familiar with during the coronavirus pandemic. Aerosols like dust and pollen are picked up naturally by the wind, which can also carry soot, smoke, and other particles from emitters such as engine exhausts, power plants, forest fires, and volcanoes. These are major contributors to air pollution.

The amount of carbon dioxide in the air and changes in average global temperature are closely linked. The increasing levels of carbon dioxide in the air are perhaps having the most significant impact on global warming and the future of the planet. Carbon dioxide comes from natural sources and from human activities. Raising animals for food is a major contributor to greenhouse emissions. Methane from cattle is equivalent to two billion tons of carbon monoxide, about four percent of all global emissions. All animals, including humans, breathe in oxygen and breathe out carbon dioxide. Carbon dioxide is also released in the natural processes of decomposition.

Our human activities also increase the amounts of carbon dioxide in the air. Before the Industrial Revolution, the natural life cycles kept carbon dioxide levels in balance. Since then, carbon dioxide emissions from human activities and the resulting atmospheric carbon dioxide levels have increased dramatically.

So what can we do to reduce carbon dioxide emissions? We can take individual actions such as seeking alternatives to aerosol deodorants and spray cleaners, reducing reliance on meat in our diets, and supporting the planting of trees. Small individual actions add up. What are some ways in which you might take steps in your daily life to contribute to the air we breathe?

We can also support the shift to cleaner energy generation. The ambitious goal of the Paris Climate Agreement, the international treaty on climate change adopted in 2015, was to limit global warming to well below 2 (preferably to 1.5) degrees Celsius, compared to preindustrial levels, and for countries to reach global peaking of greenhouse gas emissions as soon as possible and to achieve a climate-neutral world by midcentury.[26] Carbon neutrality by midcentury could be achieved by eliminating the use of fossil fuel altogether, and although this may be possible, with fossil fuels accounting for two-thirds of all energy generated worldwide, the high cost of replacement and lack of political will suggest this approach is unlikely to be successful. More likely, pathways to carbon neutrality include increasing energy efficiency, switching to electric technologies, utilizing clean electricity such as wind and solar power, and deploying a small amount of carbon capture technology.[27]

Renewable energy from wind and solar power generation is increasing rapidly, and despite dependence on the weather and the relatively high cost of development, installation, and maintenance, it is seen as the least-cost energy generation solution. Solar technology is now being incorporated in the roof design in modern buildings. Harnessing the power of the wind using large wind turbines is also a renewable, clean, and cost-effective source of energy. Wind turbines are now a common sight on high ground and offshore and are also being installed on smaller properties. Hydropower, which is electricity created by water pouring through a dam, is being used as a renewable energy source. Nuclear technology and biomass power generation are also in the mix although with more significant challenges to overcome. If the engineering challenges can be overcome, nuclear fusion could change that equation, but we are not holding our breath.

Reducing the use of fossil fuels improves the quality of the air we breathe. Maybe it is time to learn more about clean and affordable energy options and to consider solar or wind energy for your home.

SOCIAL RESPONSIBILITY

In the broadest sense, social justice relates to the distribution of wealth, opportunities, and privileges and depends on the interrelated principles of human rights, access, participation, and equity. You may already be a social justice warrior. Many of us have been taking our social responsibilities seriously and supporting social justice issues for years and may even consider ourselves activists, yet as we move beyond midlife, we may have more opportunity and capacity for taking a stand for the issues that concern us.

With the turbulence and chaos in today's world, it may be easy to hold a pessimistic perspective on many social justice issues, but we invite you to align with something more hopeful. Reverend Deborah Moldow, an ordained interfaith minister and founder of the Garden of Light, a platform for the emerging global spirituality, writes, "Something different is emerging: a new consciousness that is our best hope for planet earth to renew her invitation for us to inhabit the only home we know. At this level of consciousness we see ourselves for the first time in history—as members of one planetary family sharing one common home."[28] This is a time to curb our natural instinct to act with self-interest and focus on acting for the greater good of humanity.

We acknowledge the plethora of social justice issues people are passionate about and the multiple, often polarizing perspectives people hold. Look at these issues with curiosity and an open mind. Be curious rather than judgmental. Contemporary social justice issues include ageism and disability, poverty and economic justice, gender and racial justice, healthcare, criminal justice, environmental justice, and human rights.

Our purpose here is to highlight some of the social responsibility issues in the world to inspire you to ask yourself, "What am I passionate about? How can I contribute to the social responsibility issues people face around the world? What am I being called to do?" We know this is a broad and deep subject and we can skim only the surface here, but we hope by including them we will inspire and educate to the extent that you can take up the challenges you are passionate about.

AGEISM AND DISABILITY

In the second half of life in particular, you are likely to face the challenge of ageism or age discrimination. Ageism tends to be considered in relation to the workplace, but the way older people are represented in the media and in general conversations can also feel discriminatory. According to the University of Michigan's national poll on healthy aging conducted in association with AARP, 82 percent of Americans who are 50 and older have experienced age-based discrimination, prejudice, and stereotyping in their daily lives.[29] Have you felt unfairly treated due to your age? How did you react? Even if this hasn't happened to you, think about how you might respond in the moment, as well as the potential legal ramifications of age discrimination.

The United Nation's Open-Ended Working Group on Ageing (OEWGA) was established in 2010 to strengthen the human rights of older persons.[30] The Global Alliance for the Rights of Older People (GAROP) is an international membership organization with a mission to support and enhance civil society's engagement at national, regional, and international levels on the need for a new international instrument on the rights of older persons, helping to create the environment leading to a UN convention to protect the human rights of older persons.[31]

Progress with the development of a UN convention has been disappointingly slow. The outcome of the eleventh session of the working group in 2021 ended without positive steps forward toward the development of a convention on the rights of older persons. We can't rely on political leaders to take action, so what can we do to address problems of ageism and enhance opportunities for older people?

Ageism sucks! So says Ken Dychtwald and Robert Morison in their book *What Retirees Want*.[32] Not only is ageism bad for older people, it can also be bad for business. Marketing pitches for products and services aimed toward older people may need to be different than those made to younger people, but as longevity increases, these market messages cannot be overlooked.

Reimagining the conversation on aging, the California Master Plan for Aging makes for inspirational reading. With five goals and twenty-three strategies to build a California for All Ages by 2030, it also includes a data dashboard to measure progress and a playbook to drive local partnerships.[33] The five goal areas cover housing, health, inclusion and equity, caregiving, and economic security. The plan offers a blueprint for national and local government departments to follow and inspiration for all of us to participate in conversations that matter about discrimination based on age.

In addition to impressive initiatives like this, we can also take individual action, standing up for what we believe in and responding constructively when we read negative comments on ageism. Becoming more conscious of ageist language, increasing the awareness of others, taking action to educate, and inspiring changes in the language we use can all make a positive difference.

Aging populations, the rapid spread of chronic diseases, and improvements in measurement methodologies are all contributing to a greater focus on disabilities around the world. Disabilities affect people of all ages, but they can present increasing challenges as we age. According to a World Health Organization survey, about 15 percent of the world's population lives with some form of disability, with 2–4 percent experiencing significant difficulties in functioning.[34] In the United Kingdom, one in five people reported a disability, according to a more recent Family Resources Survey, with nearly half (44 percent) of older people above the state pension age reporting disability.[35] Similar statistics are evident in the United States, where one in four adults live with a disability, increasing to two in five people aged 65 and older, measured across six serious disability types:

- Mobility (difficulty walking or climbing stairs)
- Cognition (difficulty concentrating, remembering, or making decisions)
- Hearing (difficulty hearing)
- Vision (difficulty seeing)
- Independent living (difficulty doing errands alone)
- Self-care (difficulty dressing or bathing).[36]

Disability rights have been addressed by different governments. The UN Convention on the Rights of Persons with Disabilities (CRPD) was adopted in 2006 and has 164 signatories. It adopts a broad categorization of persons with disabilities and reaffirms that all persons with all types of disabilities must enjoy all human rights and fundamental freedoms.[37] Many countries have laws conferring basic human rights to people with disabilities. The Equality Act in the United Kingdom and the Americans with Disabilities Act in the United States provide legislation to protect the rights of people with disabilities, promising equal opportunity in public accommodations, jobs, transportation, government services, and telecommunications.

These conventions and laws have given disabled people rights but haven't necessarily changed the way society views disabled people. What can we do to better accept and support people with disabilities?

Awareness of disabilities often depends on our experience of a disability or those of friends and family. Many of us have a significant *disability awareness gap*. Learning more about the different types of disabilities may help us better understand and, where appropriate, accommodate the needs of disabled persons. This may mean supporting the representation of disabled persons in the media, feeling comfortable with disabled people alongside us in education and in workplaces, improving accessibility, and increasing our own confidence in talking about disability and impairment and in interacting with disabled people.

> "You can't see that I can't hear; it's not visible to everybody
> and they didn't understand. Now I tell people that I wear
> two hearing aids so they can understand if I don't respond."
> —**Patti Correll-Syring**, 62 years old, profoundly deaf from
> the age of ten

Sam Rau was blind from birth, and during our conversation with him, he said: "Technology has come a long way in playing a fundamental role in all of our lives and in providing comparable access to the world for people with disabilities as nondisabled individuals. However, there are still many physical and psychological barriers to people with disabilities in adequately providing value and their important contribution to that world and to living the lives they want. Until we have equal access for all regardless of age or disability and until the barriers to access are removed, there will always be a struggle, although also a journey well worth taking."

We have a responsibility for encouraging the support and inclusion of disabled people within society. Human rights advocate and president of Disability Rights International, Laurie Ahern, was a Purpose Prize winner in 2015. Disability Rights International is dedicated to promoting the human rights and full participation in society of people with disabilities worldwide. Although we may not aspire to a leading role in the field of disability, we can more actively support the inclusion of people with disabilities in all aspects of our lives.

As someone who loves walking, Paul was delighted to see how people in the United Kingdom with limited mobility and those using wheelchairs and mobility scooters are being offered accessible trails that enable them to go for a "walk" in the woods. Not all paths are suitable for those with limited mobility, but the National Trust has identified multiuse trails that enable people with mobility aids to experience nature and wildlife without having to go off the beaten track. Attention to providing an accessible countryside for everyone is a worthwhile pursuit.

Whether or not you have a disability, pause and consider how you can contribute to making the world a better place for people with disabilities. A simple action is to get to know people with disabilities and their challenges of living with a disability. Our disabilities are likely to increase as we age. What can we do to reduce our disability awareness gap and do something to help overcome the challenges of living with a disability?

DIVERSITY, EQUITY, INCLUSION, AND BELONGING

The diversity, equity, inclusion, and belonging framework is about integrating the presence, perspectives, and contributions of people representing our diverse populations. In a 2018 report on diversity in the workplace, Gallup described diversity as representing the full spectrum of human demographic differences—race, religion, gender, sexual orientation, age, socioeconomic status, physical disability—with different demographics such as lifestyles, personality characteristics, perspectives, opinions, family composition, and education level.[38]

The sense of belonging to a group applies not only to the workplace but to all walks of life, and although racism and gender equality garner higher media attention, embracing the full spectrum of human demographic differences is important to the future of humanity. We can also take a more proactive approach to cultivating our own sense of belonging.

Much has been achieved in terms of human rights for women and people of the lesbian, gay, bisexual, transsexual, and queer (LGBTQ+) community. Despite the progress that has been made, work on gender equality remains an important priority and was included as one of the United Nations Sustainable Development Goals with a focus on achieving gender equality and empowering all women and girls.

Racial injustice is deep-seated, yet many of our biases are unseen and not acknowledged. Creating a successful multiethnic society can be challenging, and racial disparities can be difficult to overcome. We can begin with greater awareness of our own perspectives. We are more alike than unalike, and we all have a responsibility to promote racial harmony and help to overcome the racial injustice that exists in our communities.

Although diversity, equity, inclusion, and belonging feature prominently in many workplace initiatives, minority groups still experience prejudices and discrimination in their lives outside of work. Larry Jacobson, an openly gay author and round-the-world sailor, talked to us about the challenges facing the gay community and entire community of LGBTQ+ people in midlife and beyond. During our conversation, Larry talked about the specific challenges of prejudice and discrimination facing the gay community, saying: "Discrimination in the workplace and when applying for jobs, visiting partners in hospital, renting homes, and moving into assisted living and care homes is always present, either overtly or just under the surface. We need to continue the education of workers and the population at large to reduce prejudice and discrimination." Examples of positive improvements can be found with greater access to 55-plus affordable housing and senior living places that are welcoming to the LGBTQ+ communities, but we need to continue to educate staff in these places and in the general public.

Other examples of positive action can be found. What examples come to your mind as you think about diversity, equity, inclusion, and belonging? What can we do to make our world more inclusive?

IDEAS FOR BEING SOCIALLY RESPONSIBLE

We have provided a brief overview of some of the issues facing our planet and our lives—and if any of these issues speak to you, we encourage you to continue the learning process on your own. You may already be taking social responsibility seriously, or you may be thinking about getting involved. Take some time to think about where you want to put your attention. How can you participate in organizations that promote well-being for all? What can you do on a global or local scale? Here are some ideas:

- Support elections of officials aligned with your values.
- Participate in activist organizations such as the Elders for Social Justice within the Elders Action Network.
- Take a leadership role in activist organizations.
- Lobby legislators as an individual or member of a group.
- Talk about the social causes that matter to you—with your family, friends, and others in your community.
- Convene conversations that matter about social causes in your local communities or online.

One resource for consciously helping humanity and addressing our social responsibilities is the movie *The Third Harmony*, based on the book by Michael Nagler that describes "nonviolence and the new story of human nature."[39] As described in the film and book, the three harmonies are harmony with the universe, harmony with all of life, and harmony within and among ourselves. Cultivating the harmony within is a place for us all to start.

LEADING CONSCIOUSLY

The crisis of leadership in the world today has perhaps never been more evident than in the state of governments around the world, both at the local and national level. Political leaders often appear more concerned about their own reelection than on making a positive difference for the people they represent. Although the media tends to accentuate the failure of leadership and amplify the negative attributes of leaders in government and business, leaders around the world are making a positive difference with local and global initiatives. While leaders in government and business have an important role to play, all of us have the opportunity and the responsibility to step forward and play our part in leading consciously.

Governmental leaders may find themselves trapped by the consequences of their public positioning. In his essay in the book *Deep Adaptation*, Jonathan Gosling notes that "admitting the atmospheric impact of coal would so threaten the self-image of Australian politicians, and the extractive industries are so significant in sustaining the economy, that denying their contribution to climate change seems to be the only pragmatic policy."[40] This is but one example, but political leaders around the world may find themselves unable to support change because of the unintended consequences of their positioning. As Bill

Wiles, a schoolteacher and probation and parole officer, said during our interview, "One way to achieve change is through the political process; having a government that's more open or accepting of things like climate change, clean air protection, and clean water could make a difference." Our role may be in taking our right to vote seriously and considering carefully how we choose to cast our votes.

Government policies matter. The work of the United Nations may be slow and laborious at times, but it influences and is influenced by national governments and international working groups. Policies, acts, conventions, and laws can all help improve our lives, but it may be business leaders who potentially have the largest influence on saving the planet. Unfortunately, according to Jeremy Lent, a researcher investigating the patterns of thought that has led our civilization to its current crisis of sustainability, "As long as governmental policies emphasize gross domestic product (GDP) growth and transnational companies pursue shareholder returns, we will continue to hurtle towards global catastrophe."[41]

Fortunately, some business leaders are stepping up with more than lip service to the nonfinancial environmental, social, and governance (ESG) criteria being applied by investment analysts. Much has been written about the shift toward stakeholder capitalism where companies embrace the concerns of employees, customers, their communities, and the planet they inhabit, as well as needs of shareholders to maximize profits. Conscious leaders in business may have much greater influence on helping humanity than leaders in government. Larry Fink, chief executive officer of BlackRock, the world's largest shareholder, which manages approximately 10 trillion US dollars on behalf of pension funds, endowments, governments, companies, and individuals, has called on firms to align with global efforts to reach net-zero greenhouse gas emissions by 2050. BlackRock expects companies to disclose a plan for how their business model will be compatible with a low-carbon economy, and it "expect[s] directors to have sufficient fluency in climate risk and the energy transition to enable the whole board rather than a single director who is a 'climate expert' to provide appropriate oversight of the company's plan and targets."[42] BlackRock wields vast shareholder voting power and has declared it could vote against company directors that fail to provide credible climate plans. Whether you think BlackRock is doing too much or isn't doing enough in helping humanity, the influence of leaders of this type of business organization is immense.

Other business leaders demonstrating their strongly felt responsibility for environmental and social change include Paul Polman, ex-CEO of Unilever and his successor Alan Jope; Bob Chapman, CEO of Barry-Wehmiller; Jesper Brodin, CEO of IKEA; Marc Benioff, CEO of Salesforce; and Chuck Robbins, CEO of Cisco Systems. Following these business leaders on social media, along with the chief sustainability officers of these and many other international organizations, can help provide insights on what is being done for the good of humanity. Understanding how organizations do—or do not—engage in social responsibility can also assist you in determining how to invest (as we noted in chapter 3).

PURPOSE, PEOPLE, AND THE PLANET

Along with choosing how to invest in businesses that support sustainability and other positive aspects of social change, we can exercise our right to vote and support elected officials locally and nationally who emphasize purpose, people, and the planet before profit. Politicians will take action that supports their reelection and, despite sometimes superficial support for environmental and social change, will actively engage if sufficient constituents bring the issues to their attention. You may even feel called to run for office yourself—and again, think local!

Another way to make a difference is to participate in the conscious capitalism movement inspired by John Mackey, cofounder of Whole Foods Market, and Raj Sisodia, professor and research scholar at Babson College. In their book *Conscious Capitalism: Liberating the Heroic Spirit of Business*, they described the four pillars of conscious capitalism as higher purpose, stakeholder integration, conscious leadership, and conscious culture.[43] Emerging terminology also includes inclusive capitalism, responsible capitalism, natural capitalism, moral capitalism, progressive capitalism, and breakthrough capitalism. Many organizational leaders are becoming more conscious of their choices with a greater focus on all stakeholders. The needs of business have to come into balance with the needs of society and the needs of nature. Leaders in government and business have a role to play, but we as individuals must play our part.

What can we do to influence leaders in governments and business to put a greater focus on helping humanity? Here are some ideas:

- Taking our right to vote seriously and consider carefully how we cast our votes

- Running for office in local or national governments

- Being a socially responsible investor and divesting our investments in fossil fuel companies and investing in companies producing green energy

- Buying products and services from socially responsible suppliers

- Being a more conscious leader

- Convening conversations that matter about conscious leadership and helping humanity

In this chapter we introduced you to some—although by no means all—of the pressing issues facing humanity and our planet and provided some suggestions for making a contribution. The feeling of overwhelm is not unusual as we consider the problems facing humanity, but we can all make a positive difference in the environmental sustainability of our planet, the social justice issues people face, and the leadership challenges in governments and business. Find something you really care about, something that makes you angry or sad, and do something about that. Set a clear personal intention, imagining what might seem to be at the edge of possibility, and map out individual or collective pathways to realize your dreams. Midlife and beyond is the perfect time to choose to live and lead more consciously and to contribute to helping humanity today and for those who come after us.

CONSCIOUS LIVING PRACTICES

Questions for Reflection

- What areas of environmental sustainability inspire you to take action?

- What aspects of social responsibility are you passionate about?

- What is your contribution to helping humanity and saving the planet?

- Where can you take a leadership role in helping humanity?

- Where can you join or convene conversations about environmental sustainability and social responsibility?

Try This

- Social responsibility embraces a multitude of opportunities to contribute. To narrow down areas of contribution you wish to make, make a list of the injustices that irritate or annoy you. Ask yourself, "What makes me cry?"

- Search the internet and local communities for existing groups taking action on causes focused on helping humanity. Consider how you can take a more conscious leadership role.

Living
Well

Bouncing
Forward

Appreciating
Money

Living with
Technology

Working
for a Living

Exploring
Purposefully

Helping
Humanity

Working for
Fulfillment

Minding
Relationships

Savoring
the World

Living Life
Creatively

CHAPTER 10

LIVING WITH TECHNOLOGY

The biggest benefit of technology to ageing is the freedom
of choice, empowering older adults to maintain autonomy,
choose the lifestyle they want, and promote dignity.

–A. VIGNESWARI AND ADRIENNE MENDENHALL

"The times they are a-changin'," sang Bob Dylan in 1964.[1] Fast-forward twenty years and Steve Jobs is using the words of the song to introduce the Macintosh computer.[2] Today the times are still a changin' with such a rapid pace that it is a challenge to keep up. How can we best live with technology?

In this chapter, we share an overview of our Conscious Living approach to technology and highlight the relevance to the 11 dimensions of our Conscious Living Wheel. We offer information, thoughts, and resources on technology to help you evolve your relationship with technology and consciously integrate it into your life. Supplemental information can be found in the Resources section.

How we perceive technology can impact our experience of using it. Our perception matters, because being knowledgeable about the current technological landscape presents possibilities for us in midlife and beyond. As we've been emphasizing throughout this book, a well-lived life is one of connection—to our purpose, to people, to places, and more. Technology is the semi-invisible platform that connects us to all those components in one way or another.

What feelings arise when you think of technology? Is it a visceral feeling of dread or an excited sense of new possibilities, or somewhere in between? Maybe you have embraced technology in some life dimension areas but not others. As you read this chapter and discover how technology relates to each dimension of the Conscious Living Wheel, we suggest asking yourself:

- What's the opportunity for me with technology here in each particular life dimension?
- What do I need to learn? Where do I need help?
- What might I need to be careful about as I proceed?

Technology touches all parts of our life—some more than others, depending on our access to it. Adjusting to technology's changes and reach is in and of itself a challenge, and this is where our Conscious Living approach comes in.

We can all see in our everyday life how much technology affects us, from checking our phones or computers in the morning, to turning off our home alarms or engaging with audible assistants, to texting and email, to ordering from the internet. Despite the fact that technology is ever present—and can seem unavoidable—we can consciously choose the degree that technology is present in our lives. Making decisions that support our values helps put technology in perspective. It's possible to remain aware of advances and updates to technology without allowing it to intrude or take over. Our approach is to acknowledge and accept the presence and speed of technology, along with awareness of advances and updates, and then to consciously decide on the level of its integration in our lives.

Having technology in our lives has advantages and disadvantages. The National Institute of Health (NIH) reports that technology has both a significant positive and negative impact on brain function and behavior, for example. Some positive impacts include increases in neural activity, memory, fluid intelligence, and other cognitive abilities and mental health benefits, particularly with the use of apps and tools to improve sleep, mood, and behaviors. Negative impacts include technology addiction, social isolation, and sleep disruption.[3] However you feel about modern technology—whether you are digitally savvy and embrace it fully or are kicking and screaming with the challenges—the key to living consciously is understanding how you can engage with it on your own terms.

A DIGITAL MINDSET

A digital mindset refers to one's approach to technology rather than one's expertise in using it. A digital mindset is basically a "set of behavioral and attitudinal approaches that enable individuals and organizations to see the possibilities of the digital era, to use its affordances for deeper personal and greater professional fulfillment."[4] The mindsets of abundance, growth, agility, comfort with ambiguity, exploration, collaboration, and diversity are considered the digital mindset's seven key characteristics.[5]

Midlife and beyond is an ideal time to reassess how we want to continue to live our lives and where we want to invest our energy and time. Technology provides us with an opportunity to enhance our lives if we are open to it, and it also presents numerous challenges.

Mary Ann Esfandiari, a retired NASA senior executive of dual careers and now a part-time consultant, credits technology for enhancing her active and engaging lifestyle. Mary Ann shared with us that she loves technology and that it saves her valuable time and makes life easier and more fun. She believes it's important to make the effort to stay current and learn how to use technology to enhance your life. Mary Ann uses a variety of tech items: for example, in her kitchen she has Wi-Fi–enabled appliances and cookware with sensors to allow her to monitor her cooking with precise temperatures and timing for delicious meals she loves to create. In her office she uses digital calendars and virtual meeting platforms such as Zoom and FaceTime. For her photography hobby she uses her digital camera to capture wildlife, and for sewing, another passion, she uses a machine with advanced features to create a variety of products. She uses voice assistants and wearable tech like her fitness tracker that measures and monitors exercise, sleep, and more. She has found new emerging technologies that can help with diagnosis, treatment, and rehabilitation of potential health issues.

Mary Ann's uses of technology may be familiar to you—or perhaps she seems more plugged in than you currently are and you're curious. Let's explore the other dimensions of our Conscious Living Wheel and see how they connect with technology and how they might enhance our lives.

EXPLORING PURPOSEFULLY

We explored our purpose, meaning, and identity in chapter 1 of this book. This exploration is mostly inner work where the influence of technology may not be as impactful. Let us be mindful, however, that technology can be a useful platform in exploring our identity using value assessment tools, character strength profiles, and other online resources for further discovery and insight.

Life purpose and meaning can be associated with being centered and connected to a purpose greater than oneself and the sense of universal connection to others. This can lead into the realm of service and spirituality. Online services to find life coaches, purpose-focused communities, and faith-based communities are some options to explore.

LIVING WELL

In chapter 2, we examined the mind and the body in midlife and beyond and issues around healthcare. Technology is widely used in this area, and here we provide some examples of where the influence of technology is having the most impact and where we may need to learn more.

The COVID-19 pandemic caused creativity to surge and merge with needs and desires, which resulted in an amplification of education technology of online learning and sharing of information and knowledge. Zoom,[6] Google Meet,[7] and other platforms provided enhanced online communication and learning. We know that lifelong learning supports building brain reserve and that the more we learn, the more brain connections we have. Many classes and clubs that were formerly in person can now be found online.

A rich variety of global sources provide opportunities for online learning called MOOCs, which stands for Massive Open Online Courses. Some of these classes are given through Coursera,[8] Udacity,[9] FutureLearn,[10] The Great Courses,[11] and Class Central.[12] Many of them provide free access. They are often affiliated with universities. Some MOOCs offer classes in multiple languages, thus expanding their global applicability.

There are also classes to calm and relax the mind and body from the stresses of the day, such as yoga, dance, drawing, music, and woodworking, which often combine an online format with downloadable booklets and recorded audiovisual instruction and discussion. Search the internet for what interests you and see what is available. Being consciously aware of how you best learn will help you choose a class format and interaction that is ideal for you.

Perhaps you're inclined to teach some classes yourself based on your interests, knowledge, and experiences. Knowing how to interact with technology and its platforms to set up and run the classes is an essential factor in being able to teach online. Eileen teaches a variety of community classes, for example, and they offer instruction and tech support for their teachers. So feel free to inquire about this option with the organization you wish to teach for.

Technology can help us live long, healthy, active lives. The Stanford Center on Longevity[13] studies life span and the ways in which science and technology can support us with aging challenges. We can benefit from common medical technology and assistive technology that allows us to be more independent, using wearable sensing and monitoring devices to detect heart rate, blood sugar, and irregular heart rhythms, and gives us the ability to call for help. Apple Watch and Fitbit are examples of wearable tech.[14] Femtech is technology designed for women's health. Thermaband,[15] a wrist band temperature sensor that detects menopausal hot flashes and responds with a cooling sensation, is another example being brought to the health arena. Apps and tools can assist us with our sleep, relaxing our mind and body, and provide access to programs and classes to augment healthy behaviors. Health technology allows us to be proactive by monitoring our behaviors that utilize diagnostics, telemedicine, and medicine management. Eileen, for example, has a very slender EKG device[16] attached to her mobile phone that can take a medical grade EKG and send it to her doctor within minutes.

Mobility aids are another way that technology can assist us. Mobility aids have traditionally included assists such as canes, walkers, wheelchairs, and chair lifts, and modernized refinements of several now include sensors and digital software built in for ease of use.[17] Wearable robotic exoskeletons allow for standing and walking for spinal cord injuries, and "exo-suits" are available for stroke rehabilitation.[18] Electric scooters provide ease and accessibility to get you around town or to places where you may have been limited from walking. Various apps for ordering rides are available, such as Uber and Lyft in the US and Cabify in parts of Europe. Although fine-tuning and safety are a way off, the advent of autonomous vehicles or driverless cars can potentially provide us with that ability in the future. These devices have various degrees of availability and cost, so it is advisable to explore and talk with your insurance company.

In addition to the technology that can motivate and monitor us to eat balanced meals, sleep well, hydrate, and exercise, there are many online ordering apps such as Door Dash, Instacart, and Uber Eats to provide essential groceries and meals. Online ordering companies such as Amazon increased significantly during the pandemic and these days can bring us almost any needed item.

Greg M. injured his back during the COVID-19 pandemic and needed physical therapy treatment. He was invited to try out a new online virtual program with a physical therapist to provide him with exercises to do within the comfort and convenience of his home. He was sent a package with a special digital tablet and sensors for his back. He placed the sensors on his back and was instructed in how to do the exercises. The sensors provided real-time feedback to indicate whether he was doing his exercises correctly or not. The program proved to be a success for both Greg and the innovators of the new emerging telehealth program that offered it. This is but one example, and future iterations and possibilities are being explored and piloted.[19]

Technology also gives us hope for body parts that may not be able to be repaired or rehabbed. The imaginative idea of 3D printers material-ized back in the 1980s[20] and has advanced to printing prosthetics, body parts, bone grafts, artificial teeth, and more.[21] NASA is even considering 3D printers to produce much-needed items in places far from Earth.

These days we also have digital access portals where we can access our health reports. You may designate others you want to have access as well. If you do not know how to use these online portals, please ask your primary care office for help, and seek out resources so that you are able to understand and use them to support your optimal well-being.

It's also important to be mindful about evaluating your screen and digital time. Digital eye strain can impact our ability to sleep, so experts recommend that we turn off our digital items several hours before going to bed. When we are at our computers or digital devices we tend not to blink as much, which can cause dry eyes. We recommend following the 20-20-20[22] rule of taking a 20-second screen break every 20 minutes to look out 20 feet away from your devices, which provides us with a break to blink more freely.

According to the authors of the article "Advancing the Aging and Technology Agenda in Gerontology," "For healthy older individuals, technology may delay or prevent the onset of disability, stimulate new activities and interests, facilitate communication, enhance knowledge, elevate mood, and improve psychological well-being. These [technological] trends have contributed to the strong conviction that technology can play an important role in enhancing quality of life and independence of older individuals with high levels of efficiency, potentially reducing individual and societal costs of caring for the elderly people."[23]

At some point in time we may need a caregiver or be a caregiver for a loved one, so it is helpful to be aware that caregiver aids and assistive technologies are widely available. Remote monitoring can help a person age gracefully in their home. For example, a family member can remotely monitor activities of a loved one with a health issue and know whether they have done such activities as taken their meds, opened the refrigerator, turned appliances off or on, or opened or closed their front door. This type of technology can provide a long-distance sense of caring for those we love and potentially lengthen the time one can physically stay in their home. The article "How Technology Will Impact Aging Now and in the Near Future" presents new technology being piloted, such as robotic care and the use of technology in creating complex algorithms to match caregivers and those needing care.[24]

APPRECIATING MONEY

Technology has transformed the way we handle money and manage our finances. You may already have an electronic wallet on your mobile phone that allows payments in stores and restaurants without the need for cash or credit cards. Even the more cautious of us may be exploring these electronic wallets. Technology also allows for online calculations with algorithms for planning. Many of these calculators relate to helping people determine if they have enough money for day-to-day expenses or for larger financial plans such as retirement. The use of artificial intelligence (AI) and robotic process automation can provide a foundation of analyzed and processed information often used by financial advisors to help clients. We still favor using the services of a qualified fiduciary certified financial planner to complement the information and calculators online, as they can advise you best on your own personal situation.

The term "fintech" refers to "the synergy between finance and technology and is used to enhance business operations and the delivery of financial services."[25] It can take a variety of forms, such as software and services that provide advanced technological methods over traditional methods to make the process more efficient. Examples of fintech are mobile assistants or apps that help users pay bills, transfer money, and receive their FICO score, as well as software that is able to detect and fight fraud and money laundering.[26] Venmo, Zelle, PayPal, and Stripe are popular payment and money transfer vehicles.[27] Other examples include Apple Pay and Google Pay. These money transfer vehicles allow for less weight in your actual wallet, more convenience, and with encryption of financial information, enhanced security. Service fintech can include crowdfunding and peer-to-peer lending such a Kickstarter or GoFundMe.[28] As with any technology use, there is always risk. Many of these companies are on alert for data breaches and scams. Our responsibility is to stay on top of our security updates and read our bills thoroughly.

Even with estate planning, you may be surprised to learn there are digital assets to consider in addition to traditional ones. Think about all the digital accounts that contain your photos, videos, art, writing, classes, emails, and website. Some of these accounts include items of personal importance as they relate to family and legacy, and others include items with monetary value such as prized photographs, manuscripts, trademarks, or even a contact list, if you own a business.

It is helpful in estate planning to make a list of your digital accounts, their contents, and their access information to increase your awareness of this platform of assets and to help you better plan for your desired intentions. The article "Digital Cheat Sheet: How to Create a Digital Estate Plan" with references to other articles raises awareness of the many digital assets that are acquired and actions needed to manage and close accounts.[29] There are now digital executors that act on your behalf to manage your digital assets in the event of your incapacity or death. They act as an adjunct capacity to a traditional estate executor and should be identified in your will. Some estate planners include this in their work. In the US, most states have enacted a path for a fiduciary to help by either the Uniform Fiduciary Access to Digital Assets Act or the Revised Uniform Fiduciary Access to Digital Assets Act.[30] Please refer to your primary estate planner, your local estate attorney, and specific state laws for your unique situation.

WORKING FOR A LIVING AND FULFILLMENT

Technology provides a vehicle for us to converse, communicate, and collaborate—which is especially useful for working, whether it's for an employer or on our own. We can work remotely with our computers and communicate using Zoom or Google Meet. We can collaborate at the same time on a document or a special project with cloud-based file sharing such as Google Drive, Microsoft Office, and Dropbox. No longer are geography and transportation big factors in teamwork. Technology can allow us to have more of a work-life balance because we are not commuting to work, which frees up more time—although it can also be a challenge to close the proverbial office door.

Technology provides an exciting opportunity to start a small niche business doing what you love to do. We prefer the view that technology is not taking away jobs but rather providing creative avenues to bring your gifts and talents into the world on your own terms. You may need a little training or technology assistance, but the path is there if you want it.

Take for example Jill Badonsky, who is a multibook author and creativity leader. She loves technology and uses it in her business to create, connect, and produce books and workshops. For her last book, she designed each page with colorful graphics to inspire her readers and had fun with drawing and selecting the format. She tells us that technology has made a difference in her life because as an introvert she can meet and engage with people on social media, which is a comfortable and fun platform for her. Badonsky also says that it's okay "if tech is not your thing and it gets in the way of your creativity. Do what works for you, yet be willing to stretch a bit and try out new things with patience."

Fred Mandell, author and creative entrepreneur, shares that he sees technology as a tool in our relationship with the world, and he feels comfortable with it and uses it every day, including social media. "I'm very selective in terms of my use of social media," he tells us. "I use LinkedIn quite a bit. I don't do Facebook. What I think about it from a professional point of view is what is the social media platform accessed by the audience I want to work with? And that will determine the selection of technology-based social media that I'll use." He adds that he's comfortable being able to learn new platforms and that he sees technology as "a tool to not only make life easier but as a platform to facilitate the growth of my business and as an interactive platform for the delivery of some of our educational offerings."

Working helps us keep up our technological knowledge and skills. If you find yourself outside of technically advanced organizations in midlife and beyond, we recommend making an intentional effort to become knowledgeable of the latest technological applications to remain relevant in today's world.

SAVORING THE WORLD

In chapter 6 we discussed where to live and where to travel, using the internet to search locally and globally. Much of the technology we have in use in our home corner of the world is already so intertwined in our lives that we may not actually notice it: we have our digital devices such as our phones and computers, and our voice and robotic assistants to wake us up, turn lights on and off, lock doors, set alarms, surveil and video the front door, keep track of the thermostat, inventory the refrigerator, vacuum our floors, and more. We may also have fall detection devices and life alert systems. New outdoor lighting, theater systems, and space heaters are also available. There is a lot going on.

Maybe you simply desire the solitude and bird songs of being outdoors and do not feel a need for these other items. Our Conscious Living approach invites us to intentionally decide how much technology we want or need to savor our environment in our home, our community, and beyond.

What inspires you in the connection between technology and savoring your world? Perhaps you enjoy digital photography, using your phone or a digital camera. If you like walking or hiking, you can access apps for trail guides in your local area and community. You can livestream music while walking or entertaining. Many communities have their own apps or websites for learning about local happenings, and there are numerous technological resources for travel around the globe.

As you travel, travel light, use technology, and support the environment in the process. Many hotels no longer offer printing services, so rely on your cell phone or tablet to provide boarding passes, reservation confirmations, maps, and digital travel books to clear space and weight in your travel gear. Cell phones can alert you to flight delays, gate changes, and luggage location if you have a smart locator. Although much of air travel is automated such as luggage tagging, passport machine readers, and security photography, there are still smiling people to assist you if needed.

LIVING LIFE CREATIVELY

The technological advances we have today were once just ideas, questions of "what if" and possibility. Technology can enhance one's creativity simply by virtue of access and exposure to the sheer volume and variety of sources and platforms to inspire and launch new ideas. For example, visiting photos from Pinterest, Google Images, or Instagram can provide inspiration and insight for novel ways of doing an activity or expressing oneself. Simply using your curiosity to ask questions on any topic in your browser will generate and connect multiple creative dots. Today there are many easy-to-use tools and techniques with creative applications. For example, Eileen uses a variety of technological apps such as Procreate to draw and illustrate in her classes and with clients. And all three of us co-authors use collaborative platforms such as Google Drive and Google Docs to write and edit, and engage in meetings on Zoom to further discuss and move forward as a team.

Mind-mapping and flow chart tools allow for linking ideas to a visual representation. There are apps and tools to create your own music and playlists. Writing on one of the free blog sites such as blogger.com can be another platform for sharing thoughts and ideas, or you can try podcasting or creating YouTube videos. For example, Joyce Cohen, a career development and midlife transition specialist, along with Vicki Thomas, a lifelong journalist, producer, and writer, merged their creative skills with technology to develop an online program they co-host called *My Future Purpose* to help people find their purposeful path.

Technology can add fun and humor to your life. For example, you could add a "green room" background for a themed Zoom gathering such as a baseball stadium for virtual game-watching with others. You can design a landscape for your backyard or use technological application to design three-dimensional objects or most anything else. See where your curiosity and interests lead you.

MINDING RELATIONSHIPS

Technology allows our relationships to expand as we connect, converse, and learn from others of diverse ages, generations, races, cultures, and customs. This fosters a sense of shared humanity with many universal themes and builds community. Multiple social media platforms can connect us with others, and they became even more popular during the COVID pandemic. To name just a few, social media platforms and apps include Facebook, Instagram, X (formerly Twitter), WhatsApp, and Meetup. Private text and photo sharing apps like GroupMe allow families and friends to strengthen their connection with a running text log that includes photos accessed by using the app as opposed to multiple emails and texts.

Perhaps you grew up meeting potential partners at school, work, or gatherings. With the loss of a partner, you may find yourself looking for a new companion, yet you may be unsure about dating again. Online dating geared to those in midlife and beyond offers another way besides classes and events to meet. See the Resources section on navigating the dating scene as well as safeguards and precautions and other useful items.

As we've repeatedly emphasized, being intentional with our time and energy is an essential component of our Conscious Living approach—and technology can help you do this. For example, if you want to read a story to your grandchild but you are not physically there, you can set up a Zoom session. Or, you can record yourself reading and showing pictures in the book so the child can access it at any time. You can play games online such as charades or have a show-and-tell to demonstrate how to do an activity like cooking a special recipe. Another way to connect with family or friends is with a themed monthly video chat. You may want to record contact information and notes on your smartphone to include special event reminders like birthdays, along with preferences for colors and gift ideas. Preplanned reminders can keep you up to date. Tapping into your imagination and your creativity will bring up more ideas to nurture your relationships.

Technological possibilities are on the horizon for sharing on another level. Virtual 3D images that appear as living persons are called holograms. Specialized technological equipment is required to produce them, and they are expensive. A hologram of a historical figure or loved one can provide a talk. Significant advancements have allowed

for people to be interviewed and the responses saved so that future generations can even interact with the hologram and ask questions, with
the responses pulled from the interviews as if in a real conversation.[31]
Once prices come down, the value of connecting to a departed family
member in this manner can be valuable in preserving their legacy and
life lessons.

Learning to use these technological platforms and applications can
be challenging, yet the earlier we start, the greater the benefit is. Find a
young person such as a grandchild to help, and watch your relationship
flourish with fun. It's another way to connect and maintain a relationship, and it builds confidence and competence for both people.

HELPING HUMANITY

In chapter 9 we looked at the environmental sustainability of our
planet, social responsibility for people, and leadership in governments
and business. The use of technology in these areas is extensive. How
does technology in these areas affect us individually in midlife and
beyond, and how can we respond?

Technology allows us to access social responsibility reports worldwide and learn from the many initiatives designed to address social
justice issues locally. We can also learn what governments and business
leaders are doing to help humanity thrive. Artificial intelligence (AI),
with its predictive and problem-solving capabilities, can be a positive
force for helping humanity.[32] Some examples include optimizing
renewable energy, developing new drugs and therapies, use of search
and rescue robots, reaching the underserved with products and services,
crowdsourcing, and sharing empowering information relevant to farm-
ers' crops.

In terms of a personal contribution, you may be interested in
using technology to coordinate an event or simply to create a legacy

document for your family such as writing about experiences and life lessons that you want to share about saving humanity. Some in midlife and beyond are downsizing and moving to small-sized living areas and buying "energy star" products that use energy efficiently. You can recycle old electronics to dedicated sites such as Gazelle.com and make a few dollars in the process. Donating books to libraries and switching to buying virtual e-books along with virtual newspaper subscriptions can reduce the number of trees cut down for printing. Small or large ways of using and supporting technology count in helping humanity and our planet.

BOUNCING FORWARD

In chapter 11, we explore resilience and the mindsets and practices that can support us in the second half of our lives. Technology in this space allows us access to online therapists, support groups, classes, educational information, digital tools, and apps to soothe our mind and bodies. The COVID pandemic provided the catalyst to provide virtual services, and the result has opened the doors to increased availability and a variety of services to support our resilience.

LIVING WITH TECHNOLOGY

Kari Cardinale, senior VP of digital and alumni strategy at the Modern Elder Academy, shared with us how growing up has a big impact on how we approach technology now. Back in the day, she says learning how to use Excel took an entire class, with updates causing further stress to the learning process. She maintains that if you are operating from that mindset of difficulty, it is time to update your thinking to maximize your benefits.

LEARNING AND UPDATING YOUR KNOWLEDGE

Dorothy Keenan, founder and executive director of GrandInvolve, admires her granddaughter's mindset of curiosity and fearlessness with computers, yet for her the pace of technology feels exponential and scary. Dorothy shares that for her to learn new digital techniques she needs to watch someone do it and then do it herself rather than someone doing it or fixing it for her, which is better for her learning and practicing. It is helpful to remember how we best learn such as seeing a demonstration and then trying it yourself or reading a how-to guide.

Today most new devices such as computers, tablets, and mobile phones come with only basic instructions. Someone who has best learned how to use something from a longer manual may find this frustrating. Shifting your mindset to being consciously open to learning how to use something can help. We also suggest being resourceful, asking for help, and being patient with yourself in the process. Knowing how we learn best is helpful, because then we can search for the method that will help us best: written information, people to teach or tutor, videos on YouTube, or other support organizations. Knowledge can often be the antidote for fears or hesitancy with new technology, and help is certainly available for learning to use technology and adding to your knowledge with various advanced levels of complexity. A variety of resources are available. For example, if you find reading with visual pictures helpful, then take a look at the vast "For Dummies" book series. Technology books become outdated quickly, so be mindful of publishing dates. See our rich Resources section.

If you wish to pursue technology knowledge and experience, then we suggest being aware and resourceful with researching and asking others about information, and finding classes for adults online and in person. It is easier to keep up incrementally with technology than starting from scratch, but it's never too late to begin.

DEVELOPING YOUR IDEAL RELATIONSHIP WITH TECHNOLOGY

We have the opportunity to continue developing our relationship with technology, and each of us can make our own choices. Here are some questions to ask to discover what's ideal for you:

- What are the websites I visit, and what do I get out of them?

- How much time and engagement with technology do I want or need?

- How much time am I on digital devices? How much time would I like to do something else?

- What are my thoughts on taking a mini break from technology, such as a "digital detox"?

We want to emphasize again that navigating technology comes with safety concerns. Be sure to not click on links in emails from people you don't know, give out personal information on social media, or give out your Social Security number or credit card numbers. New scams are invented every day, which can catch even the most sophisticated and educated person off guard, so it is worthwhile to read about scams and how to avoid them. Local police departments generally provide information and community classes on such topics.

In addition to navigating safely on the internet, knowing what to do when technology does not act as expected is also important. Here are some things to think about ahead of time that will help you develop your plan B when technology fails:

- What actions do I first need to take once my device is not operating well? Actions one may need to do with a computer are turn it off and back on, reboot it, update the latest operating system, and have the number for tech support available.

- Not everyone knows what to do with failing technology such as smart alarms or intrusion detectors. Get the information from an instruction manual or from the company's techy support and jot it down on an index card for easy reference.

- Identify who you can call upon to help you with technology challenges, and write down the names and numbers of resources you can call upon for help. Do you have an IT support person? Some might provide simple solutions, while others might provide hands-on assistance for more difficult tasks.

- Use a password manager such as One Password or LastPass to safely store your password when you need it to log in. If you write your passwords down instead, be sure you put them away in a safe yet accessible place. Share with a trusted person the location of your passwords in case of an emergency.

However you feel about technology, it will only be increasingly relevant in our lives especially with the advent of Artificial Intelligence (AI) and its potential impact—so stay updated and keep learning. Speak the language. You can enjoy technology for its opportunities and for finding technological solutions to support you in midlife and beyond. Staying updated, talking to others, taking classes, and being aware of trends and the latest security and safety guidelines can provide for optimal technological experiences.

In this chapter we presented our Conscious Living approach to technology and adopting a digital mindset. We reviewed some of the technology issues relating to the life dimensions of our Conscious Living Wheel to provide insights and illustrate ways for us to utilize technology to enhance our lives, and explained the value of learning and using technology. We hope you've been encouraged to consciously choose your own best relationship with technology and to support others.

CONSCIOUS LIVING PRACTICES

Questions for Reflection

- What mindset and approach will offer you an optimal relationship with technology?
- How might technology help you ?
- What technological apps might encourage you to lead a healthier lifestyle?
- What are some ways you can keep track of your passwords?
- What is your plan for addressing your technological challenges?

Try This

- Create your own online group of people for one of your areas of interest or to share information and resources about technology.
- Review class offerings of the Massive Open Online Classes (MOOCs) and select one course of interest to try.
- Refer to the Resources section for more ways to enhance your technological knowledge and experience.

Living
Well

Bouncing
Forward

Appreciating
Money

Living with
Technology

Working
for a Living

Exploring
Purposefully

Helping
Humanity

Working for
Fulfillment

Minding
Relationships

Savoring
the World

Living Life
Creatively

CHAPTER 11

BOUNCING FORWARD

I am no longer afraid of storms,
for I am learning how to sail my ship.
–LOUISA MAY ALCOTT

We have explored many of the challenges faced by people in midlife and beyond in the chapters of this book. One of the most important characteristics of people who were able to adapt and thrive during these life-changing challenges is *resilience*. Developing our resiliency muscle will enable us to move to places of choice, consciously steering our ship to new horizons and creating something better than before.

In this chapter we share approaches and practices for adapting to change to build up our resiliency muscle so we can indeed bounce forward for optimal well-being in midlife and beyond.

Many changes and challenges are predictable, yet we may not pay attention to them until they come closer to us as we advance on life's journey. Or if we are peripherally aware of them, we may think their impact may not be significant. The result may be that we are not prepared. We are not alone in this human experience. The good news is helpful research on change, challenge, and resilience has provided a wealth of mindsets and practices to ease our transitions, making them more manageable and smoother.

According to the American Psychological Association, resilience is "the process of adapting well in the face of adversity, trauma, tragedy, threats and even significant sources of stress—such as family and relationship problems, serious health problems, or workplace and financial stresses."[1] Resilience is said to involve "bouncing back" from difficult experiences and achieving personal growth.[2] For us, resilience is not so much about bouncing back from adversity as it is about the process of consciously bouncing forward to embrace new visions in the second half of life.

THE MIDLIFE LANDSCAPE OF CHANGES, CHALLENGES, POSSIBILITIES, AND GROWTH

As we grow older, changes occur with our physical bodies and minds as well as in the spiritual, social, occupational, financial, service, and environmental life domains. We may face huge unforeseen challenges like ill health, job loss, financial disasters, the loss of a partner or family member, or separation and divorce. How we respond to changes can allow us to remain standing, surviving, and thriving—or to fall and succumb. Navigating change and figuring out ambiguous situations can challenge us, especially as we may have more of them in the second half of life.[3]

UNCERTAINTY, FEARS, AND VULNERABILITY

Underneath uncertainty lives a multitude of fears: of the unknown, of making the wrong decision, and of our failure to handle changes well. This can make us feel vulnerable, especially if we've been in a leadership position or were the go-to person for problem-solving in the past. Fears and vulnerabilities show up in a number of life domains in our Conscious Living Wheel, and they can feel overwhelming.

We are not alone in this feeling. Uncertainty can be so uncomfortable that people will often prefer to be given some answer or information even if it is undesirable, rather than sit with uncertainty. Perhaps you can relate, such as waiting for a pathology report or an acceptance of a job offer. But uncertainty can also be a catalyst—the spark for a new life direction leading to happiness, fulfillment, and joy.

Brené Brown, author of *Daring Greatly*, defines vulnerability as "uncertainty, risk, and emotional exposure."[4] She asks: How are we going to respond? The process of responding can activate our excitement and fears at the same time. Trying something new such as starting a new life chapter, a new business, a new relationship, salvaging an old relationship, or trying out a new way of being can elicit anxiety. Our emotional exposure of not having all the answers and our fears of potential loss or failure can put our sense of self, our security, and our growth and development at stake. The good news is that resilience can be learned and developed so that we can optimally respond.

THE RESILIENCE EFFECT

Resilience is the ability to combine supportive mindsets with supportive behaviors that inspire us to move forward with hope from our changes, challenges, and adversities. A key *intrinsic* reward of being resilient is the ability to experience more joy and happiness in life. We call this "the resilience effect." The rewards of a resilient mindset affect all life domains, including restful sleep, improved immune function, better health and longevity, higher rates of happiness, improved relationships, greater work and life satisfaction, and the ability to move forward in difficult situations in support of our overall well-being.[5] Being resilient can be similar to riding a wave on a surfboard: You need to remain flexible, agile, and balance yourself in the process. In learning to be a creative problem solver, you build your balance and confidence as you ride the waves of change.

Alternatively, if we do not cultivate resilience, we may find ourselves more vulnerable and susceptible to being overcome by adversity. Being overwhelmed can impact our health, and for some can result in unhealthy practices with drugs or alcohol. These substances can impact us more significantly in midlife, as our metabolism slows so they reside in our body longer, and medicines treating underlying health conditions can interact negatively.[6] At the extreme, lack of resiliency can even lead to suicide in older adults. Risk factors related to becoming a widow or widower, health status changes, social isolation, the loss of family and friends, depression, and lack of meaning and purpose can all weigh heavily.[7, 8] Statistics show that 46.8 percent of all suicides in the United States are middle-aged adults (aged 35–64), indicating that midlife can be a time of vulnerability.[9]

Some changes associated with aging and midlife often seem on the periphery of our lives until those changes happen to those close to us or to ourselves. We may notice only small changes at first, such as neighbors and friends retiring and moving to be near their children or to smaller homes. News of friends or colleagues retiring or moving, or of a new diagnosis, disability, or death, can catch us off guard. Sometimes it is so sudden we may feel stunned and saddened about how life is changing. At the same time, we may be seeing colleagues retire and start new businesses with renewed energy and vigor or taking up new activities like teaching, sculpting, or mentoring. We may notice friends with renewed interest and zest in old pastimes and travel. All of these changes, both gradual and sudden, can at times overwhelm us—which is why cultivating resilience is so important.

How will you respond to the changes in your life? Do you have a plan?

PREPARING FOR THE PATH AHEAD

Change may be an event, while the process of adapting to it is a transition.[10] For example, a job loss is an external event, whereas the associated process involving one's interior thoughts and emotions is considered a transition. As mentioned back in chapter 1, William Bridges, author of the classic book *Transitions*,[11] notes three transition phases: the ending, the neutral zone, and the new beginning. This middle neutral zone is characterized by ambiguity, uncertainty, and discomfort. It is a period of not knowing one's direction and of questioning what's next. It usually arrives after an ending such as a job loss, retirement, or the last child leaving the nest. It has been described as a blurry, foggy, messy phase full of questions, doubt, and the striving for clarity. We humans generally like predictability, because it gives us a foundation for our daily lives and expectations. The thing is, this messy middle phase is where our creative canvas exists, where we put together pieces of what we have and what we want for our future. It takes thought, time, energy, and iteration upon iteration, yet it is where we create something even better.

So how do we get from the pause of uncertainty to the other side? What does it take to get to the stage of new beginnings? It's about how we think and set ourselves up for forward movement.

Moving Forward

- **Continual rebalancing:** "Life is about continually finding new balances and new perspectives. Your circumstances change, and then you have to start rearranging your life. One day you go from being married to being a widow, from being a full-time mother to being a grandmother. Take time to think, assess your situation, and find your new balance." —**Betty McDowall**, social justice advocate
- **Try it:** "There is no moving ahead without change and doing something different. Always be looking at what you can do differently, always assessing the way it is now and the way it could be and what you might do to get to that place. My motto is 'try it,' as you usually can go back to try something different. Do something that's going to make a difference whether it works or not." —**Dorothy Keenan**, GrandInvolve founder and positive aging advocate
- **Experience the unknown and build confidence:** "You're always going to have unknowns and challenges in your life. While taking on new challenges, take care of yourself as much as you can, but then open yourself to the experience, whatever that may be. You'll find that each new experience and challenge becomes easier and less frightening. Fear goes down and your resiliency goes up." —**Mary Ann Esfandiari**, retired NASA senior executive and Navy Commander

In each chapter of this book, we have covered aspects supporting a resilient well-being, such as consciously thinking and intentionally acting on a life purpose, proactive healthy practices, nurturing relationships, developing optimal work practices, living creativity, and more. We provide you now with enhanced supportive content to bring it all together to find your new balance and how to bounce resiliently forward into new beginnings—your next life chapter.

RESILIENT MINDSETS

The uncertainty of the neutral zone is a creatively rich and ripe time for reflection, renewal, and reinvention where each of us can envision and create the future we want. Yet it can be difficult finding clarity if we don't have a way of handling the uncertainty.

We aspire to adapt to changes and handle uncertainty with a harmonic alignment between our interior life and our exterior life. Here we present the mindsets that offer optimal freedom, flexibility, and forward-thinking that are key to resilient living in midlife and beyond. These are the conscious thinking approaches that will help you bounce forward:

- The Novice Mindset
- The Acceptance Mindset
- The Competent Mindset
- The Confident Mindset
- The Courageous Mindset
- The Well-Being Mindset
- The Positive Future Mindset
- The Resilient Mindset

THE NOVICE MINDSET

Adopting the mindset of being a novice to any change can grant us diverse viewing perspectives and enable us to think up numerous ways to adapt and be resilient to life's shifts and surprises. It is really okay to not know something! This mindset liberates us to discover new options and opportunities to choose, all of which lends itself to hope, optimism, and moving forward. The novice mindset is about cultivating a beginner's perspective of being open, curious, and willing to learn and grow.

For example, Candy Spitz, a career transition coach, found herself desiring to travel more in her fifties and was curious and open to the possibilities of combining travel with her work. She discovered that travel and life coaching was doable. Through a series of steps, she stopped her full-time therapy work to coach individuals. She now happily travels extensively and coaches clients. As she tells her clients, "We never know what we will like until we try different things. Self-growth does not just stop when we reach a certain age, and we have the opportunity to grow in different directions."

Bob Ruggiero retired from being a teacher and moved into being a tour guide as a good fit for his skills, interests, and lifestyle. When the COVID pandemic hit, priorities became clearer. His husband had already decided to retire earlier than planned. With travel opportunities suddenly halted, Bob too decided to free himself from work and spend more time with his spouse. As things returned to somewhat more normal, he was open to taking life a little more slowly by traveling, savoring the world, and having life experiences filled with hobbies, play, family, and more.

THE ACCEPTANCE MINDSET

Research tells us that accepting change as part of life is foundational to cultivating resilience. Acceptance allows our energy to move from fighting a change to investing in the energy of adapting, being creative, and thriving in spite of it. We can also accept that it is natural to initially react to change with discomfort, because it poses a threat to our status quo. Moving beyond our comfort zone is where the learning, growing, and creativity exist.

Writer Ann McKerrow, who has weathered the storms of her husband's rare brain tumor, shares with us that "life is full of challenges, and the constant is life changes, so adopt a mindset of expecting and adapting to change." She accepted the uncertainty and worked on researching treatments and being her husband's spokesperson. Today she reports that her husband's treatment was successful, and they have begun to travel again.

Kathy McEvoy, an entrepreneur, not only survived but thrived after the loss of both her parents at an early age; she also recovered from a serious car accident and later from breast cancer. She emphasizes how the advice she received from Fran, her father's cousin, provided her with an important tip for resilience: "Accept this situation and figure out how to move on, because challenges are going to happen to you the rest of your life. The way to deal with it is to accept and move beyond it the fastest way you can in your own way." Acceptance, determination, self-responsibility, and having a future vision are all part of Kathy's resilience.

THE COMPETENT MINDSET

A positive psychology perspective flips the focus from what is not working to what *is* working and positive. It provides a realistic reframe to launch forward with realistic optimism, which refers to balancing out the negative and positive in situations and leading with an optimistic mindset and a realistic sense of actions that need to occur. It is an acceptance of the situation itself, then deciding how best to move forward from the base of what is working. Sheryl Sandberg, previous Facebook CEO who found herself suddenly a widow, shares in her book *Option B: Facing Adversity, Building Resilience, and Finding Joy*[12] that changing the narrative from what we are not to who we are is a shift in thinking that opens the door to what might be possible and provides support for the path ahead. Research reveals that optimism is strongly correlated with resilience and increased longevity.[13] The competent mindset focuses on what is working.

Dorothy Keenan, founder of GrandInvolve, shares that a recent illness that landed her bedridden for weeks led her to understand the importance of seeing the beauty in everyday things and what was already working for her. "Something very simple, like looking out a window and seeing butterflies, can be calming," she shares.

THE CONFIDENT MINDSET

We can become more aware of what is and isn't working for us, giving us a sense of what will work for us now and in the future. We can also become more aware and appreciative of our capacities and our strengths.

By looking to our past, we can see how we have encountered uncertainties before. How did we handle them? What qualities, strengths, and skills did we develop as a result? Our experiences tell us how we have moved forward and provide indications of what we can rely on for the future.

Mary Ann Esfandiari, a retired NASA senior executive and Navy Commander, shares that her technical and resiliency skills she had gained over the years as a leader did not initially kick in with the loss of her husband and soul mate of 43 years; she needed time to absorb and accept the profound sadness of her new reality. Because Mary Ann is a self-described fixer and problem solver, she found it especially difficult to accept that she could not save her husband from his severe medical condition nor herself from the sadness of losing the love of her life. Slowly, with time and the help of a grief counselor, she began to reengage her resilience. She went back to the encouraging and calming self-talk she used while learning challenging physical skills in the navy. Although still dealing with the loss of her husband, today she is back to cooking, engaging with friends, confidently taking on projects of interest, and has discovered some newfound friends who enjoy similar activities.

THE COURAGEOUS MINDSET

If we want something, we often have to reach for it—whether it be a pen on the table, our phones, or something much bigger, such as an opportunity for a fascinating position or starting our own business, or simply starting to date again. The bigger the reach, the more the effort, risk, and discomfort with uncertainty and the potential of failing are. If all goes well the reward is big, too. Whether you receive a big reward or not, you can be assured you will learn lessons to move you forward. Becoming more comfortable with discomfort can enable us to grow and move closer to the reward of enhanced living in midlife and beyond. Who knows what doors may be opened from our stretching and reaching beyond our usual pattern?

We suggest thinking of possible small steps as small risks that can boost confidence and build up a repertoire of lessons. Margie Warrell, a global authority on living with courage, states that the more we move out of our comfort zone and into the courage zone, the more we build capability, grow influence, and can take on bigger challenges.[14]

Expecting and accepting gray areas and being open to exploring possible paths are part of the process of getting to clarity. This leads to learning what works for you and to cultivating comfort and confidence with ambiguity and uncertainty.

Brené Brown suggests activating our courage and being okay with the discomfort of our attempts to do something new imperfectly. "We must dare to show up and let ourselves be seen," she says. "This is vulnerability. This is *daring greatly*."[15] The mindset precedes any actions. Trying new ventures can indeed be scary, yet moving forward despite fears and getting beyond fear can be fulfilling, exciting, and provide a sense of achievement.

Accepting and embracing uncertainty and showing our vulnerability allows us to be a learner, fostering self-growth and development and the building up of our resilience muscle as we navigate the second half of life. Being mindful and practicing this way of thinking is the way forward to reaping the rewards of being resilient.

THE WELL-BEING MINDSET

Our Conscious Living Wheel contains key areas of what makes up a well-lived life. Keep these areas in focus for making conscious, intentional decisions that will support you in midlife and beyond. Developing a sense of well-being can help us with bouncing forward in times of stress.

Kathy McEvoy, a successful executive, developed breast cancer and received a midlife wake-up call. She realized she had to make changes in order to survive and thrive. She rethought her priorities and made the intentional decision to focus on her health and family and be the project manager for her optimal well-being rather than a corporate entity. She quit her successful job, focused more on health and people, received treatment, and became healthy again. True to her new focus, she later launched Celebrate in Pink, a responsible partyware company that celebrates a return to optimal well-being. Her company donates a portion of profits to help women through their breast cancer journey.

THE POSITIVE FUTURE MINDSET

The positive future mindset focuses on seeing the future as holding opportunities for happiness and well-being. It includes a positive mindset with characteristics such as optimism, gratitude, and integrity. It also includes attitudes about positive aging. A study of 60 96-year-old individuals revealed that those who had a positive attitude toward aging were more resilient to stress.[16] An entire movement is devoted to amplifying this positivity in the media with more inclusivity of midlife and beyond individuals. The Age Friendly Vibes greeting card company is another example of changing the passé narrative on aging and adopting a positive aging-living mindset.[17] Morton Shaevitz, psychologist and co-author with Ken Blanchard of *Refire! Don't Retire: Make the Rest of Your Life the Best of Your Life*, recommends the mindset of accepting and embracing the "new normal" of some limitations of aging with a resilient spirit, which shows up in one's attitude and actions in living a full and active life.[18] Self-growth, understanding, empathy, and wisdom are some of the rewards of aging.

Bruce Frankel, president of the Life Planning Network, shares that "aging is wonderful. It allows us—and has allowed me—to accept imperfection, and that is a lovely freedom." He saw firsthand how his mother role-modeled giving up perfectionistic behaviors, which allowed her to return to painting late in life and, as a result, receive several commissions.

THE RESILIENT MINDSET

The resilient mindset embraces all of the previous mindsets. Michaela Haas, author of *Bouncing Forward: The Art and Science of Cultivating Resilience*, states: "Acceptance, openness, flexibility, patience, mindfulness, empathy, compassion, resourcefulness, determination, courage and forgiveness are all part of a resilient mindset. These are the qualities we can train in. Maybe there is a 'resilience makeup' after all. We just cannot buy it in the store."[19]

Amanda Ripley, author of *The Unthinkable: Who Survives When Disaster Strikes—and Why*, says: "Resilience is a precious skill. People who have it tend to also have three underlying advantages: a belief that they can influence life events; a tendency to find meaningful purpose in life's turmoil; and a conviction that they can learn from both positive and negative experiences."[20]

Shawn Perry is founder of *The Senior Zone*, a popular radio station that provides information and support to those in midlife and beyond. He shares with us that he used determination and persistence to overcome his resistance to the unknowns as he created and charted an entirely new career. He figured it out as he went along. He didn't know the radio business and wasn't a journalist or polished speaker, but he was motivated by passion for his goal. He stretched himself and was optimistic in his purpose, patience, and willingness to learn, do the work, and be resourceful. He took a financial pinch initially, yet his resilient tenacity helped him succeed.

We can foster more of these qualities into our thinking by giving ourselves a number on a scale of 1 to 10 of where you are now with these qualities. We can then determine what would be the easiest next step to take to move it to a higher number.

Respecting Each Person's Unique Experience

We acknowledge there are some deeply impactful, painful, and devastating situations of adversity and trauma, and we do not look upon these situations lightly nor offer up simple universal formulas. We do, however, offer what we and others have learned about resilience and coping strategies in the hopes it will provide value in navigating some of the more common challenges of the second half of life.

We are all unique in how we perceive and experience situations. No matter how we categorize an event or situation, research tell us that it is the individual's perception of it that can put them at risk for challenges and health issues.[21] In the words of Brigadier General Rhonda Cornum of her experience as a prisoner in the Iraq War, as told by author and interviewer Michaela Haas: "You can't judge trauma from the outside."[22]

For more in-depth and individualized care, consult with professionals specializing in trauma.

RESILIENT LIFE PRACTICES

Resilient life practices are actions or strategies that complement mindsets. Practices involve the doing, and mindset involves the being. Intentionally adopting a mindset and then applying it in the form of an activity allows for the integration of the two, which results in living a resilient life. Following are 10 activities to get you started.

FORTIFY YOURSELF WITH HEALTHY PRACTICES OF SELF-RENEWAL

Change can cause us to be anxious and fearful of the unknown. Basic health practices such as eating nutritionally, hydrating, getting fresh air and exercise, and ensuring restorative sleep and reflective time provide a firm well-being foundation for adapting to the changes in midlife and beyond. In addition, mindsets partnered with actions relevant to mindfulness, self-care, self-compassion, and self-acceptance have been shown to be beneficial because they help protect your energy by calming the mind and body and building resilience.[23] Some of these practices include finding the joy and the humor in your days and putting your findings in a gratitude journal. The serenity prayer,[24] mostly famous for its abridged version, "God, grant me the serenity to accept the things I cannot change, the courage to change the things I can, and wisdom to know the difference," can also raise awareness of where and how much to invest one's energy, as it relates to affecting and accepting change. These healthy practices remain helpful in everyday life for preventing overwhelm and burnout.

PAY ATTENTION TO YOUR INTUITION

Perspectives and values can shift. For example, you may enjoy and value working full time yet find that you do not have time for the family activities you also value. By being flexible, you might discover that you can work part time and have the opportunity to be available for unexpected situations and more spontaneous fun.

Fred Mandell, a successful entrepreneur we've referenced in several chapters, shares how paying attention to your intuition can boost your resilience and fulfillment by uncovering your inspiring "why" for life direction, purpose, and relevant decision-making. "There is that logical thought process that is part of the way in which you make life choices," he explains. "The other is, I think, this thing called emotions, passion, things in the gut, things that you know, in other ways, than the pure mind that can get you to. That's where I think some courage and resilience come in. Because at the end of the day, something could logically make sense. But if you're not feeling it in your gut, I don't think it's sustainable. So much of how we go about making decisions has been programmed into us through our education, our training, our life experiences, etc. One of the things that I think is exciting about this stage in life is it gives us the opportunity to step back from all of that and take a fresh look and challenge our own assumptions. About not simply who we are but how we go about deciding who we are going to be."

We suggest you actively check in with your intuition for matters that relate to important values, purpose, and passion and write down that response. Include it as part of the criteria for making decisions.

KEEP VISIBLE REMINDERS OF YOUR SUCCESSES AND STRENGTHS

Challenges in midlife and beyond may be different from earlier challenges, yet there are lessons learned from these experiences. Reminders of these lessons provide concrete evidence of past survival and success so that we can apply them going forward. Having a handy reminder reinforces our confidence in our abilities. We suggest making these reminders visible by jotting them down on Post-it Notes or notecards, printing them out, or putting them on a screen saver.

Also consider these questions for further insight, which can help you shift the focus to what you are learning and how that process can help you proceed and thrive:

- How do I currently deal with change, ambiguity, and risks?
- How have I successfully handled change in the past? What strengths did I use?
- Does ambiguity in certain life areas bother me more than others?
- What will make it easier to live with uncertainty within midlife and beyond?
- What might I learn about myself from dealing with ambiguity?

Dorian Mintzer has a different type of visible reminder of her successes: her family. She took a risk by changing direction in life and choosing to remarry. With an older spouse and having a child later in life, she flourished and managed the challenges with skills she learned along the way from her own experiences and those shared from others. She credits frequent moves in her younger years to helping her know she can adapt and learn time and time again and that she can not only survive, but thrive.

EASE OUT OF YOUR COMFORT ZONE

It is in our best interest to acquire new techniques, skills, and coping practices to enhance our repertoire of being adaptable and flexible. Adding an element of fun and creativity makes learning new skills easier.

Eileen teaches a class called "Resilience and Self-Care for Caregivers" that advises attendees to anticipate change, along with practical resilience tips and techniques and how to create a self-care kit. Items in the kit can include mindset reminders, a list of resilient activities to choose from, supportive people and resources to reach out to, and much more. One of the resilience techniques from the class is referred to as "serenity snacks," which combines three activities that make a virtual "snack sandwich," with two simple pleasant activities representing the bread and the inside middle being an activity requiring stretching or being courageous. The combinations could represent anything in your life, such as the simple activities of taking a walk in nature and visiting a friend, enclosing the more challenging activity of attending a widowers gathering or taking a sailing class. What serenity snack might you create for yourself? What small steps can you take to ease out of your comfort zone toward new interests?

Kathy McEvoy shares that she created a plan for midlife and beyond by asking herself how she could ease forward from a comfortable to a more enhanced active life. She created her "compass question" that she kept asking herself: "What do I want to wake up doing every day?" She followed her dream to a community in North Carolina, where she resides in comfortable temperatures, plays pickleball, cycles, and is engaged in being a volunteer for SCORE (Senior Corps of Retired Executives), which helps people in starting and building their businesses. Try asking yourself what you want to wake up doing every day as a way to ease forward.

TAKE SMALL RISKS

Resilience is not just about handling the unforeseen events along our lifelong journey but also about being able to try out new ways of thinking and behaving that help us move forward to vitality and growth. It's about moving toward new interests and passions that enrich and enhance our lives. In order to get there, we often need to challenge ourselves to face our fears and take risks. Taking small risks as steps forward can benefit us because it can make the unfamiliar a bit less scary, and changing directions with small steps is easier to do.

Elizabeth Mahler, a professor at Northeastern University, shares an insightful and inspirational perspective on risk. She says that stepping out to try a new path is a risk—and so is staying where you are no longer happy. She suggests stepping away to gain perspective. She practices "metacognition," which means observing your thought processes without judgment to see what insights you may have. If you can think about what and how you think in a more objective way, you can see the patterns of your approach that work and don't work and make shifts accordingly. Elizabeth took small, cumulative risks in deciding to pursue a university degree in pastoral counseling and discovered it was not a well-aligned path for her, so she went in another direction, earning a graduate degree in human and organizational learning. She integrated what she learned from pastoral counseling when appropriate, and her directional change resulted in her being very happy and fulfilled as a university professor. "After you have lived a certain amount of time," she says, "you know you have survived challenges and you can do it again."

Identifying and facing our fears allows us to be aware and prepared for those predictable potential changes so that we can make optimal choices for ourselves. Our lives are finite; we may not want to think about the fact of the end of our life yet, and that is often why wills are not written, advance directives are not directed, and so forth. We understand this perspective, and at the same time we know there is value in understanding that the future is closer than it seems and that it is important to take small steps to realize your potential and goals.

Some of the changes we face are practical and others more existential. As with most of life, there are areas that can frighten us and those that free us. Being frightened of losses or changes can be balanced with the freedom and flexibility to be who we are and to try out new ways of being, doing, and relating without the worry of others' perceptions. We take a risk by trying out a new step. We learn from it and recalibrate expectations and next steps as needed. We learn from what did not go well and apply those lessons going forward. These lessons are valuable. Moving through a challenge both in our thinking and acting gives us a sense of fulfillment that we stretched, we learned, and have grown—and that we have indeed accomplished something important in the process.

BALANCE RISK WITH REWARDS

We suggest using a continuum to gauge your perception of risk and potential benefits. For example, you can assign various activity levels of taking a risk a value from 1 to 10. If you feel confident taking a risk with a low value of 3, you can move forward with some benefit and little risk. The higher-value activities incur more risk and potential benefit, yet they might not be to your comfort level or sense of balance or harmony. What will playing it safe cost you? What will taking a risk cost you? We can take small, cumulative steps in spite of uncertainty.

Minimize or reduce risk by doing due diligence and being resourceful. Talk with those who have knowledge and experience. Consider talking with a certified financial planner on building a financial buffer or financial reserve to ensure stability during transitions.

We've discovered time and time again that taking some type of movement forward, whether in a small or large way, often leads to joy-filled results. Bruce Frankel, president of the Life Planning Network, found himself at age 51 taking what he called an existential risk by leaving a successful career in journalism at *USA Today* and then *People* magazine and going back to school to follow his calling to poetry. After having cancer and a heart attack he realized life was ephemeral, and it ultimately clarified for him what he wanted and needed to do.

In terms of taking risks, Bruce found that he was not jumping off the metaphoric bridge; it was more accurately described as moving from one room to another, just lifting his feet across the threshold. With planning, evaluation, and taking small risks forward, he has landed in a much happier spot. "Resilience is all about finding solutions, creating alternates, figuring out and following what is important to you," he tells us.

Jill Badonsky shares that being older is a risk reducer for her, as she has more trust and acceptance of the ambiguity of trying new things, and she has survived and thrived getting out past her comfort zone. It has been a huge growth experience that has been exhilarating and rewarding beyond her initial expectations. She finds that the rewards can often be surprising, which adds to the delight.

BUILD YOUR CARING COMMUNITY

We look to people, groups, and organizations for information and resources. This leads us to think of our supportive networks and what connections we have or want to have or need to have for our well-being as we make decisions for midlife and beyond.

Being resourceful and having a supportive social network is part of being resilient. Building our social support network can take a variety of routes, from in-person to virtual, and can be found in community interest groups, faith communities, classes, volunteer groups, and more. Including various age ranges in your social network for different perspectives and talents can enhance the relationship for all people involved. Friends who find joy in life are optimistic, caring, and provide humor to bring lightness to our journeys.

PREPARE AND PLAN

The Life Planning Network is a national group of professionals in the United States that help individuals and groups navigate the challenges and opportunities of the second half of life. Being prepared for some of the predictable life events can give us a sense of ease we're deciding on the right risks to take. Tapping our creativity helps develop flexible options too. Information and self-reflection add to the formation of a vision and the establishment of goals and plans. This builds our resilience and confidence with handling uncertainty, change, and challenges. In being proactive, we have ideas and information of how to handle an issue ahead of time, giving us a buffer of confidence, knowledge, and time to understand optimal decisions without the stress of an emergent or impending critical decision.

No matter where we are in our sense of resiliency, a multitude of skills identified by resilience experts, psychologists, and thought leaders can build our resiliency muscle or add to our resiliency toolbox.

As the American Psychological Association points out, resilience is a process that evolves through experience and learning skills. Once we know the skill and apply it, it becomes easier to step forward. Resilience is a skill we learn and integrate with practice into our lives.

MOVE FORWARD THROUGH THE BIG LIFE HURDLES

But what if the challenges ahead look difficult, painful, and over-whelming? Sometimes the only way to the other side is through it: accepting the situation and pushing forward, despite the discomfort, pain, and uncertainty.

We can do everything right yet despite it all, something out of the blue hits us hard. Brian Hill is one such person who was living a healthy and happy life when he was shockingly diagnosed with late stage 4 oral cancer. Not having a lot of options, he accepted his situation and courageously went through and survived extensive and exhausting treatments. He got through it with his supportive wife, his community, and his perseverance to move on and help others. As a result, his life purpose evolved to raise awareness and support those with oral cancer. Brian utilized his medical experience from Vietnam and his knowledge and years in the healthcare support system to uniquely be the ideal person to found the Oral Cancer Foundation.[25]

The ABCDE model for building resilience[26] is a model that embraces the mindsets and practices presented in this chapter. The ABCDE model was developed by Paul T. Wong, an internationally acclaimed psychologist. It is an easy-to-understand approach that can be applied to both cognitive and behavioral resilience. The approach is as follows:[27]

- **A**ccept what cannot be changed.
- **B**elieve that life is worth living and affirm core values.
- **C**ommit to relevant goals and actions.
- **D**iscover something new about self and life.
- **E**njoy and evaluate positive outcomes and progress.

As explained by Paul Wong, "The ABCDE module provides cognitive and behavioral resilience. Positive and realistic thinking enables one to make sound decisions and judgments. Acquiring the habit of persistence and flexibility enables one to persevere with courage, fortitude, and resourcefulness. Success in overcoming difficulties further increases one's cognitive resilience; one learns to attach positive meanings and attributions to adversity, perceiving them as challenges and opportunities, rather than threats, to becoming better and stronger."[28] The model provides a series of sequential steps that one can take to bounce forward from the hurdles that life can present.

JOIN OR START A RESILIENCE CIRCLE

The resilience circle concept was noted in an article by Elizabeth White for Next Avenue, a media platform dedicated to providing innovation, inspiration, and big thinking on the potential of older Americans.[29] Her article evolved into the book *55, Underemployed, and Faking Normal: Your Guide to a Better Life*.[30] She introduced the resilience circle concept as a way to build a supportive, caring environment focused on issues related to aging and living a good life on a limited income. Building a resilience circle can be adapted beyond unemployment and limited income to include specific areas such as the loss of a partner, health challenges, and aging issues.

You can find a resilience circle offered by healthcare organizations, life coaches, and mental health professionals. If you cannot find one in these categories, then we suggest looking for conversation circles that focus on resilience. Or you can start one of your own: for example, by asking friends, family, and colleagues, or you could start one online, such as on Meetup. We advise keeping the circle small and confidential, with simple plans such as meeting at someone's home or meeting online. See Elizabeth's book for more details.

Resilience circles and the sharing of similar experiences can provide help and hope. This can be the case especially when it seems there are limited choices and the only way to the other side is through the hardship. They build individual and community resilience.

Resilience is a learnable life skill. In this chapter, we introduced the resilience effect relating to the benefits and shared ways to build up your resilience muscle with mindsets and practices. We encourage you to integrate these into your life in hopes that they will help you bounce forward, adapting to any challenge in midlife and beyond with hope, purpose, and resilience. See our Resources section for a mnemonic or acronym as a helpful reminder of resilience practices.

CONSCIOUS LIVING PRACTICES

Questions for Reflection

- What mindsets would you like to try out or adopt to augment your resilience?
- What is a fear or concern relating to uncertainty in midlife and beyond where these mindsets could help you?
- What life dimension on the Conscious Living Wheel do you feel you are the most resilient to, and why do you think this is so?
- What are some of the benefits of resilience that inspire you?
- What are some practices that you would like to try to build your resilience?

Try This

- Start a resilience journal: write about what has worked for you in the past and what you have learned from your challenges.
- Identify one small step/small risk you could take in an area of your concern.

CONCLUDING
THOUGHTS

Let choice whisper in your ear and love murmur
in your heart. Be ready. Here comes life.

—MAYA ANGELOU

Your new life awaits. You may have experienced an unexpected crisis, or you may be meandering comfortably on your journey through life and beginning to look to the future. Wherever you are on life's journey, now is the time for conscious choices about your future direction. Some of the aspects of the Conscious Living Wheel explored in this book may resonate more than others—it's for you to choose what is important to you now. Wherever you are on your journey, we hope we have been able to educate and inspire you to set clear intentions and take responsible actions with a focus on living consciously in the second half of life.

We began this book at the center of the Conscious Living Wheel. Purpose is the core, the heart center from which all other aspects of the wheel radiate. We hope you have been able to discover your purpose in life and answer the questions, "Why am I here?" and "Who do I choose to be?" With a clear purpose, we can embrace the challenges of any aspects of the Conscious Living Wheel.

Nurturing our mind and body was the focus of the Living Well aspect of the wheel. What we eat and drink has a significant impact on our health and well-being. Our rest, relaxation, and restorative sleep together with our focus on fitness also affect our physical health. We also need to be attentive to our mental health. Our mindset matters. Stimulating the mind through self-growth and lifelong learning can be complemented with practices for soothing the mind through meditation and time spent in nature and with family and friends.

Living consciously requires us to be more conscious about our money: making it, saving it, managing it, spending it, and leaving it behind. In addition to these money practices, we have looked at our beliefs about money, our relationships with money, and that difficult-to-answer money question, "How much is enough?" Shifting our mindset from worrying about money to Appreciating Money can help establish positive inner beliefs about money and do the outer practical work of financial management.

Working will likely remain an important feature of the second half of our lives. People are living longer and working longer, some because they have to and others because they want to. In the chapters on Working for a Living and Working for Fulfillment, we have explored different options to continue and enhance our existing careers along with entrepreneurial choices to make money and to make a contribution, volunteer, and give back to our chosen communities.

Where we live and where we visit was explored in the chapter on Savoring the World. We looked at the opportunities for living in different countries or different environments, the importance of work and volunteering, and recreational and community activities where we choose to live. Inspiration for conscious travel together or solo, spiritual or inner journeys, and even virtual holidays online was offered.

In the chapter on Living Life Creatively we explored the value of consciously living life with imagination, curiosity, courage, and cheer as an attitude and a way of life. Beyond traditional thinking of creativity as art, we have explored how to develop our creative potential everywhere with mindsets and practices, processes and skills, and pathways and plans.

Mutually caring relationships are increasingly important in the second half of life, yet we often find our relationships are in transition as we explore new adventures and opportunities. In the chapter on Minding Relationships, we explored close relationships with a spouse or life partner, the loss of a close relationship, and embracing new relationships. We explored family and intergenerational relationships and the challenges of going solo in midlife and beyond.

The second half of life often provides opportunities for making a difference in the lives of others and in our communities and the wider world. In the chapter on Helping Humanity, we explored three broad areas where we can make a contribution: the environmental sustainability of our planet, social responsibility for people, and leadership in governments and business. We have offered insights into how you may be able to find your unique contribution to helping humanity today and for those who come after us.

Technology is advancing at an ever-increasing pace. Being aware and knowledgeable about the current and emerging technological landscape presents possibilities for living consciously. In the chapter on Living with Technology, we have explored how technology impacts how we live consciously in each of the elements of the Conscious Living Wheel.

We all need resilience to adapt and thrive when responding to challenges in the second half of life. In the chapter on Bouncing Forward, we have suggested mindsets and practices to help build your resilience muscle in readiness for the challenges you may face. We hope the RESILIENCE mnemonic shared in the Resources section will serve as a reminder for practices that will help you prepare for the path ahead and be ready for bouncing forward into a more positive future.

Living consciously in the second half of life requires Attention, Intention, and Action (A-I-A). Attention comes from awareness of ourselves, others, and the world around us. Setting intentions based on our purpose and identity can help us translate awareness into positive, responsible action. We, the authors of this book, have enjoyed our journey through the writing and publication of *Midlife, New Life*, and hope you are inspired to continue your exploration of the aspects of our Conscious Living Wheel. We invite you to live more consciously in the second half of life.

RESOURCES

There are numerous resources available to assist you on your journey to Conscious Living in the second part of your life, and we can't list them all here. In addition to the books and articles you'll find in the notes, following are resources we find especially valuable when we work with our clients. Please also visit our website at midlifenewlife. net, where you can find links and download helpful tools.

CHAPTER 1: EXPLORING PURPOSEFULLY

CONSCIOUS LIVING MANIFESTO

In the Exploring Purposefully chapter, we included ideas on vision, mission, purpose, identity, core values, and guiding principles. Although each are independently helpful, bringing these elements together in a single representation of who we are and where we want to be can enhance our dream of living consciously. Consider writing a personal Conscious Living Manifesto as a declaration of your vision, mission, purpose, core values, beliefs, and intentions, expressing who you are and how you wish to show up in the world.

A Guide to Developing your Conscious Living Manifesto is available from the authors via the *Midlife, New Life* website: https://www. midlifenewlife.net.

VALUES AND STRENGTHS ASSESSMENT TOOLS

- Barrett Values Centre: https://www.valuescentre.com
- Clifton Strengths Assessment from the Gallup organization: https://www.gallup.com/cliftonstrengths/
- Values in Action Character Strengths profile from the Institute on Character: https://www.viacharacter.org

CHAPTER 2: LIVING WELL

- Inspiration for living well and living fully: Randy Pausch's 2008 Carnegie Mellon University Commencement Speech, May 18, 2008. The following site has the transcript and video: https://lanredahunsi.com/randy-pauschs-2008-carnegie-mellon-university-commencement-speech/

SOURCES TO SUPPORT LIFELONG LEARNING

Some sources are referred to as MOOCs. (Massive Open Online Courses)

Massive=large number of people can take at once;
Open=free, affordable or open enrollment;
Online=via internet;
Courses=classes with possibilities for certification.

- National Resource Center for Osher Lifelong Learning Institutes (at Northwestern University). This site can direct you to OLLI in your state: https://sps.northwestern.edu/oshernrc/about/osher-lifelong-learning-institute-network.php
- Road Scholar: https://www.roadscholar.org
- Master Class: https://www.masterclass.com
- Smithsonian: https://www.si.edu/learn

- Class Central: https://www.classcentral.com (good access to many courses)
- Coursera: https://www.coursera.org
- Edx: https://www.edx.org
- The Great Courses: https://www.thegreatcourses.com
- FutureLearn: https://www.futurelearn.com
- Udacity.com: https://www.udacity.com

- Project Big Life in Canada, https://www.projectbiglife.ca, provides online life-expectancy calculators run by researchers, clinicians, data scientists, and developers to educate the public on the impact of their lifestyle choices. They also provide calculators for sodium consumption, dementia, cardiovascular disease, and more.

- The Conversation Project provides help with starting conversations about your wishes for care for any potential illness, disability, or death, https://theconversationproject.org.

- Baseline Balance is a personal assessment tool kit created to help people spark change in their lives. Baseline Balance's self-assessment questions center around Diet + Exercise + Emotion. For more information, read the book *Baseline Balance: Live A Happier, Balanced Life*, or visit http://www.baselinebalanced.com/.

- The Blue Zones: https://www.bluezones.com

CHAPTER 3: APPRECIATING MONEY

- Bari Tessler, financial therapist, author, and founder of The Art Of Money: https://baritessler.com/

- Dr. Brad Klontz has authored five books on the psychology of money and created the Klontz Money Script Inventory (KMSI) assessment tool. For more information, visit: https://www.yourmentalwealthadvisors.com/our-process/your-money-script/.

- George Kinder, life planning guru and often considered the father of financial life planning, offers three reflective life planning questions. Learn more at https://www.kinderinstitute.com/george-kinder/.

- A classic text that could not be overlooked in thinking about our money beliefs is Napoleon Hill's *Think and Grow Rich*. Hill presents a well-known verse reminding us of the law of auto suggestion based on our thoughts that begins with: "If you think you are beaten, you are. If you think you dare not, you don't. If you like to win, but you think you can't, it is almost certain you won't" and ends with "The man who wins is the man WHO THINKS HE CAN!"

CHAPTER 4: WORKING FOR A LIVING

- Jobs for Older and Experienced Workers: https://www.workforce50.com/

- An online community for those that want to recruit folks 50 and older: https://www.seniors4hire.org/

- Test yourself by assessing your strengths at https://gallup.com and skills at https://www.skillscan.com/.

CHAPTER 5: WORKING FOR FULFILLMENT

- Adopt a Grandparent: https://www.adoptagrandparentprogram.com/

- Big Brother Big Sisters of America: https://www.bbbs.org/

- Blue Zones Project: https://www.bluezones.com/services/blue-zones-project/

- The Eden Alternative: https://www.edenalt.org/
- The Enneagram: https://www.enneagraminstitute.com/
- The Modern Elder Academy: https://www.modernelderacademy.com/
- Skillscan.com: work and life values assessment

CHAPTER 6: SAVORING THE WORLD

- The most comprehensive listing of property caretaker positions is published by a friend of 2Young2Retire, *The Caretaker Gazette*. Since 1983, the newsletter has been published in print every two months and is also now online with email updates sent to subscribers. For more information, contact Gary Dunn via the website www.caretaker.org.
- Home Swap Membership Site Example: https://www.lovehomeswap.com/how-it-works
- *Right Place, Right Time: The Ultimate Guide to Choosing a Home for the Second Half of Life* by Ryan Frederick

CHAPTER 7: LIVING LIFE CREATIVELY

- Jill Badonsky, an internationally known creativity expert and humorist, inspires creativity using playful muses to share creativity principles in her book: *The Nine Modern Day Muses (and a Bodyguard): Ten Guides to Creative Inspiration*, expanded third edition (San Diego, California: Renegade Muses Publishing House, 2010). The expanded version has a "dream recover" section that applies to the second half of life. Other books include *The Muse Is In: An Owner's Manual to Your Creativity* and *The AWE-MANAC: A Daily Dose of Wonder*, https://themuseisin.com/workshops-trainings.

- Michael J. Gelb is a pioneer in the fields of creative thinking, innovative leadership, and executive coaching, and is considered a leading authority on the application of genius thinking to personal and organizational development. His books include *Creativity On Demand, How to Think Like Leonardo da Vinci*, and *Innovate Like Edison*. Learn more at https://michaelgelb.com/.

- Conscious Living Conversation Circles: http://www.midlifenewlife.net/

CHAPTER 8: MINDING RELATIONSHIPS

- The National Widowers' Organization is a resource with articles, peer-to-peer support information, and data on how to start your own group. For more information, visit their website at http://nationalwidowers.org/.

- Soaring Spirits International: https://soaringspirits.org/

- Foster Grandparent: https://www.friendsprogram.org/programs/foster-grandparent/general-information

CHAPTER 9: HELPING HUMANITY

- Elders Action Network: a nonprofit organization in the United States dedicated to education and activism aimed at achieving greater social and environmental justice in American society: https://eldersaction.org/

- For more information about facilitating more loving conversations about our predicament, read *Deep Adaptation: Navigating the Realities of Climate Chaos*, edited by Jem Bendell and Rupert Read.

- World Water Law: https://www.codes.earth/waterlaw

CHAPTER 10: LIVING WITH TECHNOLOGY

- Inspiration for living with technology as we age: Sofiat Akinola, "What Is the Biggest Benefit Technology Will Have on Ageing and Longevity?" World Economic Forum, March 20, 2021, see section "The Freedom of Choice," A. Vigneswari and Adrienne Mendenhall, https://www.weforum.org/agenda/2021/03/what-is-the-biggest-benefit-technology-ageing-longevity-global-future-council-tech-for-good/.

Here are some additional resources from general to specific to explore and seek help:

- Public libraries
- Senior centers
- High school students
- Technology coaches or tutors
- Tech classes at adult education centers in the local community and community colleges
- Technology programs and podcasts such as *This Week in Technology*, hosted by the tech guys, Leo Leporte and Mikah Sargent. https://twit.tv/shows/ask-the-tech-guys
- Senior tech clubs, which provide a large variety of free, easy classes on different types of technology and their use. In Australia, there is the Australian Senior Computer Clubs Association: https://www.ascca.org.au.

FREE TUTORIALS AND SUPPORT

- GCFGlobal.org (https://edu.gcfglobal.org/en/topics/) provides help to millions around the world to learn the basic skills for living and working in the 21st century. They provide free, informative, self-paced tutorials on basic computer, tablet, phone, and internet skills, along with using Microsoft and Google programs and much more.

- Generations online (http://www.generationsonline.com) provides free, easy digital help for seniors in using digital devices and navigating the internet.

- CyberSeniors.org (https://cyberseniors.org) bridges the digital divide and connects generations using technology training and support by high school and university student

- The organization OATS (Older Adults Technology Services), https://oats.org was founded by Tom Kamber in 2004 in the US to help seniors learn to use technology to improve their functioning in the digital world. OATS evolved to include being a social impact organization garnering global influence on how we age. OATS joined AARP as a charitable affiliate in 2021, allowing for what they describe as "a fuller-scale mission of helping seniors utilize technology without restraint of geography, socioeconomic level, education, or age."

  » Senior Planet, https://seniorplanet.org is the "flagship program of OATS from AARP" which focuses on connecting older adults to technology and creating a thriving vibrant. community. It has been described as the resource for older adults who want to stay engaged with what's new and what's next. It has in person centers and on-line offerings.

    – Senior Planet Community, https://community. seniorplanet.org is a virtual social place where seniors can connect and share common interests

- New and emerging technology: The annual Computer Electronic Show (CES) in January might be of interest—or at least the write-up of it—to see what is new and emerging with technology.
- For online dating: GreatSeniorLiving.com (https://www.greatseniorliving.com/articles/online-dating-for-seniors)

SAFETY GUIDES

- Online safety guide link: https://www.safetydetectives.com/blog/the-ultimate-internet-safety-guide-for-seniors/
- Link to check for data breach of your info: https://haveibeenpwned.com

DIGITAL ESTATE PLANNING

- "Digital Cheat Sheet: How to Create a Digital Estate Plan," Everplans, accessed August 22, 2023, https://www.everplans.com/articles/digital-cheat-sheet-how-to-create-a-digital-estate-plan

RECYCLING DIGITAL DEVICES

Divert your used digital devices from landfills for refurbishing/reuse. Some places provide cash, which can be used to donate to help the environment.

- https://www.epa.gov/recycle/electronics-donation-and-recycling
- https://www.recycleyourelectricals.org.uk/donate-electrical-goods/

- https://www.gazelle.com
- https://money4mytech.co.uk/bulk-sales

CHAPTER 11: BOUNCING FORWARD

RESILIENCE PRACTICES MNEMONIC

R	Risk and Reward	Balance risk and reward
E	Empower	Empower yourself with concrete reminders of your own resilience and your successes
S	Self- Renewal	Fortify yourself with healthy practices of self-renewal
I	Intuition	Pay attention to your intuition with values, passion, & purpose
L	Life Lessons	Take small risks; reap life lessons and rewards
I	Impact	Imagine the impact of resilience on your future
E	Ease	Ease out of your comfort zone with fun & creativity
N	Navigate	Navigate and move forward through big life hurdles
C	Communities	Build your caring communities; join or start a resilience circle
E	Every Day	Prepare and plan every day

ACKNOWLEDGMENTS
AND GRATITUDE

Writing this book was harder than expected, but our highly collaborative writing journey has been more rewarding than we could have imagined. It is for this reason we start by acknowledging our fellow authors on this journey. We are grateful for the insights, inspiration, and support offered by each other. This was a truly collaborative experience.

The origins of *Midlife, New Life* can be traced back to Marika and Howard Stone and their groundbreaking book *Too Young to Retire: 101 Ways to Start the Rest of Your Life,* first published in 2003. Although *Midlife, New Life* is a very different book from theirs, we are grateful for the early inspiration of these two pioneering Purpose Prize fellows. The authors of *Midlife, New Life* are all graduates of the 2Young2Retire facilitator certification program originally developed by Howard Stone and appreciate the groundbreaking work of Marika and Howard Stone that led to our book-writing journey.

The image for the Conscious Living Wheel was inspired by the Convening Wheel in Craig and Patricia Neal's *The Art of Convening* book, which supports the conversation circles we have described.

We are grateful to Fred Mandell and Kathleen Jordan, co-authors of the book *Becoming a Life Change Artist: 7 Creative Skills to Reinvent*

Yourself at Any Stage of Life, for their permission to use elements of their Creative Process and Skills in chapter 7, Living Life Creatively.

We recorded interviews with more than fifty people during the research phase of this book-writing journey. Insufficient space meant that many stories and quotations could not be included, but we are grateful for all the insights shared during the research phase. Following is a list of people whose stories and quotations we have included in the book and people who have influenced and supported our book-writing journey:

Story and quotation contributors: Larry Ackerman • Jill Badonsky • Mike Bernhardt • Kari Cardinale • Nancy Collamer • Patti Correll-Syring • Jim Currie • Glenys and Brian Davison • Mary Ann Esfandiari • Bruce Frankel • Alain Gauthier • Nadine Hammoud • Brian Hill • Kathy Holly • Steve Jacobs • Larry Jacobson • Dorothy Keenan • Donna Kraus • Dee Kyne • Richard Leider • Elizabeth Mahler • Claude Morency • Fred Mandell • Don Maruska • Betty McDowall • Kathy McEvoy • Ann McKerrow • Marc Miller • Dorian Mintzer • Susan O'Neil • Monty Patch • Shawn Perry • Gregory Peters • Ron Pevny • Dawn Pratt • Sam Rau • Hilary Rowland • Bob Ruggiero • David Shriner-Cahn • Candy Spitz • Michael Stuart • David Treece • Bill Wiles

People who have significantly influenced our thinking about living consciously in midlife and beyond: Moira Allen • Jill Badonsky • Dan Buettner • Jack Canfield • Kari Cardinale • Bob Chapman • Gene Cohen • Chip Conley • Joan Ditzion • Bill Gates • Ken Dychtwald • Chris Farrell • Bruce Frankel • Marc Freedman • Michael Gelb • Jane Goodall • Kerry Hannon • Paul Hawken • Jack Levine • Dorothy Keenan • David Korten • Jeremy Lent • Elizabeth Mahler • Fred Mandell • Wendy Marx • Dorian Mintzer • Craig and Patricia Neal • Paul Polman • Karen Sands • Martin Seligman • Simon Sinek • Candy Spitz • Lynne Twist • Margaret Wheatley

Others who supported our book-writing journey, including people interviewed but not quoted: Brian Ashley • Michael Banks • Al Boyce • Katie Garnett • Johnnie Godwin • Steven Kowalski • Rita Losee • Lynn Ruth Miller • Renee Robinson • Patrice Robson • Don Woerner

Editors and early draft reviewers: Larry Ackerman • Jill Badonsky • Kari Cardinale • Nancy Collamer • Patti Correll-Syring • Joan Ditzion • Debra Englander • Kerry Hannon • Kathy Kane • Richard Leider • Elizabeth Mahler • Mary McDowall • Dorian Mintzer • Betsy Pickren • Sam Rau • Laura Siner • Candy Spitz • Larry Spoont • Tracy Wallace • everyone at Greenleaf Book Group

From Eileen: To my dear husband, Tom, a special thank-you for your unending support, kindness, patience, humor, and exquisite culinary skills as I typed away on my computer for endless hours. You are truly the wind beneath my wings.

Heartfelt appreciation to my dear family, friends, colleagues, clients, and those we interviewed for sharing your inspiration, insight, lightness, and laughter.

From Sandy: To my three wonderful daughters, Melissa, Brooke, and Leah, for your endless encouragement and for cheering me on, especially during the tough times. And to my husband, Russ, a huge thank you for your belief in me when I didn't always believe in myself, giving me time and space to write, making dinners and supporting me through each step of this process. I am grateful every day for your love and support.

From Paul: I am grateful for everyone who has supported this book-writing journey and who listened patiently to updates on progress, the challenges and frustrations, and the exciting development milestones. Family and friends, conversation circle members, my coaching clients, my 2Young2Retire community, and my coaches, mentors, and trusted advisors, thank you for sharing the journey with me.

Finally, to you, the reader. We are grateful for your willingness to read what we have written. We hope we have in some way inspired you to live more consciously in midlife and beyond.

NOTES

INTRODUCTION

1. Paul Ward, *The Inner Journey to Conscious Leadership: Ten Practices for Leading Consciously* (Bloomington, IN: Balboa Press, 2018).

2. Marika and Howard Stone, *Too Young to Retire: 101 Ways to Start the Rest of Your Life* (New York: Penguin, 2004).

CHAPTER I

1. Lewis Carroll, *Alice's Adventures in Wonderland* (London: Macmillan, 1865).

2. Simon Sinek, *Start with Why: How Great Leaders Inspire Everyone to Take Action* (New York: Portfolio, 2006).

3. Viktor E. Frankl, *Man's Search for Meaning: An Introduction to Logotherapy* (Boston: Beacon Press, 1959).

4. James Hollis, *Finding Meaning in the Second Half of Life: How to Finally, Really Grow Up* (New York: Gotham Books, 2005).

5. Gregg Levoy, *Callings: Finding and Following an Authentic Life* (New York: Harmony Books, 1997).

6. Richard J. Leider, *The Power of Purpose: Find Meaning, Live Longer, Better*, 3rd ed. (Oakland, CA: Berrett-Koehler, 2015).

7. Interview with Larry Ackerman, February 20, 2020. To learn more about identity mapping and the thinking behind these eight questions, visit Larry's website at https://www.larryackerman.com/ and read his book *The Identity Code: The 8 Essential Questions for Finding Your Purpose and Place in the World* (New York, Random House, 2005).

8. William Bridges, *Transitions: Making Sense of Life's Changes*, revised 25th Anniversary Edition (New York: Da Capo, 2004).

9. The Captain Tom Foundation, accessed June 19, 2023, https://captaintom.org/.

10. Margaret J. Wheatley, *Who Do We Choose to Be? Facing Reality, Claiming Leadership, Restoring Sanity* (Oakland, CA: Berrett-Koehler, 2017).

CHAPTER 2

1. World Health Organization, Preamble to the Constitution of the World Health Organization as adopted by the International Health Conference, New York, June 19–22, 1946; signed on July 22, 1946, by the representatives of 61 States (Official Records of the World Health Organization, no. 2, p. 100) and entered into force on April 7, 1948 [Health definition], https://www.who.int/about/accountability/governance/constitution

2. Age Wave, "The New Age of Aging: A Landmark Age Wave study" 2023, page 13. Agewave.com reports. https://agewave.com/wp-content/uploads/2023/08/08-07-23-Age-Wave-The-New-Age-of-Aging-Report_FINAL.pdf

3. Lauren Medina, Shannon Sabo, and Jonathan Vespa, *Living Longer: Historical and Projected Life Expectancy in the United States*, 1960 to 2060 Population Estimates and Projections, Current Population Reports, US Census Bureau report, p. 25-1145, February 2020, https://www.census.gov/library/publications/2020/demo/p25-1145.html

4. Pili Roberto and Petretto Donatella Rita, "Genetics, Lifestyles, Environment and Longevity: A Look in a Complex Phenomenon," *Open Access Journal of Gerontology & Geriatric Medicine* 2, no. 1 (2017), p1-5, https://juniperpublishers.com/oajggm/pdf/OAJGGM.MS.ID.555576.pdf. Axel Skytthe et al., "Longevity Studies in GenomEUtwin," in *Twin Research and Human Genetics*, Volume 6 , Issue 5 , 01 October 2003, pp. 448 – 454, DOI: https://doi.org/10.1375/twin.6.5.448

5. Alvin Powel, "Ellen Langer's State of Mindfulness," *Harvard Gazette*, October 1, 2018, https://news.harvard.edu/gazette/story/2018/10/ellen-langer-talks-mindfulness-health/

6. Carol Dweck, *Mindset: The New Psychology of Success* (New York: Ballantine Books, 2016) p. 2–3.

7. "Thinking Positively about Aging Extends Life More Than Exercise and Not Smoking," *Yale News*, July 29, 2002, https://news.yale.edu/2002/07/29/thinking-positively-about-aging-extends-life-more-exercise-and-not-smoking

8. Courtney E. Ackerman, "What Is Flourishing in Positive Psychology?" updated February 17, 2023, https://positivepsychology.com/flourishing/.

9. Dr. Martin Seligman on his PERMA Theory, University of Pennsylvania, Positive Psychology Center, PERMA Theory of Well-Being and PERMA Workshops, https://ppc.sas.upenn.edu/learn-more/perma-theory-well-being-and-perma-workshops.

10. "Positive Ageing," Positive Psychology Institute, accessed June 12, 2023, https://www.positivepsychologyinstitute.com.au/positive-ageing.

11. "Suicide and Older Adults: What You Should Know," National Council on Aging (NCOA), September 7, 2021, https://www.ncoa.org/article/suicide-and-older-adults-what-you-should-know

12. Elizabeth Blackburn and Elissa Epel, *The Telomere Effect: A Revolutionary Approach to Living Younger, Healthier, Longer* (New York: Grand Central, 2017).

13. Robert C. Atchley, "A Continuity Theory of Normal Aging," *The Gerontologist* 29, no. 2 (April 1989): 183–190, https://doi.org/10.1093/geront/29.2.183.

14. "Mindfulness Exercises," Mayo Clinic, accessed June 19, 2023, https://www.mayoclinic.org/healthy-lifestyle/consumer-health/in-depth/mindfulness-exercises/art-20046356

15. "Keeping Your Brain in Tiptop Shape," *Washington Post*, November 27, 2018, https://www.washingtonpost.com/national/health-science/keeping-your-brain-in-tiptop-shape/2018/11/23/8e37cf08-cd78-11e8-a3e6-44daa3d35ede_story.html

16. Jane E. Brody, "The Secret of 'Cognitive Super-Agers,'" *New York Times*, October 21, 2021, https://www.nytimes.com/2021/06/21/well/mind/aging-memory-centenarians.html

17. "Sleep Deprivation Increases Alzheimer's Protein," National Institutes of Health (NIH), April 24, 2018, https://www.nih.gov/news-events/nih-research-matters/sleep-deprivation-increases-alzheimers-protein

18. Kendra Cherry, "What is Neuroplasticity?" Verywell Mind, November 8, 2022, https://www.verywellmind.com/what-is-brain-plasticity-2794886.

19. "Cognitive Super Agers Defy Typical Age-Related Decline in Brainpower," NIH National Institute on Aging, July 31, 2020, https://www.nia.nih.gov/news/cognitive-super-agers-defy-typical-age-related-decline-brainpower

20. Here is a site to start you off: https://www.projectbiglife.ca.

21. "Doctor-Patient Relationship Improves Your Health," Harvard Health, June 12, 2014, https://www.health.harvard.edu/staying-healthy/doctor-patient-relationship-improves-your-health

22. Dan Buettner, *The Blue Zones: 9 Lessons for Living Longer from the People Who've Lived the Longest*, 2nd ed. (Washington, DC: National Geographic, 2012).

23. "Water: How Much Should You Drink Every Day?" Mayo Clinic, accessed June 19, 2023, https://www.mayoclinic.org/healthy-lifestyle/nutrition-and-healthy-eating/in-depth/water/art-20044256

24. "Water: How Much Should You Drink Every Day?"

25. "Why Is Physical Activity So Important to Health and Well-Being?" The American Heart Association, January 14, 2017, https://www.heart.org/en/healthy-living/fitness/fitness-basics/why-is-physical-activity-so-important-for-health-and-wellbeing

26. The American Heart Association, "Why Is Physical Activity So Important?"

27. Matthew Thorpe, "How to Fight Sarcopenia (Muscle Loss Due to Aging)," Healthline, May 25, 2017, https://www.healthline.com/nutrition/sarcopenia.

28. Mary MacVean, "'Get Up' or Lose Hours of Your Life Every Day, Scientist Says," *Los Angeles Times*, July 31, 2014, https://www.latimes.com/science/sciencenow/la-sci-sn-get-up-20140731-story.html

29. Buettner, *Blue Zones*.

30. Courtland Milloy, "'Ageless Wonder' Seeks to Be a Model for Senior Health," *Washington Post*, August 18, 2021.

31. "Does Medicare Cover Annual Physical Exams?" AARP Medicare Question and Answer Tool, accessed July 1, 2023, https://www.aarp.org/health/medicare-qa-tool/does-medicare-cover-physical-exams/

32. "Oral Cancer Facts," Oral Cancer Foundation, accessed June 19, 2023, https://oralcancerfoundation.org/facts/.

33. "Complementary and Alternative Medicine," NIH: National Cancer Institute, accessed June 19, 2023, https://www.cancer.gov/about-cancer/treatment/cam.

34. These may be challenging conversations to begin with family members, so available resources provide guidance. See free conversation starter guides from The Conversation Project: https://theconversationproject.org.

CHAPTER 3

1. Lynne Twist, *The Soul of Money: Transforming Your Relationship with Money and Life* (New York: Norton, 2017).

2. Peter Diamandis and Steven Kotler, *Abundance: The Future Is Better Than You Think* (New York: Free Press, 2012).

3. Lion Goodman, Clear Your Beliefs Program, https://clearyourbeliefs.com/.

4. "Free E-Book," Sonia Ricotti, accessed June 19, 2023, https://soniaricotti.com/.

5. T. Harv Eker, *SpeedWealth: How to Stop Earning a Living and Start Creating Wealth* (eBook, 2016), https://harvekeronline.com/speedwealth-book-old/; T. Harv Eker, *Secrets of the Millionaire Mind: Mastering the Inner Game of Wealth* (New York: Harper Business, 2005).

6. Twist, *The Soul of Money*.

7. Robert Skidelsky and Edward Skidelsky, *How Much Is Enough?: Money and the Good Life* (New York: Other Press, 2013).

8. Twist, *The Soul of Money*.

9. Jack Canfield, *The Success Principles: How to Get from Where You Are to Where You Want to Be* (London: Thorsons, 2005).

10. *Finances in Retirement: New Challenges, New Solutions: A Merrill Lynch Retirement Study, Conducted in Partnership with Age Wave* (Bank of America Corporation, 2017), https://agewave.com/what-we-do/landmark-research-and-consulting/research-studies/finances-in-retirement-new-challenges-new-solutions/.

11. Catherine Collinson, Patti Rowey, and Heidi Cho, "A Precarious Existence: How Today's Retirees Are Financially Faring in Retirement. A Transamerica Report," Transamerica Institute, 2018, https://www.transamericaretirementstudies.org/docs/default-source/retirees-survey/tcrs2018_sr_retirees_survey_financially_faring.pdf.

12. Thorstein Veblen, *The Theory of the Leisure Class* (1899; Project Gutenberg, 1997), https://www.gutenberg.org/cache/epub/833/pg833-images.html.

13. Olivia Mellan and Sherry Christie, *Money Harmony: A Road Map for Individuals and Couples* (Washington, DC: Money Harmony Books, 2014).

14. Twist, *The Soul of Money*.

CHAPTER 4

1. Stephen Hawking, *Worklife*, BBC, March 2018, https://www.bbc.com/worklife/article/20180314-stephen-hawkings-advice-for-a-fulfilling-career.

2. Marc Miller, Career Pivot; Interview with Marc Miller, September 24, 2019, https://careerpivot.com/2019/careers-2nd-half-life/.

3. Bob Buford, *Half Time: Moving from Success to Significance* (Grand Rapids, MI: Zondervan, 2015), 35–36.

4. Richard J. Leider and David A. Shapiro, *Work Reimagined: Uncover Your Calling* (Oakland, CA: Berrett-Koehler, 2015).

5. "Meet Amy LaBelle of LaBelle Winery," BostonVoyager, May 1, 2018, http://
    bostonvoyager.com/interview/meet-amy-labelle-labelle-winery-amherst-nh/.

6. Gary Burtless and Joseph Quinn, "Retirement Trends and Policies to Encourage
    Work Among Older Americans," chap. 18 in *Ensuring Health and Income Security
    for an Aging Workforce* (Kalamazoo, MI: W.E. Upjohn Institute for Employment
    Research, 2001), 375–415, DOI: 10.17848/9780880994668.

7. Marc Freedman, *Encore: Finding Work That Matters in the Second Half of Life*
    (New York: Public Affairs, 2007).

8. Barbara A. Butrica et al., "The Disappearing Defined Benefit Pension and Its Impact
    on the Retirement Incomes of Baby Boomers," *Social Security Bulletin* 69, no. 3
    (2009), https://www.ssa.gov/policy/docs/ssb/v69n3/v69n3p1.html.

9. Kim Parker and Eileen Patten, *The Sandwich Generation: Rising Financial Burdens
    for Middle-Aged Americans* (Washington, DC: Pew Research Center, 2013),
    https://assets.pewresearch.org/wp-content/uploads/sites/3/2013/01/Sandwich_
    Generation_Report_FINAL_1-29.pdf.

10. Ken Dychtwald and Robert Morison, *What Retirees Want: A Holistic View of Life's
    Third Age* (Hoboken, NJ: Wiley and Sons, 2020).

11. Jeff Haden, "A Study of 2.7 Million Startups Found the Ideal Age to Start a
    Business," *Inc.*, July 16, 2018, https://www.inc.com/jeff-haden/a-study-of-27-
    million-startups-found-ideal-age-to-start-a-business-and-its-much-older-than-you-
    think.html.

12. Kerry Hannon, *Never Too Old to Get Rich: The Entrepreneur's Guide to Starting a
    Business Mid-Life* (Hoboken, NJ: Wiley, 2019), pages 7–9.

13. Caroline Castrillon, "Why It's Time to Consider a Portfolio Career," *Forbes*,
    September 15, 2019, https://www.forbes.com/sites/carolinecastrillon/2019/09/15/
    why-its-time-to-consider-a-portfolio-career/.

14. Wendy Marx, *Thriving at 50+: The 7 Principles to Reinvent and Rebrand Yourself*
    (New Degree Press, 2020).

15. David Zak, "Why a 70-Year-Old Retiree Went Back to Work as an Intern,"
    Fast Company, September 20, 2016, https://www.fastcompany.com/3062378/
    the-oldest-intern.

16. Chip Conley, *Wisdom @ Work, The Making of a Modern Elder* (New York: Currency,
    2018); A mentern combines the roles of a mentor and an intern, often experienced
    professionals "looking to share their knowledge with a younger workforce, while
    learning additional skills from different age groups of peers and partners," https://
    www.mentern.com/mentern-com.html.

17. Lindsey Pollak, *The Remix, How to Lead and Succeed in the Multigenerational Workplace* (New York: Harper Business, 2019).

CHAPTER 5

1. Sam Horn, *Someday Is Not a Day in the Week: 10 Hacks to Make the Rest of Your Life the Best of Your Life* (New York: St. Martin's Press, 2019).

2. Richard J. Leider and David Shapiro, *Who Do You Want to Be When You Grow Old?: The Path of Purposeful Aging* (Oakland, CA: Berrett-Koehler, 2020).

3. "More Americans Working Past 65," AARP, April 22, 2019, https://www.aarp.org/work/employers/americans-working-past-65/.

4. Marc Freedman, *Encore: Finding Work That Matters in the Second Half of Life* (New York: Public Affairs, 2007).

5. Marci Alboher, *The Encore Career Handbook: How to Make a Living and a Difference in the Second Half of Life* (New York: Workman, 2013).

6. Jim Emerman, Nancy Peterson, and Betsy Werley, "Purpose in the Encore Years: Shaping Lives of Meaning and Contribution," Encore.org and Stanford University, PEP-Briefs, Pathways to Encore Project, 2018, 2–3, https://encore.org/wp-content/uploads/2018/03/PEP-Full-Report.pdf.

7. Alboher, *Encore Career Handbook*.

8. Joshua David Stein, "Sandy Hook Promise's Mark Barden Will Never Stop Fighting," Fatherly.com, updated December 14, 2022, https://www.fatherly.com/life/mark-barden-sandy-hook-promise-gun-violence.

9. Chris Farrell, *Purpose and a Paycheck: Finding Meaning, Money, and Happiness in the Second Half of Life* (New York: HarperCollins, 2019).

10. Credits to Lesah Beckhusen, M.S., President and Developer, www.skillscan.com.

11. Cynthia Vinney, "Understand Maslow's Theory of Self-Actualization," ThoughtCo., September 21, 2018, https://www.thoughtco.com/maslow-theory-self-actualization-4169662.

12. Vicky Levy, "Giving Back: Attitudes and Behaviors Across the Lifespan," AARP Research, updated February 2020, https://www.aarp.org/research/topics/life/info-2019/volunteer-attitudes-behaviors-lifespan.html.

13. Levy, "Giving Back."

14. Before Giving to a Charity, Federal Trade Commission, https://consumer.ftc.gov/articles/giving-charity.

CHAPTER 6

1. "Original Blue Zones Explorations," Blue Zones, accessed June 19, 2023, https://www.bluezones.com/exploration.

2. "Global Ecovillage Network," Ecovillage, accessed June 19, 2023, https://ecovillage.org/.

3. A comprehensive listing of property caretaker positions is published by a friend of 2Young2Retire, *Caretaker Gazette*. Since 1983, the newsletter has been published in print every two months, and is also now online with email updates sent to subscribers. For more information, contact Gary Dunn via the website: www.caretaker.org.

4. "A Quick Guide to How It Works," Love Home Swap, accessed June 19, 2023, https://www.lovehomeswap.com/how-it-works.

5. Jonathon Day, Travel Care Code, https://travelcarecode.org/.

6. "Playa Viva," Regenesis, accessed June 19, 2023, https://regenesisgroup.com/project/playa-viva/.

7. "Begin Your Regenerative Journey," Regenerative Travel, accessed June 19, 2023, https://www.regenerativetravel.com/.

8. Paul Ward, *The Inner Journey to Conscious Leadership: Ten Practices for Leading Consciously* (Bloomington, IN: Balboa Press, 2018).

9. "Circles of Air & Stone: Finding a Dream Worth Living," Quest for Vision, accessed June 19, 2023, https://www.questforvision.com/.

10. Journeys of the Spirit (website), accessed June 19, 2023, https://journeysofthespirit.com/.

11. Dorobo Safaris (website), accessed July 15, 2023, https://www.dorobosafaris.com/.

12. "Welcome," the Explorers Passage, accessed June 19, 2023, https://explorerspassage.com/.

13. "You Have the Power to Build a Better World," Roots and Shoots, accessed June 19, 2023, https://www.rootsandshoots.org/.

14. "2041 Foundation" (Robert Swan), 2041 Foundation.org, accessed June 19, 2023, https://www.2041foundation.org/.

CHAPTER 7

1. Carl Sagan, *Cosmos* (New York: Ballentine Books, 2013), 2.

2. "What Is Creative Aging?" Lifetime Arts, accessed June 19, 2023, https://www.lifetimearts.org/creative-aging/.

3. Dr. Gene Cohen, "The Creativity and Aging Study: The Impact of Professionally Conducted Cultural Programs on Older Adults," April 30, 2006, https://www.arts.gov/sites/default/files/NEA-Creativity-and-Aging-Cohen-study.pdf.

4. Elizabeth Gilbert, *Big Magic: Creative Living Beyond Fear* (New York: Riverhead Books, 2015), 12.

5. Abraham H. Maslow, "A Theory of Human Motivation," *Psychological Review* 50, no. 4 (July 1943): 370–396, https://www.academia.edu/9415670/.

6. Mihaly Csikszentmihalyi, *Flow: The Psychology of Optimal Experiences* (New York: Harper Perennial Modern Classics, 2008).

7. Mihaly Csikszentmihalyi, *Creativity: The Psychology of Discovery and Invention* (New York: Harper Perennial Modern Classics, 2013).

8. Gary Wolf, "Steve Jobs: The Next Insanely Great Thing," Wired.com, February 1, 1996; Note: This is the specific direct quote from the source on Steve Jobs, https://www.wired.com/1996/02/jobs-2/

9. Modern Elder Academy (website), accessed June 19, 2023, https://www.modernelderacademy.com.

10. Julia Cameron, *The Artist's Way: A Spiritual Path to Higher Creativity*, 25th Anniversary Edition (New York: TarcherPerigee, 2016).

11. Julia Cameron with Emma Lively, *It's Never Too Late to Begin Again: Discovering Creativity and Meaning at Midlife and Beyond* (New York: TarcherPerigee, 2016).

12. Fred Mandell and Kathleen Jordan, *Becoming a Life Change Artist: 7 Creative Skills to Reinvent Yourself at Any Stage of Life* (New York: Avery, 2010).

13. Mandell and Jordan, *Becoming a Life Change Artist*.

14. Gene Cohen, *The Creative Age: Awakening Human Potential in the Second Half of Life* (New York: Quill, 2001), 24.

15. Steven Pressfield, *The War of Art: Break Through the Blocks and Win Your Inner Creative Battles* (New York: Black Irish Entertainment, 2012).

16. Jill Badonsky, *The Muse Is In: An Owner's Manual to Your Creativity* (Philadelphia, PA: Running Press, 2013).

CHAPTER 8

1. Liz Mineo, "Good Genes Are Nice, but Joy Is Better," *Harvard Gazette*, April 11, 2017, https://news.harvard.edu/gazette/story/2017/04/over-nearly-80-years-harvard-study-has-been-showing-how-to-live-a-healthy-and-happy-life/.

2. Vivek H. Murthy, *Together: The Healing Power of Human Connection in a Sometimes Lonely World* (New York: Harper Collins, 2020).

3. Kathlyn and Gay Hendricks, *Conscious Loving Ever After: How to Create Thriving Relationships at Midlife and Beyond* (Carlsbad, CA: Hay House, 2015).

4. Hendricks and Hendricks, *Conscious Loving Ever After.*

5. Marta Zaraska, *Growing Young: How Friendship, Optimism and Kindness Can Help You Live to 100* (Canada: Appetite by Random House, 2020).

6. Susan L. Brown and I-Fen Lin, "The Gray Divorce Revolution: Rising Divorce Among Middle-Aged and Older Adults, 1990–2010," *Journals of Gerontology Series B: Psychological Sciences and Social Sciences* 67, no. 6 (November 2012), 731–741, doi:10.1093/geronb/gbs089.

7. "How Death and Divorce Compare in Degrees of Loss and Stages of Grief," *Sonyan White* (blog), September 26, 2017, https://www.sonyanwhitecoaching.com/how-death-and-divorce-compare/.

8. Benjamin Gurrentz and Yeris Mayol-Garcia, "Marriage, Divorce, Widowhood Remain Prevalent Among Older Populations," Census.gov, April 22, 2021, https://www.census.gov/library/stories/2021/04/love-and-loss-among-older-adults.html.

9. Ann Brenoff, "There Is No One Right Way to Be a Widow. I'm Proof of That," AARP, July 24, 2019, https://www.aarp.org/disrupt-aging/stories/info-2019/breaking-the-widow-rules.html.

10. Sharon Hyman, "We've Been Together 23 Years and Never Lived Together. Here's Why It Works," Today, December 16, 2021, https://www.today.com/health/essay/living-apart-together-sharon-hyman-relationship-rcna8781.

11. Clare Ansberry, "More Older Couples Stay Together Because They Live Apart," *Wall Street Journal*, July 28, 2019, https://www.wsj.com/articles/more-older-couples-stay-together-because-they-live-apart-11564311602.

12. Kathy Simpson, "A Grandparent's Role with Grandchildren," The Hartford, Extra Mile, February 14, 2023, https://extramile.thehartford.com/family/grandparenting/grandparenting-role/.

13. Susan Krauss Whitbourne, "Five Types of Grandparents and How They Shape Our Lives," *Psychology Today*, February 16, 2010, https://www.psychologytoday.com/intl/blog/fulfillment-any-age/201002/five-types-grandparents-and-how-they-shape-our-lives.

14. Brittne Nelson-Kakulla and Patty David, "2018 Grandparenting Study," AARP, April 2019, https://www.aarp.org/research/topics/life/info-2019/aarp-grandparenting-study.html.

15. "Census Bureau Releases New Estimates on American Families and Living Arrangements," US Census Bureau, November 29, 2021, https://www.census.gov/newsroom/press-releases/2021/families-and-living-arrangements.html.

16. Sara Zeff Geber, *Essential Retirement Planning for Solo Agers: A Retirement and Aging Roadmap for Single and Childless Adults* (Coral Gables, FL: Mango Publishing Group, 2018).

17. C. S. Lewis, *The Four Loves* (Orlando, FL: Harcourt, 1988).

18. Kathleen Coxwell, "Making Friends in Retirement (and Before)," the New Retirement website, March 5, 2020, https://www.newretirement.com/retirement/making-friends-after-retirement/.

19. Deb Taylor, "Engage at Every Age: The Benefits of Intergenerational Relationships," Senior Community Services, May 1, 2018, https://seniorcommunity.org/engage-every-age-benefits-intergenerational-relationships/.

CHAPTER 9

1. Global Footprint Network (website), accessed June 19, 2023, https://www.footprintnetwork.org/.

2. David Korten, "Ecological Civilization: Choice Point for Humanity," Living Economies Forum, April 27, 2018, https://davidkorten.org/ecological-civilization/.

3. "Global Climate Highlights 2022," Copernicus Climate Change Service, accessed June 19, 2023, https://climate.copernicus.eu/global-climate-highlights-2022.

4. World Meteorological Organization (website), accessed December 17, 2023, https://wmo.int/media/news/july-2023-confirmed-hottest-month-record.

5. Bill Gates, *How to Avoid a Climate Disaster: The Solutions We Have and the Breakthroughs We Need* (New York: Alfred A. Knopf, 2021).

6. "Soil Erosion and Degradation," World Wildlife Fund, accessed June 19, 2023, https://www.worldwildlife.org/threats/soil-erosion-and-degradation.

7. Leah Penniman, "Black Gold," in *All We Can Save* (New York: One World, 2020), 301–310.

8. Soul Fire Farm (website), accessed June 19, 2023, https://www.soulfirefarm.org/.

9. Gates, *How to Avoid a Climate Disaster*.

10. Mike Joy, "Food for Healing," in *The New Possible: Visions of Our World beyond Crisis* (Eugene, OR: Cascade Books, 2021),163–170.

11. Gates, *How to Avoid a Climate Disaster*.

12. Stephanie A. Malin, Stacia Ryder, and Mariana Galvão Lyra, "Environmental Justice and Natural Resource Extraction: Intersections of Power, Equity and Access," *Environmental Sociology* 5, no. 2 (2019), 109–116, DOI: 10.1080/23251042.2019.1608420.

13. World Water Law (website), accessed June 19, 2023, https://www.codes.earth/waterlaw.

14. Laura Parker, "How the Plastic Bottle Went from Convenience to Curse," *National Geographic*, August 27, 2019, https://www.nationalgeographic.co.uk/environment-and-conservation/2019/08/how-plastic-bottle-went-miracle-container-despised-villain.

15. Paul Hawken, ed., *Drawdown: The Most Comprehensive Plan Ever Proposed to Reverse Global Warming* (New York: Penguin, 2017).

16. The Great Bubble Barrier (website), accessed June 19, 2023, https://thegreatbubblebarrier.com/en/.

17. Tide Turners Plastic Challenge, UNEP, accessed June 19, 2023, https://www.tide-turners.org/.

18. "Drinking Water," World Health Organization, June 14, 2019, https://www.who.int/news-room/fact-sheets/detail/drinking-water.

19. "Ensuring Prosperity in a Water-Stressed World," World Resource Institute, accessed June 19, 2023, https://www.wri.org/our-work/topics/water.

20. Hawken, *Drawdown*.

21. Water Aid (website), accessed June 19, 2023, https://www.wateraid.org/.

22. Water Is Life (website), accessed June 19, 2023, https://waterislife.com/.

23. Water (website), accessed June 19, 2023, https://water.org/about-us/.

24. Charity: Water (website), accessed June 19, 2023, https://www.charitywater.org/about/scott-harrison-story.

25. Don Maruska, "Solve Climate Change Now," accessed June 19, 2023, https://donmaruska.com/solve-climate-change-now/.

26. "The Paris Agreement," United Nations Climate Change, accessed June 19, 2023, https://unfccc.int/process-and-meetings/the-paris-agreement/the-paris-agreement.

27. James H. Williams et al., "Carbon-Neutral Pathways for the United States," *AGU Advances* 2, no. 1 (March 2021), https://doi.org/10.1029/2020AV000284.

28. Rev. Deborah Moldow, "Spirituality in the Twenty First Century: A Quiet Revolution," in *Our Moment of Choice: Evolutionary Visons and Hope for the Future* (Portland, OR: Beyond Words, 2021).

29. "National Poll on Healthy Aging" conducted by the University of Michigan, July 2020, https://www.healthyagingpoll.org/reports-more/report/everyday-ageism-and-health.

30. "United Nations Open Ended Working Group on Ageing," UNDESA, accessed June 19, 2023, https://social.un.org/ageing-working-group/.

31. Global Alliance for the Rights of Older People (website), accessed June 19, 2023, https://rightsofolderpeople.org/.

32. Ken Dychtwald and Robert Morison, *What Retirees Want: A Holistic View of Life's Third Age* (Hoboken, NJ: Wiley, 2021).

33. "Master Plan for Aging," California for All, accessed June 19, 2023, https://mpa.aging.ca.gov/.

34. "World Report on Disability 2011," World Health Organization, accessed June 20, 2023, https://www.who.int/teams/noncommunicable-diseases/sensory-functions-disability-and-rehabilitation/world-report-on-disability.

35. "UK Family Resources Survey, Financial Year 2019 to 2020," Gov.UK, March 25, 2021, https://www.gov.uk/government/statistics/family-resources-survey-financial-year-2019-to-2020/family-resources-survey-financial-year-2019-to-2020.

36. "Disability Impacts All of Us" CDC, May 15, 2023, https://www.cdc.gov/ncbddd/disabilityandhealth/infographic-disability-impacts-all.html.

37. "Convention on the Rights of Persons with Disabilities (CRPD)," United Nations, accessed June 20, 2023, https://www.un.org/development/desa/disabilities/convention-on-the-rights-of-persons-with-disabilities.html.

38. Ella Washington and Camille Patrick, "Three Requirements for a Diverse and Inclusive Culture," Gallup, September 17, 2018, https://www.gallup.com/workplace/242138/requirements-diverse-inclusive-culture.aspx.

39. Michael Nagler, *The Third Harmony: Nonviolence and the New Story of Human Nature* (Oakland, CA: Berrett-Koehler, 2020).

40. Jonathan Gosling, "Leadership and Management in a Context of Deep Adaptation" in *Deep Adaptation: Navigating the Realities of Climate Chaos* (Cambridge, UK: Polity Press, 2021), 218.

41. Jeremy Lent, "Envisioning an Ecological Society," in *The New Possible: Visions of Our World Beyond Crisis* (Eugene, OR: Cascade Books, 2021), 3–12.

42. Jessica McDougall and Danielle Sugarman, "Climate Risk and the Transition to a Low-Carbon Economy," Harvard Law School Forum on Corporate Governance, March 2, 2021, https://corpgov.law.harvard.edu/2021/03/02/climate-risk-and-the-transition-to-a-low-carbon-economy/.

43. John Mackey and Raj Sisodia, *Conscious Capitalism: Liberating the Heroic Spirit of Business* (Boston: Harvard Business School Publishing, 2014).

CHAPTER 10

1. Bob Dylan, "The Times They Are A-Changin'" (lyrics), accessed June 20, 2023, https://www.bobdylan.com/songs/times-they-are-changin/.

2. Andy Hertzfeld, "The Times They Are A-Changin'," Folklore.org, January 1984, https://www.folklore.org/StoryView.py?story=The_Times_They_Are_A-Changin.txt.

3. Gary W. Small et al., "Brain Health Consequences of Digital Technology Use," *Dialogues in Clinical Neuroscience* 22, no. 2 (June 2020): 179–187, https://www.ncbi.nlm.nih.gov/pmc/articles/PMC7366948/.

4. Sahana Chattopadhyay, "7 Characteristics of a Digital Mindset," Learnnovators, accessed August 27, 2023, https://learnnovators.com/blog/7-characteristics-of-a-digital-mindset/.

5. Chattopadhyay, "Digital Mindset."

6. Zoom (website), https://zoom.us.

7. Google Meet (website), https://apps.google.com/meet/.

8. Coursera (website), https://www.coursera.org/.

9. Udacity (website), https://www.udacity.com/.

10. FutureLearn (website), https://www.futurelearn.com/.

11. The Great Courses (website), https://www.thegreatcourses.com/.

12. Class Central (website), https://www.classcentral.com/.

13. Stanford Center on Longevity (website), accessed June 20, 2023, https://longevity.stanford.edu/.

14. Kinza Yasar and Ivy Wigmore, "Wearable Technology," TechTarget Network, accessed July 11, 2023, https://www.techtarget.com/searchmobilecomputing/definition/wearable-technology

15. Suzanne Bearne, "The Tech Helping Women Manage the Menopause," BBC News, March 13, 2023, https://www.bbc.com/news/business-64899189.

16. Kardia (website), accessed June 20, 2023, https://www.kardia.com/kardiamobile/.

17. "Smart Walkers (Rollators) for the Elderly," Innovation Toronto, accessed June 20, 2023, https://innovationtoronto.com/2015/10/smart-walkers-rollators-for-the-elderley/.

18. ReWalk (website), accessed June 20, 2023, https://rewalk.com.

19. Clifford A. Reilly et al., "Virtual Reality-Based Physical Therapy for Patients with Lower Extremity Injuries: Feasibility and Acceptability," *OTA International* 4, no. 2 (May 18, 2021), https://pubmed.ncbi.nlm.nih.gov/34746664/

20. Joseph Flyntt, "A Detailed History of 3D Printing," 3dInsider.com, accessed July 15, 2023, https://www.3dinsider.com/3d-printing-history/.

21. Tony Hoffman, "3D Printing: What You Need to Know," *PC Magazine*, updated July 1, 2020, https://www.pcmag.com/news/3d-printing-what-you-need-to-know.

22. "20/20/20 Rule," American Optometric Association, accessed June 20, 2023, https://www.aoa.org/AOA/Images/Patients/Eye%20Conditions/20-20-20-rule.pdf.

23. Richard Schulz et al., "Advancing the Aging and Technology Agenda in Gerontology," *The Gerontologist* 55, no. 5 (October 2015): 724–734, https://doi.org/10.1093/geront/gnu071.

24. "How Technology Will Impact Aging Now and in the Near Future," USC Leonard Davis School of Gerontology, accessed June 20, 2023, https://gero.usc.edu/students/current-students/careers-in-aging/How-Technology-Will-Impact-Aging-Now-and-the-Near-future/

25. CFI Team, "Fintech (Financial Technology)," CFI, updated December 7, 2022, https://corporatefinanceinstitute.com/resources/wealth-management/fintech-financial-technology/

26. Alyssa Schroer, "Fintech Banking: 17 Fintech Banks and Neobanks to Know," Built In, March 24, 2023, https://builtin.com/fintech/fintech-banking-examples.

27. Sam Daley, "Fintech. What is Fintech? Financial Technology Definition," Builtin, September 2, 2022, https://builtin.com/fintech.

28. "What Is Fintech? Examples of Types, Products & Regulations," Finances Online, accessed June 21, 2023, https://financesonline.com/what-is-fintech/.

29. "Digital Cheat Sheet: How to Create a Digital Estate Plan," Everplans, accessed August 22, 2023, https://www.everplans.com/articles/digital-cheat-sheet-how-to-create-a-digital-estate-plan

30. Betsy Simmons Hannibal, "The Revised Uniform Fiduciary Access to Digital Assets Act (RUFADAA)," https://www.nolo.com/legal-encyclopedia/ufadaa.html

31. Lesley Stahl, "Artificial Intelligence Preserving Our Ability to Converse with Holocaust Survivors Even After They Die," CBS News, March 27, 2022, https://www.cbsnews.com/news/holocaust-stories-artificial-intelligence-60-minutes-2022-03-27/

32. Ashish Sukhadeve, "Artificial Intelligence for Good: How AI Is Helping Humanity," *Forbes*, February 9, 2021. https://www.forbes.com/sites/forbesbusinesscouncil/ 2021/02/09/artificial-intelligence-for-good-how-ai-is-helping-humanity/ ?sh=21846f03366b

CHAPTER 11

1. "Building Your Resilience," American Psychological Association (APA), updated February 1, 2020, https://www.apa.org/topics/resilience/building-your-resilience.

2. American Psychological Association, "Building Your Resilience."

3. Tara Parker-Pope, "How to Build Resilience in Midlife," *The New York Times*, July 25, 2017, https://www.nytimes.com/2017/07/25/well/mind/how-to-boost-resilience-in-midlife.html.

4. Brené Brown, *Daring Greatly: How the Courage to Be Vulnerable Transforms the Way We Live, Love, Parent, and Lead* (New York: Avery, 2012), 34.

5. "Ramp Up Your Resilience!" Harvard Health Publishing, November 1, 2017, https://www.health.harvard.edu/mind-and-mood/ramp-up-your-resilience; Jeremy Sutton, "What Is Resilience, and Why Is It Important to Bounce Back?" Positive Psychology, January 3, 2019, modified April 19, 2023, https://positivepsychology. com/what-is-resilience/.

6. "2019 National Survey of Drug Use and Health," Substance Abuse and Mental Health Services Administration, accessed June 21, 2023; Stacy Mosel, "Alcohol & Aging: Impacts of Alcohol Abuse on the Elderly," American Addiction Centers, updated October 20, 2022, https://americanaddictioncenters.org/ alcoholism-treatment/elderly

7. Ismael Conejero et al., "Suicide in Older Adults: Current Perspectives," *Clinical Interventions in Aging* 13 (2018): 691–699, https://doi.org/10.2147%2FCIA. S130670

8. Marnin J. Heisel and Gordon L. Flett, "Do Meaning in Life and Purpose in Life Protect Against Suicide Ideation Among Community-Residing Older Adults?" in *Meaning in Positive and Existential Psychology* (New York: Springer, 2014), https://doi.org/10.1007/978-1-4939-0308-5_18.

9. "Disparities in Suicide," Center for Disease Control and Prevention, accessed June 21, 2023, https://www.cdc.gov/suicide/facts/disparities-in-suicide.html.

10. William Bridges, *Transitions: Making Sense of Life's Changes*, revised 25th Anniversary Edition (New York: Da Capo, 2004).

11. Bridges, *Transitions*.

12. Sheryl Sandberg and Adam Grant, *Option B: Facing Adversity, Building Resilience, and Finding Joy* (New York: Alfred A. Knopf, 2017).

13. Lewina O. Lee et al., "Optimism Is Associated with Exceptional Longevity in 2 Epidemiologic Cohorts of Men and Women," *Proceedings of the National Academy of Sciences* 116, no. 37 (September 10, 2019): 18357–18362, https://doi.org/10.1073/pnas.1900712116

14. Margie Warrell, "Why Getting Comfortable with Discomfort Is Crucial to Success," *Forbes*, April 22, 2013, www.forbes.com/sites/margiewarrell/2013/04/22/is-comfort-holding-you-back/

15. Brown, *Daring Greatly*, 2.

16. Jennifer A. Bellingtier and Shevaun D. Neupert, "Negative Aging Attitudes Predict Greater Reactivity to Daily Stressors in Older Adults," *Journals of Gerontology, Series B: Psychological Sciences & Social Sciences* 73, no. 7 (September 20, 2018):1155–1159, https://doi.org/10.1093/geronb/gbw086.

17. Age Friendly Vibes (website), https://agefriendlyvibes.com.

18. Morton H. Shaevitz, "Aging, Resilience and the New Normal," *Psychology Today*, April 4, 2017, https://www.psychologytoday.com/us/blog/refire-don-t-retire/201704/aging-resilience-and-the-new-normal

19. Michaela Haas, *Bouncing Forward: The Art and Science of Cultivating Resilience* (New York: Enliven, 2016), 9.

20. Amanda Ripley, "Resilience," in *The Unthinkable: Who Survives When Disaster Strikes—And Why* (New York: Three Rivers Press, 2009), 91.

21. "Trauma," Mind, accessed June 21, 2023, https://www.mind.org.uk/media-a/4149/trauma-2020.pdf

22. Haas, *Bouncing Forward*, 54.

23. Badri Bajaj and Neerja Pande, "Mediating Role of Resilience in the Impact of Mindfulness on Life Satisfaction and Affect as Indices of Subjective Well-Being," *Personality and Individual Differences* 93 (April 2016): 63–67, https://doi.org/10.1016/j.paid.2015.09.005

24. Bob Hinds, "The Serenity Prayer: A Blueprint for Living," LinkedIn, July 25, 2017, accessed August 30, 2023, https://www.linkedin.com/pulse/serenity-prayer-blueprint-living-bob-hinds-dba-acata/

25. Brian Hill founded the Oral Cancer Foundation (OCF), https://
oralcancerfoundation.org, which has grown into an amazingly abundant source of
information and dedicated support 24/7.

26. Paul T. P. Wong and Lillian C. J. Wong, "A Meaning-Centered Approach to
Building Youth Resilience," in *The Human Quest for Meanings: Theories, Research,
and Applications*, 2nd ed., (New York: Routledge, 2012), 585–617, http://www.
drpaulwong.com/documents/HQM2-chapter27.pdf.

27. DrPaulWong.com; Wong and Wong, "A Meaning-Centered Approach to Building
Youth Resilience," p. 603.

28. DrPaulWong.com, p. 361; Wong and Wong, "A Meaning-Centered Approach to
Building Youth Resilience," p. 607.

29. Elizabeth White, "Jobless After 50? Start a Resilience Circle: 'Advice from Fifty-Five,
Unemployed and Faking Normal'," Next Avenue, December 2, 2016. https://www.
nextavenue.org/jobless-50-start-resilience-circle/

30. Elizabeth White, *55, Underemployed, and Faking Normal: Your Guide to a Better Life*
(New York: Simon & Schuster, 2019).

INDEX

dreaming, 17
drifting apart, 181–182
Dunn, Gary, 285
Dweck, Carol S., 32
Dychtwald, Ken, 216
Dylan, Bob, 229

E

earth, climate change, 204–206
eating, 42–43
ED (erectile dysfunction), 48
Eden Alternative, 285
educational health programs, 51
Eker, T. Harv, 62–63
EKG devices, 234
Elders Action Network, 286
Elders for Social Justice, 221
electricity, 205, 213
electronic wallets, 64, 237
emergencies, health, 49–50
emotional health, 35–39
    practices to soothe mind, 37–39
    self-growth and lifelong learning, 36–37
empty nesters, 175, 180
Encore (Freedman), 113
encore years, careers in, 113–118
ending phase, 255
end-of-life issues, 134, 187
engagement (PERMA Model), 33
Enneagram, 285
entrepreneurship, 118–121
    becoming entrepreneur, 97–100
    connecting with other entrepreneurs, 121
    social entrepreneurship, 119–121
environmental, social, and governance (ESG), 223
environmental sustainability, 203
Epel, Elissa, 35
Equality Act, 217
equity, 219–221
erectile dysfunction (ED), 48
Esfandiari, Mary Ann, 20–21, 202, 232, 256, 260
ESG (environmental, social, and governance), 223
estate planning, 79, 134, 238, 289

estrogen, 42
existential risk, 270–271
expatriates, 132
expenditures, 67, 70
experience, 98, 156
Explore, Experience, and Expand Your Creativity class, 155
The Explorers Passage, 145
extraction, 205

F

faith-based communities, 125, 156
Family Resources Survey, 217
Farrell, Chris, 118
fears, 253
Federal Trade Commission, 125
fee-only financial advisors, 80
Femtech, 234
fertilizers, 205, 210
fiber, 42
fiduciaries, 80
55-plus communities, 137, 221
final salary pensions, 91–92
financial advisors, 79–81
    selecting, 80–81
    trusted resources, 81
financial donations, 126
financial freedom, 57, 68–69
financial planners, 60, 70, 237, 270
financial power of attorney, 79
Finding Meaning in the Second Half of Life (Hollis), 12
Fink, Larry, 223
fintech, 237–238
fire, climate change, 210–211
Fitbit, 234
fitness and movement, 44–47
fixed mindset, 32
flourishing, 33, 175
Flow (Csikszentmihalyi), 153
flow chart tools, 242
flow state, 153
fluid creative process, 163
"For Dummies" book series, 246
forest bathing, 39
fossil fuels, 143, 211–213
Foster Grandparent, 192, 286

I

ideas
    collecting for potential creativity, 160
    for social responsibility, 221–222
identity, 21–24
    mapping questions for finding purpose,
        15–16
    reinvention, 24–25
    shifts in, 23–24
    transitioning, 19–20
    work and sense of, 86
imagination
    creativity versus, 150
    fueling, 159–160
impact, moments of, 23
improv classes, 155–156
inclusion, 104, 219–221
inclusive capitalism, 225
income
    increasing, 70
    multiple streams of, 100–101
    tracking, 67
independent living disability, 217
inflammatory-producing foods, 39
informal volunteering, 123
inner journeys, 144–145
Insight Timer app, 38
Institute on Character, 282
Intention (A-I-A), 31
intergenerational relationships, 195–196
The Intern, 103
internet safety, 247–248
*An Introduction to Sustainable Tourism and
        Responsible Travel* (Day), 141
intuition, paying attention to, 90–91,
        265–266
inventure expeditions, 144
investments, growing, 70
It's Never Too Late to Begin Again
        (Cameron), 156, 159–160

J

Jacobs, Steve, 88, 202
Jacobson, Larry, 137–138, 220–221
Jobs, Steve, 155, 229

Jope, Alan, 224
Jordan, Kathleen, 162
journeys, spiritual or inner, 144–145
Journeys of the Spirit, 145
joy factor, creative aging, 153–154

K

Keenan, Dorothy, 50, 115, 140, 246, 256,
        260
Kinder, George, 284
Klontz, Brad, 283
Klontz Money Script Inventory (KMSI)
        assessment tool, 283
Know the Signs programs, 116–117
knowledge
    learning and updating, 246
    self-knowledge, 175–177
Korten, David, 203
Kotler, Steven, 58
Kraus, Donna, 38, 154, 183–184
Kyne, Dee, 206–207

L

LaBelle, Amy, 90
LaBelle Winery, 90
Langer, Ellen, 32
leading consciously, 222–225
learning knowledge, 246
legacy document, 244–245
legacy of money consciousness, 79
legal paperwork, 51
Leider, Richard, 15–16, 90, 144
Lent, Jeremy, 223
Leporte, Leo, 287
Lerman, Liz, 157
Levine, James, 45
Levoy, Gregg, 14
Levy, Becca, 33
Lewis, C. S., 17, 194
LGBTQ+ community, 137–138, 220–221
life expectancy, 30, 41, 77, 91
life lessons, 155–158
life list, 53–54
Life Planning Network, 157, 272

reset button, 92–94
switching careers, 95–97
working longer, 91–92
World Health Organization (WHO), 30,
        208, 217
World Meteorological Organization, 203
World Ocean Day, 207
World Resources Institute, 208, 210
World Vision Clean Water program, 208
World Water Law, 206, 286
World Wildlife Fund, 204

Y

yoga, 38, 45, 233

Z

Zaraska, Marta, 180

ABOUT THE AUTHORS

EILEEN CAROSCIO, CSC, RN, MSN

Eileen is a multicertified coach, consultant, and a registered nurse. She is passionate about helping individuals to achieve their goals and live their best life. Referred to as the "midlife muse," she engages you beyond your titles, jobs, and formalities to get to the core of what will enrich your midlife, making it more meaningful and magical.

She is a thought leader in midlife management. She teaches adult education classes and provides coaching to clients of a prominent financial firm. She is the local life planning network (LPN) membership chair and has held past leadership positions at the national level. She is an advocate of positive aging and has co-led the ALPA program (Advocacy Leadership for Positive Aging).

Eileen has a bachelor of science degree in nursing from Catholic University and a master of science degree in nursing from Marymount University. She is a member of Sigma Theta Tau, the national nursing society, with over 35 years of experience in a wide span of nursing areas.

After 25 years as a registered nurse, Eileen augmented her career to include coaching. Eileen began coaching in 2005 and is a member of the International Coaching Federation (ICF). She established Passageways Coaching in 2007, offering coaching, consulting, classes, and workshops on midlife navigation, creativity, and resilience.

Eileen holds certifications as a Myers Briggs Type Indicator facilitator, a Success Unlimited Network coach, Life Change Artist coach, Visual Coach, Kaizen-Muse creativity coach, KMI Master Mind facilitator, Modern Day Muse Group facilitator, and 2 Young 2 Retire workshop facilitator. She is also an authorized facilitator for the "Now What? 90 Days to a New Life Direction" coaching program.

Eileen lives with her husband in the Maryland-DC-Virginia region and works remotely around the globe. Eileen has a fondness for foxes and can often be found with a camera capturing their antics and escapades. She loves to immerse herself in nature, kayaking along a lake or hiking a trail. Learn more about Eileen at www.passagewayscoaching.net.

SANDY DEMAREST

Sandy is an executive career and a retirement lifestyle and leadership coach, trainer, and speaker who leverages her experience to help organizations and mid-late-stage workers transition to new chapters. She specializes in training and coaching programs focusing on Engage as You Age, From Fulltime Career to Fulltime Life, and Create Your Next Meaningful Chapter. Her greatest gifts and joy are helping individuals, couples, and small groups craft their next chapter to make the most of the years ahead. Sandy is the founder and owner of Demarest Directions, providing coaching, training, and retreats.

Sandy started her career in social work after earning a degree in social welfare and psychology from Ohio Wesleyan University and extensive coursework in social work from Fordham University. For the past 25 years, Sandy has worked in career development. She later transitioned to coaching with certifications as a Career Management Coach, Executive Leadership Coach, and Strengths-Based Coach from The Academies. She is also a Certified Retirement Options Coach.

After ten years working with leaders and professionals embarking on their next life and work challenges, the last five years have been a time of change and reassessment for Sandy. Against the backdrop of the pandemic, there has been another opportunity for personal self-reflection and reassessment. She appreciates now more than ever that life is short, and we often live our best lives in our later years. Sandy has a renewed sense of urgency to live each day with purpose, joy, and gratitude and to help others do the same by embracing the freedom to create their future.

Sandy believes life is filled with adventures and often seeks new opportunities to learn and grow. She recently became certified as a barre instructor, bringing her energy and love of health and fitness to others. Another new adventure for Sandy has been the creation of Rewire Retreats for women as they transition to new chapters.

Sandy gives back to her community in a variety of ways, including leading the business education committee at her local chamber and being active on the world service committee at her church.

Sandy lives in Amherst, New Hampshire, with her husband, Russ, and they both enjoy traveling and spending time with their three grown daughters and family. She can often be found on the coast of New Hampshire or Maine enjoying a long walk on the beach.

Find out more about Sandy at www.demarestdirections.com and www.linkedin.com/in/sandydemarest/.

PAUL WARD, PhD

Paul is an international conscious leadership and conscious living coach, author of *The Inner Journey to Conscious Leadership*, and a host of conscious conversation circles. He is sometimes referred to as the consciousness whisperer. Paul is the principal owner of the coaching, consulting, and training company 2Young2Retire, LLC, offering impactful life transitions coaching and facilitator certification training.

Born in England, his spirit of adventure has taken him around Europe and the Americas practicing his craft as designer, engineer, marketer, business leader, visioneer, facilitator, and coach. Farther afield, walking among the indigenous tribes and the animals of the Serengeti has provided deep appreciation of the need to find guides for adventures and spiritual journeys, and for personal and organizational transformations.

Paul has masters and doctoral degrees in organization and management and has spent more than 30 years consulting to large and small organizations in Europe and the Americas. He is a certified conscious business change agent and a certified professional co-active coach, credentialed by the International Coaching Federation.

Paul has served on not-for-profit boards in the fields of mental health and chemical dependency and as president of the board of trustees for his local church. He is a hot-air balloon pilot and operated a commercial balloon rides business in upstate New York.

Jim Dethmer, co-founder of The Conscious Leadership Group, says of Paul in the foreword to his book, "When it comes to Conscious Leadership, Paul Ward is an astronomer and a biologist—he looks through both a telescope and a microscope. His book gives the reader a big picture overview of the subject as well as practical, specific details on how to live and lead consciously."

Paul divides his time between West Palm Beach, Florida, and Portsmouth, England.

Find out more about Paul at

www.drpaulward.com
www.2young2retire.com